LIFE'S CAREER—AGING

LIFE'S CAREER - AGING
Cultural Variations on Growing Old

edited by
BARBARA G. MYERHOFF
ANDREI SIMIĆ

SAGE PUBLICATIONS   **Beverly Hills**   **London**

Copyright © 1978 by Sage Publications, Inc.

For information address:

SAGE PUBLICATIONS, INC.
275 South Beverly Drive
Beverly Hills, California 90212

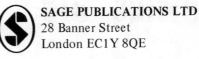

SAGE PUBLICATIONS LTD
28 Banner Street
London EC1Y 8QE

Printed in the United States of America

Library of Congress Cataloging in Publication Data

Main entry under title:

Life's career—aging.

   (Sage series on cross-cultural research and methodology ; 4)
     Bibliography: p. 247
     1. Old age—Addresses, essays, lectures. 2. Aging —Social aspects—Addresses, essays, lectures. 3. Cross-cultural studies—Addresses, essays, lecture.
     I. Myerhoff, Barbara. II. Simić, Andrei.
   HQ1061.L478   301.43'5   77-14268
   ISBN 0-8039-0867-9

FIRST PRINTING

CONTENTS

ACKNOWLEDGEMENTS

This work is in part the result of a project originated at the Andrus Gerontology Center at the University of Southern California in 1972, and forms part of a five-year study funded by the National Science Foundation (#APR 7521178) and administered by Professor Vern Bengtson in the Laboratory for Social Organization. The anthropological component of the investigation, "Ethnicity and Aging," constituted a section of a larger study, "The Social and Cultural Contexts of Aging."

The personnel of the anthropology component varied somewhat over time, as did the objectives of the research. One segment of the study, the library survey, was not brought entirely to fruition though it was worked on diligently by many competent individuals including Professor Jay Abarbanel, Denise Leeper Lawrence, and Thomas Sheehan. Our editorial consultant, Julia Kessler, aided in the preparation of this collection from its incipiency to its completion. Many secretaries and research assistants have worked long and hard in the course of the investigation, Sherrie Wagner first among them.

Work on this project was facilitated by a seminar conducted at the University of Southern California in the spring of 1973 in the Department of Anthropology (then Sociology and Anthropology). Led by Professor Abarbanel, attended by Cuellar, Moore, Myerhoff, Simić, and Vélez, and many anthropology students, it allowed us to develop many of our notions and examine the extant literature on aging together. The university and the department deserve our gratitude for providing the opportunity for exploring our mutual interests in a supportive, open setting. The three major themes which run through these writings—aging as a career, the concern with continuity, the significance of sex differences in aging—are primarily the result of Moore, Myerhoff, and Simić's ongoing discussions.

Andrei Simić
Barbara Myerhoff

Chapter 1

INTRODUCTION:

Aging and the Aged in Cultural Perspective

Andrei Simić

This volume brings together the research of five anthropologists, each of whom considers old age and aging in relation to a particular cultural environment. Each carried out field work among a people with whom he or she was long familiar in both the academic and personal sense. The investigations sought to discover common themes punctuating the lives of informants, similar threads of experience and meaning transcending more superficial cultural and situational differences. In other words, they were concerned not only with variation, but, perhaps more importantly, with the definition of universals as well.

The project, funded by the National Science Foundation through the Andrus Gerontology Center at the University of Southern California, led three of the group to exotic regions of the world. Sally Moore traveled to the slopes of Mt. Kilimanjaro in Tanzania to work among the semi-tribal Chagga; Andrei Simić sojourned in village and urban settings in rapidly modernizing Marxist Yugoslavia, and then returned to the United States to derive comparative materials from among Yugoslav-Americans in Northern California; and Carlos Vélez shared the daily lives of older Mexicans who had uprooted themselves from traditional rural settings in order to follow their adult children into a newly developing slum settlement not far from Mexico City.

AUTHOR'S NOTE: *I am indebted to Barbara Myerhoff, with whom this chapter was developed, and who critiqued it at length many times in the course of its preparation.*

Barbara Myerhoff remained in the United States, focusing on a small community of very old Jewish-Americans from the East European *shtetl* living in cultural isolation in the Southern California beach town of Venice. José Cuellar studied the question of aging among Mexican-Americans in the context of several voluntary associations within the very large and complex Chicano settlement in East Los Angeles.

What is perhaps the most unusual aspect of this research is that, with the exception of Moore, each participant carried out field work among a group to which he or she was personally tied by bonds of ethnicity. The significance of this is manifold, and as Nash and Winthrob (1972) have noted, the self-identity and social role of the investigator are as much a part of the ethnographic description and analysis as are ostensibly detached scientific observations. In this instance, bicultural identities made it possible to assume at the same time the role of an insider with its concomitant insights, sensitivities, privileges of membership, and natural biases; and that of an outsider, a trained anthropologist committed to a position of objectivity. This particular ethnic dimension of the project recalls the words of Dell Hynes (1974: 67):

> Knowledge about people is a resource, like control of oil and of armies: Nations cannot accept permanent inferiority in this regard . . . the proper role of the scientist, and the goal of his efforts, should not be "extractive," but mediative. It should be to help communities be ethnographers of their own situations, to relate their knowledge usefully to general knowledge, not merely to test and document. Such a role could be the safeguard of both the intellectual and ethical purposes of the science itself.

The selection of the particular field settings was thus in no sense random or fortuitous, but the direct result of the personal identities and past professional experience of the investigators. Not only was the element of co-ethnicity a salient factor, but each of us had chosen a culture in which he or she had previously worked as an anthropologist, and the present studies are not the result of a single period of research; rather, they represent the cumulative effort of a number of contacts and an extensive background of ethnographic and linguistic knowledge. At the same time, the cultures considered constitute a fairly broad sample of the contemporary spectrum of worldwide societal types. In this respect, their diversity admirably corresponds to the need to explore aging in vividly contrasting situations.

At one end of the cultural continuum lie the Chagga. While they are in no stereotypic sense "primitives," nevertheless they have only recently emerged from a tribal past, and are just now beginning to enter the main currents of world economic and political life in the context of socialist and nationalist development in Africa. The Chagga belong to that segment of the world's population that approximately a generation ago freed itself from colonial domination. Yet, in spite of the tremendous impetus for modernization and the influence of a more impersonal and bureaucratic form of society, the Chagga have managed to maintain many aspects of their traditional, preindustrial heritage, including a strong emphasis on lineal kinship organization.

Yugoslavia and Mexico lie somewhat further along the road to modernization, though, like the Chagga, both have retained a notably agrarian character in spite of massive urbanization. For example, though Yugoslavia has experienced a recent Marxist revolution with its concomitant stress on social reform and industrial development, it still manifests many remnants of an earlier culture based on patrilineal clans and large extended households (*zadruge*) which at one time made up the basic social and economic units in the society. Both Mexico and Yugoslavia can be characterized as *intermediate societies* in that they lie somewhere near the midway point between the least and the most economically developed nations. However, in Mexico, modernization is occurring within a modified capitalist, free-enterprise system. Here, as in Yugoslavia, strong elements of traditional life persist.

Contrasting markedly with Tanzania, Yugoslavia, and Mexico is the United States, which lies fully at the other end of the spectrum as a totally industrialized and urbanized country lacking a significant rural segment within its population. Nevertheless, even in such a contemporary context, the levels of participation in the fruits of industrial-urban culture vary widely among the various subgroups within the society. The diversity of the American experience is underscored by the lives of Mexican and Jewish Americans in Southern California. Both Cuellar and Myerhoff describe groups that can be characterized as being *in* our society but not totally *part* of it, inasmuch as their beginnings and continued cultural orientations lie in traditions rooted elsewhere. While these older people certainly share many common problems with other elderly Americans, at the same time their experience belies the myth of the melting pot.

The questions addressed by our research can be stated simply enough. What can the experience of older people in Africa, the Balkans, Mexico, and the United States tell us about common problems and challenges generated by the aging process? What is the inevitable in aging, and what manifestations are simply cultural elaborations? In what way can knowledge derived from other societies help us build a more relevant and humane social policy in regard to the aged in our own country? For example, how can we help the aged cope with such obstacles as declining physical strength, shifting relationships with family and kin, and changing sex-roles in later life? What kinds of different solutions to these same vexing problems can we encounter in the cultures we have chosen to study?

Clearly, these questions are commonplace and even obvious, but the answers and methods of determining them are extremely complex. Looking first to the existing anthropological and sociological literature, we found no really adequate treatment of these problems and a paucity of cross-cultural materials dealing specifically with gerontological concerns. Outside anthropology, most of the available research on aging was treated in either a demographic or statistical manner, ignoring its qualitative aspects. The few anthropological studies in this field pointed principally to the fact that aging was a phenomenon that evidenced considerable cross-cultural variability and constituted an area of ethnological research meriting further attention.

Anthropology's late commitment to gerontology provides another instance of the discipline's tendency to be a follower of history rather than its prophet. In 1972, when the contributors to this volume were invited to participate in a multidisciplinary cross-cultural study of aging, none of them had given any significant thought to the subject as a topic of real ethnological interest. Nevertheless, the signs that aging and the aged were becoming objects of broad social concern should have been evident. In this respect, American attitudes had been changing radically for at least several decades. At one time, not too long ago, older people were regarded—and, indeed, viewed themselves—simply as a loosely defined category of persons otherwise integrated into an age-heterogeneous society, and identifying most closely with the interests of their own families. However, of late a new self-perception and stereotyping has emerged competing with older values in response to growing feelings of marginality and alienation on the part of many senior people, who increasingly regard their place in society in terms of their common experience and needs. In other words, the aged have shifted significantly in their orientation, from an image of a *noncorporate category* to that of a *group*. Thus, age has become a principle for corporate organization and the basis for social, economic, and even political demands. In part, this process has been stimulated and encouraged by the emergence and high visibility of so-called "oppressed" ethnic, racial, and sexual minorities. Perhaps the feminist movement is the most analogous, inasmuch as it too has involved the transition from a categorical identity to one of a corporate nature transcending, and in some cases even supplanting, previous familial and heterosexual identities.

It was inevitable that anthropology would eventually take note of such a profound and widespread shift in the orientation of many older Americans, and in so doing, speculate on its significance in light of ethnographic data from other cultures. In all fairness, it would be erroneous to suggest that the aged have somehow been overlooked completely in the accounts of anthropologists; however, rarely have they provided a pivotal focus for the collection of data and the formulation of theory (cf. Clark, 1967).

Nevertheless, there have been notable exceptions to this generalization. For example, intergenerational relationships and seniority provide dominant themes in the classic and moving account of peasant life in traditional Ireland by Conrad Arensberg (1937), and in Hart and Pilling's (1960) description of the gerontocratic Tiwi of Melville and Bathurst Islands off the north coast of Australia. Similarly, the rich literature on African age-graded societies should be included in anthropology's contribution to the field of gerontology. Nevertheless, most ethnographic sources including material on the aged are not the deliberate product of a specific problem orientation concerned directly with the question of aging, but rather the incorporation of data of gerontological interest has been the inevitable by-product of anthropology's so-called "holistic" approach, by which cultures are perceived in their totality as functionally integrated systems.

The earliest attempt to systematize and compare existing ethnographic information about the aged was that of Leo Simmons, who in 1945 published *The Role of the Aged in Primitive Society*. In this work, he investigated the range of adjustments to old age in different physical and cultural environments and sought to discover any observable universal trends. Drawing on the resources of the Yale Human Relations Area Files, he analyzed 109 cultural traits relating to the position of the aged in 71 ostensibly primitive societies. His analysis focused on formal social status as related to cultural and economic variables. For example, he demonstrated that older women more frequently retained property rights than men in hunting-and-gathering societies, while the reverse appeared to be true in agrarian communities. However, a major drawback to this approach relates to the inherent difficulties in the use of secondary sources whose comparability cannot be established, and whose original intent did not relate to the resolution of these particular issues. In spite of such limitations, a number of provocative ideas did emerge from this and a later study of his which appeared in 1960. In the latter work, Simmons proposed a set of criteria by which aging could be compared cross-culturally. He suggested that for most people success in aging related to their ability to make a place for themselves in society where they could grow older and achieve fulfillment through strategic participation as long as possible. Simmons concluded that there were five wishes shared by older people everywhere: to live as long as possible; to hoard waning energies; to keep on sharing in the affairs of life; to safeguard seniority rights; and to have an easy and honorable release from life.

Simmons' generalizations about aging reassert the essential and most basic task of anthropology—the discovery of universals underlying the complex elaborations specific to given cultures. At the same time, the very broadness of his assumptions will allow for a wide range of variation in their realization, symbolization, and interpretation from society to society. Nevertheless, the ultimate identification of such phenomena in one context will help our recognition of them in another, and to understand exotic experience is to shed light on our own. The work in this book shares Simmons' goal of discovering basic general principles in the aging process, but at the same time it also strives to elucidate the manner in which such universals are generated and realized in dynamic terms. This has been attempted through the collection of field data oriented primarily to the resolution of this specific problem.

A recent anthology edited by Cowgill and Holmes (1972) suggested in both a positive and a negative sense the direction future ethnological research might profitably take. In their collection of essays, such diverse peoples as the Bantu and the Norwegians provide an inventory of hypothetical universals and variables related to aging. For example, the editors propose that the following characteristics are to be found everywhere:

(1) The aged are a minority.
(2) Older females outnumber their male peers.
(3) Widows form a high proportion of older populations.
(4) Every society classifies some people as old, and prescribes appropriate behavior toward them on the part of others.
(5) With old age, there is a shift from participation in economic production to sedentary, advisory, or supervisory roles.
(6) Some older people continue to assume positions of leadership.
(7) The relationship between older people and adult children is characterized by mores prescribing some form of mutual responsibility.
(8) All societies value life and seek to prolong it, even in old age.

At the same time, Cowgill and Holmes emphatically underscore the malleability of the aging process, proposing a list of twenty-two cross-cultural variables. Summarized succinctly, they hypothesize a negative correlation between participation, status, and satisfaction in aging on the one hand, and modernization on the other. In contrast, they also observe that the numbers of aged persons, and their chances for longevity, are positively correlated with the level of modernization. While these contentions certainly point the way to the formulation of problems testable in the field, they nevertheless focus on intangibles and static structures, omitting from consideration the nature of the social processes that underlie and generate them.

Moreover, it should be pointed out that the entire concept of modernization is an elusive one that the editors themselves find difficult to define. For some it is measured by per capita income, for others by level of education, the degree of urbanization, or the extent of industrialization. In spite of these admitted difficulties in defining the exact characteristics that designate a society as "modern," the conclusions of Cowgill and Holmes bear a strong Rousseauian stamp perceiving "modernization" as a more or less homogeneous and negative phenomenon. Significantly, some two decades before the appearance of this anthology, Oscar Lewis (1952), on the basis of a study of rural migrants in Mexico City, had concluded that urbanization could not be defined as a single negative process, but rather as one that differed according to the specific historical and cultural context in which it occurred. Similarly, our chapters here will demonstrate that aging is not necessarily a less satisfying experience in so-called "developed" societies, but simply one posing different obstacles and problems to be overcome. Moreover, it will also be shown that elements of traditional life can indeed thrive in an urban-industrial environment, and meaningfully affect and structure the lives of older persons.

The pessimistic view of modernization also permeates much of the literature dealing with aging in our own society, which, in spite of its obvious heterogeneity, is treated generally as if it were uniform. The dominant theme is that of *alienation*, and what emerges as a common thread is the perception of aging as a personal and social "problem." For instance, Clark (1967) suggests that one of the principal reasons for anthropologists' neglect of the field of aging is that they have the same aversion to the subject that characterizes American society at large. It would appear that the ramifications of such attitudes for gerontological research have been either neglect or negative stereotyping. Not only have the models of aging been mostly pejorative; a number of them have also made claims of universality, though evidence for such an assumption is totally lacking.

For example, Cumming and Henry (1971), in their influential study of a largely white middle-class sample from Kansas City, assert that there exists a direct relationship between aging and decreased interaction within a social system, a theory they label *disengagement*. Similarly, in another American study, Anderson (1972) proposes the concept of *deculturation*, a process by which older persons gradually assume a "cultureless" role, one in which they somehow exist and function outside the major body of tradition that constitutes the daily patterns of younger persons. These ideas are essentially two sides of the same coin of personal alienation—supposed to occur almost inevitably in one's later years as the inescapable result of the very act of growing older. In the former case, Cumming and Henry are addressing themselves essentially to structural and interactional characteristics, while in the latter Anderson is concerned with ideas and values as well. While there appears to be no real argument with the fact that these manifestations reflect a segment of contemporary life in the United States and the way some older Americans undoubtedly evaluate their position, the attributing of universality even within our own society must be challenged. In this respect, the tendency to project our own experience on others is rooted in ethnocentrism, and even anthropologists are frequently susceptible to perceiving their own cultural environment, uncritically, very much as a "natural" or "god-given" system.

Certainly it would be erroneous to suggest that all gerontological research has cast a foreboding and gloomy shadow on the aging experience, since there is ample ethnographic evidence of the variability of behavior and attitudes in respect to growing old. At the same time, this variability does not negate the discovery of universals, but simply underscores the fact that they cannot be discerned from the study of a single culture. The value of such theories as those of disengagement and deculturation is that they can provide a fruitful comparative basis for the investigation of aging in the context of a spectrum of possible behavior.

Another correlate of the perception of aging as a deprived and unhappy experience in American society is the supposition that the aged once enjoyed greater security and contentment as part of large extended families at an earlier period in our history, or do so now in more "backward" tribal and peasant societies. This stereotype is one of growing old with respect, power, and affection, that of a later life essentially devoid of intergenerational conflict, alienation, and loneliness. The fault with this model lies primarily in its partial truth. Indeed, there is considerable evidence that in many primitive and agrarian cultures, older people remain deeply and actively embedded in ongoing sets of interpersonal relationships, usually of a kinship nature, in which they frequently occupy pivotal and significant positions. However, the belief in universal satisfaction in harmonious intergenerational relationships under such conditions is to an extent illusory. Among the first to observe this was LeVine (1965), who described the intergenerational tensions typifying extended family structures in Africa. While the author recognized many beneficial functions fulfilled by such extended family relations in African and Asian societies, he also pointed to a growing body of ethnographic and anecdotal evidence that in such cultures there existed evident manifestations of fear, tension, and conflict within cohesive kinship groupings. Similarly, the essays in this present volume demonstrate that one of the salient aspects of group engagement and dynamics consists of dissatisfaction (or potential dissatisfaction), veiled competitive hostility, and/or open conflict.

If one were called upon to select a single theme underlying past gerontological literature, it might be characterized as an attempt to discover and evaluate levels of contentment. This in itself is a reflection of a kind of ethnocentrism in that it seems very much part of the American middle-class mentality to suppose that any state other than that of contentment is somehow untenable. Of course, the effort to identify the presence of happiness is empirically and methodologically difficult, perhaps impossible. This problem is part of a broader one related to the perception and demonstration of the existence of certain emotional states as concomitant with specific observable external manifestations. For example, in tribal societies where seniority and lineality constitute basic principles of social organization, we have tended to idealize the positions occupied by older persons as symbolic of a lasting state of satisfaction derived from the culmination of a lifetime of valued participation and accumulated power. In contrast, one also might interpret with equal credibility the status of such elders in terms of virtually empty ritual and symbolic honors devoid of genuine respect and feelings of real affection on the part of others. To evaluate old age in terms of contentment, particularly given the almost ubiquitous expressions of discontent among people of all ages, offers little promise of real enlightenment.

While any attempt to measure levels of contentment from culture to culture seems patently unproductive, it has been axiomatic in anthropology that the viability of cultures in part relates to their ability to satisfy the physical and psychological needs of their members. However, this, too, raises as many questions as it proposes to solve. For instance, in no known society do all its members have equal access to valued possessions, statuses, and modes of behavior, that is, everywhere "good" and desired (even needed) things are distributed differentially. This suggests that cultures may also differ in terms of the degree to which nonmaterial values are attainable by their individual members. Examining this idea in the context of American culture, Margaret Clark (1972) describes a paradoxical and maladaptive framework in regard to the aged. On the basis of a study conducted in San Francisco, she concludes that morality in our society is intimately bound to the value of self-reliance, and therefore there can rarely be any prolonged dependence between generations. Thus, given the growing dependency of later life, the cultural problem posed is insoluble according to the author. What she ignores is the fact that most cultures continue to operate in the presence of numerous paradoxes, and that these contradictions are often resolved as part of the process that continually generates new values within any society. For example, in the American case, it is entirely justified to presume that many older people have been able to achieve the illusion of independence by turning in their dependency to such relatively new, nonkinship institutions as pension funds, voluntary associations, public and private social services, and the like.

This volume attempts to escape from the trap of dealing with such questions as the presence of absence of contentment and the relative viability of one culture vis-à-vis another. Rather, the authors have strived to apply criteria to the collection and analysis of their data sufficiently concrete and observable as to be amenable to valid cross-cultural comparison. This work is the result of over three years of study and research in an attempt to reconcile diverse cultural solutions to the problem of growing old in terms of some common underlying structure typifying the process everywhere. The commitment of anthropology to the discovery of such deep structures cannot be reiterated enough, and were there not such universal themes, any attempt to interpret and synthesize the life experiences of peoples so different as the Chagga and Eastern European Jewish immigrants in California would be a futile exercise in the collection of exotica.

The anthropological literature was not explicitly very informative as to what the universal themes in aging might be. Rather, we were compelled to look between the lines for hints, commonplace observations, and intuitive insights. A major problem was the fact that aging, though a definable temporal and biological phenomenon, in its sociocultural aspects subsumes a multiplicity of attitudes, values, and modes of behavior. Moreover, old age per se, though recognized everywhere, is in reality simply part of a relatively undifferentiated biological continuum through time, whose culturally determined segments are defined by different kinds of markers in every society. Some of these markers are chronological, some existential, and still others dependent on external events such as the birth of a grandchild, the death of one's parents, or the receipt of an inheritance. In the same way, the comparative assessment of the relative position of older people from society to society poses an equally perplexing problem. Certainly, the mere enumeration and contrasting of formal statuses occupied by the aged, and of ritual signs of respect paid them, are not sufficiently adequate measures and may in fact be utterly misleading. For example, power takes many forms, some economic, others political, symbolic, or ritual. It may be overt or covert; intentional or fortuitous; formal or informal; permanent, intermittent, or transitory; manipulative or contractual. Power may stem from the structural attributes of the society or may be the unpredictable product of affect or good fortune. Frequently it exists invisible to the outside observer in totally unfamiliar constellations.

The question of power provides but one instance of the subtleties inherent in cross-cultural comparison. Moreover, here, too, are evident the difficulties of defining and describing such an elusive and abstract quality as power while remaining entirely within the scope of formal structures and expressed values. A dependence on such normative models has rendered much of anthropological research inordinately static, since it has resulted in a stress of those aspects of sociocultural life that are permanent rather than on the ever-changing configurations of beliefs and activities that also form a segment of our common experience. While there has been no failure on the part of anthropologists to recognize change as an intrinsic attribute of culture, they have found it difficult to deal with, and have preferred to construct synchronic models in the so-called "ethnographic present." In other cases where social change has provided the principal focus of analysis, more often than not change has been conceptualized as a shift from one integrated set of forms to another, much as the movie camera creates the illusion of movement by the rapid projection of a sequence of motionless frames. For instance, studies of the life cycle and aging have often assumed the same kind of instantaneous shift from one stereotypic life phase to another, each with its own particular syndrome of enduring characteristics (cf. Goody, 1971). This criticism is not intended to deny the utility of such an approach, since cultures certainly display many relatively lasting aspects, and continuity constitutes one of their most basic characteristics. On the other hand, in focusing attention on what survives the passage of time rather than the way forms are generated, transformed, and integrated, we tend to obscure another equally important dimension of social life, that of *process* (cf. Barth, 1966). Static models, in spite of their many positive attributes for cross-cultural comparison and even some kinds of prediction, give little hint as to the way individuals actually manage their lives in the face of varying levels of unpredictability that characterize every interactional situation. In respect to the study of gerontology, old age and aging certainly exist in a matrix of cultural forms, but aging and the experience of being old also have an essentially processual facet that demands analysis on its own terms.

Anthropology of late has increasingly treated its subject matter in dynamic rather than static terms. This approach does not negate previous analytic viewpoints, but simply constitutes an expansion of the vision of social and cultural life. This shift has entailed the stating of new problems and the asking of different kinds of questions, one of the most important of which has been the nature of the fit between culture and behavior—that is, the relationship between values and real life. To what degree can any cultural model predict the actions of society's members, or the exigencies which may arise in the almost infinite variety of social encounters? Clearly, any explanation of the relationship of process to values and structure involves a somewhat circular but necessary reciprocity. On the one hand, we construct abstractions of cultures from the behavior of individuals, most often from the statements of informants, but also from a variety of empirical evidence, and on the other, we take these models to be indicators of what we may anticipate modal behavior to be. Once such a model emerges we tend to see it as static and predictive. Thus, cultures assume the aspect of a replicative mechanism somewhat analogous to the manner in which genetic codes reproduce cells in certain set forms. What is evident is that the analogy is either a false one, or one so differing in degree as to lack utility. A more reasonable approach, and the one taken by these present studies of aging, is that culture is one of a number of resources and constraints present in the human environment, one that channels behavior but does not determine it, a force to be negotiated and manipulated rather than to be simply accepted at face value. Stated in another way, these essays depict people acting in relation to their cultures, but not necessarily in accord with them. Thus, the individual is perceived not simply as a passive subject, but also as an active and somewhat unpredictable ingredient in the interplay between relatively static mores and ever-changing situations.

Not only may questions be raised about the all-pervasiveness and stability of culture, but also regarding its internal consistency. The classic functionalist concept has been that culture constitutes a highly integrated and balanced system whose various interlocking parts respond with sensitivity to changes that may occur in any one of them. This viewpoint was epitomized by Ruth Benedict (1934) in her famous *Patterns of Culture*. She proposed that integration occurs in each culture within the matrix of a single transcendental theme that permeates the entire society and its constituent institutions. Thus, for Benedict, each separate culture exhibits a distinct orientation consisting of a unified set of values molding life in a single pattern. Despite the ubiquity of such ideas in ethnologic thought, they have nevertheless been the subject of considerable skepticism. In fact, at least a generation before the rise of functionalist theory in anthropology, German sociologist Max Weber had characterized society as an equilibrium between opposing forces rejecting any attempt to interpret social structures as wholes. For him, sociology was the study of the understandable behavior of individuals in society (cf. Bendix, 1962: 260-267). More recently, anthropologist Victor Turner has argued the issue in the following way (1967: 196):

> From the point of view of social dynamics a social system is not a harmonious configuration governed by mutually compatible and logically interrelated processes. It is rather a set of loosely integrated processes, with some patterned aspects, some persistencies of form, but controlled by discrepant principles of action expressed in rules of custom that are often situationally incompatible with each other.

In a not dissimilar view from that of Turner, Hammel (1964) has applied the concept of *entropy*, drawing an analogy from the physical sciences. He identifies culture as a series of messages corresponding to statuses in a social system. Certain ways of speaking, appearing, and behaving are thus regarded appropriate to, and consistent with, given positions in a society, and as such tend to structure and render predictable specific relationships. However, the congruence of culture and society is never absolute, and, in fact, if energy is not invested in the system, the relationship will become increasingly diffuse and disparate over time. Thus, as the result of the normal sociocultural process, there develops an inevitable widening of the gulf between the social structure and the ideas that govern it unless corrective action is taken.

Nevertheless, in spite of all efforts to maintain reasonable levels of correspondence, all cultures will be characterized by varying degrees of inconsistency, redundancy, and ambivalence. Hammel further suggests that in every cultural system there exists a capacity for defining certain relationships rapidly and precisely, and others not at all. On the one hand, there is a psychological strain for consistency, for the definition of relationships, for stability of position, and on the other, a reasonable degree of entropy assures a necessary manipulability of the social process. Hammel concludes that in general the forces of consistency must outweigh those of uncertainty and ambiguity; were this not so, society could not function at all.

The human input in both the creation and manipulation of culture is perhaps most dramatically described by Geertz in metaphorical form (1973: 5):

> Believing, with Max Weber, that man is an animal suspended in webs of significance he himself has spun, I take culture to be those webs, and the analysis of it to be therefore not an experimental science in search of law but an interpretive one in search of meaning.

It is in just this way that the work in this book sees people making and negotiating meaning in constantly changing circumstances, and using cultural materials as the fabric from which to spin new "webs."

NOTE ON METHODS

The life history method used here has a long tradition in anthropology. It is an especially useful, even essential tool in studying problems of culture and personality, role analysis, deviance, socialization, values, and social-cultural change. It is one of our few regular means of attending to questions of chance and accident in studying human behavior and culture, as Langness (1965) points out in his excellent summary and critique of the method.

It should be added that this approach is particularly pertinent in the study of aging for several reasons. First, the extended personal history of the elderly makes a historical approach especially apt, for the elderly are often engaged actively in interpreting and reviewing their lives. Their concern with integrating the past and with relating external public events to personal history must be reflected in ours. Second, as Moore points out, when aging is regarded as a cumulative process we can only understand this movement by attending to the history of an individual's life. Third, Simić's view of elders as winners and losers, focusing as it does on idiosyncratic successes and failures at aging, and on the role of good and bad luck, also requires a life historical approach. Finally, when aging takes place in life-term arenas (Moore), where social discontinuity is marked, cultural norms concerning aging and the aged are shifting and ambiguous. Norms are fluid, and maximum opportunities exist for individual innovation, exploitation, and experimentation. Resourcefulness of individuals may be maximally exercised and often becomes very influential in accounting for differential success in aging as a career. This expertise in growing old is idiosyncratic and unpredictable on the basis of cultural knowledge. Only a life-historical approach sensitizes us to the ways in which the elderly experiment with cultural materials to manage their circumstances. Vélez's concept of historical versus ahistorical families is also clearly derived by the use of this approach. Myerhoff's description of dramas of honor depends too on the historical perspective, since these are opportunities for individuals to stage and enact selections from their past history.

Thus, some of the most important themes and concepts explored throughout this volume—*aging as a career, winning and losing, limited-term arenas, historical versus ahistorical families*, and, of course, the most general question of *continuity*—are all dependent on the use of the life-historical approach.

CHAPTER 2

OLD AGE IN A LIFE-TERM SOCIAL ARENA:

Some Chagga of Kilimanjaro in 1974

Sally Falk Moore

It is early in the morning. Consider the pensive, wrinkled old man who cuts banana stems for the goats in his garden on Kilimanjaro. What might this 75-year-old Chagga tell us about the great changes he has seen in his lifetime? And the turbanned, barefoot market woman in her sixties, walking erect under a heavy headload, smiling and chatting with her companions? What does she say? What is her life like? Just what, in fact, is it like to grow old in Africa today? To ask these questions is not only to ask something about Africans, but about anyone living through rapid cultural change.

Persons living in a swiftly altering world find that their social roles change as they perform them. In some respects, it is a bad dream: What seems to be one thing, turns out to be another as soon as it is attained. Each stage of growing older is a matter of arriving at something quite different from what it was for the age group just before. Being old seems to these Chagga not at all what they thought it would be like when they were looking at older people in their youth. Clearly, some of that change is to advantage, yet some has come to seem a total cheat. The two old people described here remember themselves as having been slavishly obedient and deferential to their elders in youth, ever comforted by the thought that their turn to dominate would arrive with age. They express keen disappointment that modernization has now deprived them of the privileges and regard they expected.

In such matters, there are of course serious problems of sorting the culturally unique from the psychologically universal. Perhaps the perspective of a child on the powers of his elders is in all societies seriously distorted, and in adulthood no one ever sees himself as actually having become as powerful as the giant adults he once looked to when he was little. There is always some sense that the real change has been in the social scene and not in oneself. Yet in how many societies does one hear it said that "young people are not respectful and obedient as they used to be"? If there have indeed been enormous changes in the society that can be seen and measured, such may appear to confirm the personal perspective. But in hearing the story of a life, or in seeing an old man or an old woman in the course of their mundane activities in a rapidly changing setting, we may justly ask in what framework their experiences should be analyzed. What happened in the past is bound to be a subjective account, a view of the past strongly colored by the present. What is happening at the moment is more accessible to field observation, and only part remains hidden from view, yet its full meaning to those experiencing it must take account of the past as well as the moment. Given what one knows historically of what has happened in Chagga society from public documents and records, to what extent can the perspective of the old people of this generation who have lived through those events, enlarge one's understanding of the social process through which their cohort has passed?

The importance of time is evident when any attempt is made to analyze the situation of old people. The old themselves epitomize its passage. A description of the structure of their society now, at this moment, does not suffice to describe their experience or place. Thus, only a framework of analysis that focuses on things that happen *over time* can give a full sense of the meaning of their present.

Two such time-based themes are particularly useful: one, continuities and discontinuities of role and setting over the course of life; the other, the operation of cumulative processes—i.e., accumulating power, property, social relationships, reputation and the like. Cultural ideas and norms relating to lifelong continuity are often fairly self-evident. A Chagga woman whose children are grown may ask for a grandchild to keep, in order that "a woman never be without a child." There is a culturally provided continuity in this. A Chagga man who has been a farmer all his adult life, and who dies, still cultivating his garden, has no significant occupational discontinuity to bear. He does not face, in that respect, the kind of break that a modern African clerical worker experiences on retirement, or that his Chagga grandfather experienced when he was moved out of the warrior age-grade and into the grade of elders. Occupational discontinuities are not the exclusive invention of industrial societies, and can take place in many very different settings.

There are, of course, many other kinds of discontinuities over the course of life, some of them the products of cultural and social change—for example, among the Chagga, the introduction of cash crops where they did not exist before, or the introduction of Christianity which produced major before-after cleavages in some life-histories. The discontinuities brought about by such changes are quite different in kind from the discontinuities mentioned earlier, because these modern innovations are breaks with the past experienced by one cohort only, and are not traditional parts of the life cycle. But they are discontinuities nonetheless.

The second theme, that of cumulative processes, is more than a matter of continuity. It raises questions about movement in a direction. Does a man's property increase, and then increase again, as seniority increases? Does his authority over his juniors increase with age? Does he accumulate experience that is socially valued and become wiser or more skilled and sought after over time?

Both continuities/discontinuities, and cumulation of various kinds may take place in an individual's *social relations,* and this may well be the most important element of all, both analytically and experientially. A Chagga man who now lives in the same village he has lived in all his life, with the same kin and neighbors, may have experienced great *cultural* change in his life, and yet have had as much *social* continuity as is possible in a life. A Chagga woman who has left her natal home in the village to live with her husband a mile away on the other side of the same village has experienced some minor social discontinuity, but it is certainly very slight compared with the experience of her son, who has emigrated to the city to become a laborer and to live among strangers from other tribes.

Social relationships may be accumulated over time, and at one point or another they may be lost and broken off. They may become more intense— i.e., the cumulation over time may be in the intensifying and strengthening of the relationship in terms of emotional investment, common experience, long-term exchanges. Thus, cumulation may be of numbers of relationships, or of kind and quality of relationship, or both. But social ties may be destroyed as well as built. They may be lost through disputes, death, emigration, and the like. In each society the continuities/discontinuities and the cumulations/losses are different in content, in significant events, in style.

Another way of looking at the matter of social relations is to say that the arenas of social activity available to people differ from one society to another. The social arenas in which people can play out their lives, the circles of persons among whom their views, their actions, their reputations matter, vary very much from one society to another. In no society can the personnel in the social arena be precisely the same throughout life. The fact of death and the succession of generations makes that impossible. But there are societies in which the sequence of generations is the principal factor that alters the personnel of the social arena, and all other factors are subordinate and lesser interferences.

Such is the structure of some very stable, small-scale traditional villages. In such a village, most people enter by being born, and leave by dying. A very few individuals move in or out in the middle of life. Such a *life-term arena* has quite a different character from more temporary ones. A job in a modern city may provide a social scene to which a person belongs for the time of employment, entering it as an adult, leaving on retirement. The extent to which there is social continuity over a life, and the opportunities for cumulation in relationships are very closely connected with an individual's membership in limited-term or life-term social arenas.

Where the factors that determine entrance to or exit from a social arena are major emotional or physiological life crises, the arena itself is bound to be quite different from one which does not involve these. It follows that even the character of a voluntary association of "senior citizens" in an industrial society is bound to be deeply affected, if the principal mode of exit is death. Hence, not only are the questions of temporariness or durability of a social arena important, but the way in and the way out are also diagnostic features.

Not all "traditional" societies have fully stable life-term social arenas. There are African societies in which a village is a temporary assemblage of persons which reorganizes periodically. In such a society, it is normal for individuals to live in a number of villages in the course of a lifetime. Birth and death are not the only ways—nor even necessarily the major ways—in which people enter and leave such villages. But among the Chagga of Kilimanjaro, where land is permanently renewed by manuring, and hence can be permanently under cultivation by generation after generation of the same family, there is a remarkable amount of local residential stability in the older areas of settlement. Today, even the educated men who go to work in the cities for years at a time usually leave their wives and children behind on the mountain. That is their permanent home, to which they will return.

The local subvillage is the social arena to which they look. They entered it when they were born. They expect to die there. Meanwhile, their farmer brothers live out their whole lives in the subvillage. There has been some movement and some emigration because of population pressure and land shortages, but nevertheless, those who have plots of land in the old areas of settlement are usually the descendants of those who were there before. Consequently even for those who go to the city to work for a while, there is a strong sense that the subvillage is the principal life-term social arena of those who were born there.

News of a death travels fast on the mountain. And if there is anything unusual in the circumstances, it becomes a subject of much discussion and speculation. The death of a man named Marunda will serve here to introduce the particular customary ways in which the lives of Chagga men are tied to culturally defined, life-term social arenas with important implications for the aging.

Then, having established the general ambience that surrounds seniority and localized lineage, a description will follow of the life of Siara, a man in his mid-seventies, who has experienced the whole range of rapid alterations that have taken place in his society since 1900. Yet, having lived all his years on the same plot of land, surrounded by the same families of kinsmen and neighbors, he has, despite profound cultural changes introduced by missionaries and colonial governments, experienced a reassuring amount of social continuity. Far from seeming to be full of abrupt innovations, his life story is so focused on social relations with kin that the background of modernization seems quite secondary, and his life seems one of great continuity. His particular history is an instructive indication of the specific kinds of events and cumulative processes that give old age its character among the Chagga today.

Then, because the lives of Chagga women are quite different from the lives of Chagga men, we will describe a visit with a woman in her sixties on the occasion of her presentation with a new grandchild, and the general routine of her current life. Taken together, these two portraits should dispel once and for all any sentimental notion that an old age surrounded by kin and lifelong neighbors is by definition a blissful one. It is certainly not lonely, but it has its painful side, as well as its satisfactions. But even more than that, the two portraits should suggest some of the characteristics of life-term social arenas, by implication suggesting foci for exploring the more temporary ones that are familiar in our own society.

THE MORAL OF THE DEATH OF MARUNDA

A few years ago I heard that nearby, in a mud-walled, tin-roofed cabin in the subvillage of R _____, a man had died. He had been ill only a few days. I was told that he had suffered terribly with fever, and when death came his mouth was hugely swollen and his lips were cracked and bleeding. He was not very old by American standards—perhaps in his fifties. It was the talk of the neighborhood. In the beer shop, a structure with a tin roof, and some benches, but no walls, two old men told me about it. They sipped banana beer from their calabashes as they did every afternoon, and talked about the reasons Marunda had died. They said it was because, many years earlier, he had eaten the paternal portion of slaughter meat, the *kidari,* of his father. His father had cursed him and had subsequently died without forgiving him.

Such a curse can be withdrawn if proper amends are made. A son may beg forgiveness in a variety of ways. He may send a goat to his father with a leaf of *dracaena* around its neck. In Kichagga, the language of the people of Kilimanjaro, dracaena is called *sale.* It is ubiquitous in Chagga land because it is used as a boundary plant. Its meaning, however, is more than utilitarian.

Sale was traditionally planted in the place in the banana garden where the skulls and bones of the ancestors were kept. Each new burial was marked by the planting of a new sale broken off from the one planted at the time of a previous death. Thus, the generations of plants reproduced the generations of men. The leaf can be used to mean, "Do not enter without permission." It may be placed at the entrance of a hut at the time of a childbirth or of circumcision. As a boundary marker, it plainly has the same significance. Hallowed by its connection with the ancestors, it is made effective by their spirits, which may be angered by a violation of boundaries they have made, or any disruption that displeases them within the patrilineage of their descendants. The law of the father should not be broken. Contrition may be shown by sending him a goat and sale. The old men with the calabashes of beer say that these days respect is broken all the time. Things are not as they used to be.

Marunda could have sent a goat with a leaf of sale to his father, but he did not do it soon enough. A curse can be undone by the living, but once the father was dead, the evil remains. By not begging forgiveness soon enough, Marunda had lost his chance. Nothing happened to him right away. His death with swollen lips came many years later. It was the manner of his death that made plain that his father's curse had killed him. It was a warning to others. No son should presume to take his father's portion of meat, ever.

The reasons why a Chagga son cannot eat the slaughter share that is rightfully his father's, and the reasons why a father's curse can kill are imbedded in Chagga traditional ideology, a set of ideas handed down from the past. But there are many new ideas, too. The Chagga are a modern African people involved in a cash economy through the sale of coffee, many of them literate, some in two or three languages–Kichagga, Swahili, and English. Even the least-educated Chagga farmer has heard the voices of the outside world talking to him out of the transistor radio of a neighbor, or at the bar. More often, those voices talk to him from the pulpit of the church and from the platform of the ward political meeting. Buses go by him on the road, and most have ridden on such buses at some time in their lives. They have all heard of America. Americans, they know, go to the moon. But the government radio also tells them that there is poverty in America, the richest country in the world. There are speeches to be heard about the socialist ways at meetings, and on the radio. Socialism, they are hearing, will one day end poverty.

These are fingers reaching into an exclusively Chagga world. Kilimanjaro is a Chagga mountain. They have never let anyone from any other tribe own land in their villages. The foreign settlers took some lands and so did missions, but the Chagga were more successful in resisting other Africans. There are today about 400,000 Chagga. In the more lush parts of the mountain, they live in a situation of urban density, 950 or more per square mile. Their houses are hidden in the middle of banana gardens whose boundaries are marked with living fences of green sale plants. The houses are of three kinds: some of grass in beehive or haystack shape, the oldest traditional variety; some greater number, rectangular cabins of wattle and daub, with tin roofs. The third kind is still newer, and only the salaried can afford it, a cement-floored cinder-block, *hausi ya bloki.* Outhouses are hidden in the gardens and these, too, vary in elegance, from a simple pit with boards over it surrounded by a screen of dried leaves, to modern cement-floored structures, with a hole in the floor. There is no running water or electricity in the houses, but in the last ten years, the government has piped water from the forest streams to public taps in each subvillage. Before that, the Chagga built irrigation ditches, which still run from the mountain streams in a tangle of narrow channels between the garden plots.

In the gardens, surrounding each house, under the bananas and the coffee bushes, the women grow beans, cassava, and other vegetables. Many families also grow maize, and beans and millet on auxiliary plots down at the foot of the mountain, quite far from where they live. The bananas, beans, and cassava are to eat; coffee is to sell. Though some few men have salaried jobs, coffee remains most families' only reliable source of cash. And the coffee money belongs to the men.

In fact, the land itself traditionally belongs to the men. Their wives and children live on it with them, but the children, the bananas, and the coffee are all the men's. The vegetables, beans, and other products cultivated in the ground belong to the women. These, together with the bananas, are the principal foods on which Chagga farm families subsist. Each household is also likely to have a goat or two, and perhaps a tiny silky-haired sheep, to slaughter and eat on a day of feasting, or in the event that someone falls ill. When there is cash available, especially during coffee harvest time, meat may also be bought at the butcher shop.

In the old days, days that older people remember well, most families also had a cow or sometimes even two or three, for milk and calves. But now fodder is more and more difficult to obtain as the land is full of people, and there are few open spaces between the gardens. There is a shortage of land, especially for growing things to eat, since the coffee has taken up much space. In most places, a woman must several times a week go far down the mountain to the steppe to cut grass, and must walk the long distance up the mountain with a heavy load on her head to keep the hungry cattle fed. It is enough to do the gardening in the banana grove (*kihamba*), and to cultivate the extra patch of land on the steppe (*shamba*) and to look after the children and fetch water and firewood to cook with, which must be done every day. A cow is too much for many women to manage; yet there are still a number who have them. The men tend the bananas and coffee, the feeding of goats. They do some of the heavy work on the shambas and build the houses. The rest of the gardening and animal tending, all the domestic work, is largely left to the women.

Of a hundred households I surveyed in 1969 in one subvillage, only eight can be counted as having no animals at all (for five of these there was no information obtainable). Of the eighty-seven households that had beasts of some kind, none had more than four head of cattle or eight goats. The total number of beasts in these eighty-seven households in 1969 was as follows:

146   cattle

239   goats

25   sheep

5   households with chickens

The animals fattened at home are the only truly suitable ones for the payment of bridewealth and for lineage slaughtering and feasting.

Despite the fact that the Chagga have taken up a new and modern life in many respects, as is evident, they continue to observe many of their traditional customs in relation to slaughtering. The local explanation of Marunda's death makes it abundantly evident that it remains an activity heavy with meanings that go far beyond the gustatory. Slaughtering is a major ritual symbol of the minimal local patrilineal group. At that lowest level of organization, lineage is of daily importance in Chagga lives. In the areas of old settlement, brothers and male cousins and their paternal uncles and grandfathers all live on contiguous plots of land. One kinsman's banana-coffee garden lies right next to that of another. Their wives come from other patrilines, frequently from the same subvillage. Rights to land are handed from generation to generation in the patriline. Not only one's life, but one's livelihood comes from patrilineal kin. When men gather together a few times a year to slaughter an animal, they are ritually celebrating their relationship as patri-kinsmen, and they remember the immediate ancestors from whom they are descended. Only males attend. The feast is held at the invitation of the owner of the animal (or animals) to be killed. Whether the descendants of a grandfather are assembled, or the larger number of descendants of some great grandfather or other depends upon how much meat is available. These days, fewer people have cattle than formerly. The more usual sacrificial animal today is a sheep or a goat, and the usual slaughtering feast involves the sons and grandsons of one man or two. There are usually many more men who bear the lineage or patri-clan name in the same village than ever meet for a slaughtering feast. They may assemble in a large group for a beer drink, but slaughtering is usually confined to a small sub-branch of closely related men.

No beast is ever killed and butchered by its owner, possibly for fear its spirit might recognize him, since it was raised in his house, possibly because the butchering must be done with absolute fairness in a way that does not favor the host, or serious bad feelings may result. Instead of killing and cutting up his animals himself, each man has a slaughtering partner in the lineage, usually a brother or a cousin, with whom he exchanges this service. In the old days, before the animal was killed it was dedicated to a particular spirit ancestor. Each man present put a bit of spittle between its horns while it was still alive, but I am told this is no longer done. Immediately after an animal is killed, an artery in its throat is cut to obtain blood before its body turns cold. The blood is collected in a bowl, as is blood taken from the lungs and heart when the beast is butchered. Some of this blood is reserved for the owner, but most of it is eventually consumed by the assembled kinsmen at the slaughtering place itself. They share in drinking the blood and in some special portions of meat which are cooked on the spot.

After being killed and bled, the animal is skinned and the internal organs are removed. Every part of the beast is the particular right of a particular kinsman, or his wife, mother, sister, or daughter. Each man eventually takes a large share of meat home to his household and distributes it to the women and to friends and neighbors as he sees fit. The butchered cuts are allocated in a traditional manner which has to be adhered to, or misfortune will follow— namely, the fate of Marunda of the swollen lips. The *kidari* is given to the eldest man of the lineage branch. It is considered the most important portion and consists of the breast-bone and the surrounding meat from the throat to the navel. The second most important share is the *ngari* and consists of the middle ribs and the hump. It goes to the next senior man, and so on. Everyone is given a small part of the heart, lungs, liver, and intestines along with his large slaughtering share. Great care is taken to give each man his proper cut and no more or less than his proper share of those other portions of the animal that are divided into small pieces and distributed to everyone present. Everyone is vigilant about getting his due.

The cut which must be eaten at the slaughtering place is called the *kiuno*, the loin, and this is done by seniority, eldest first. Thus, from the first slaughtering feast a man watches as a small boy to the last he attends before he dies, he is served his portion after his elder brother and before his younger brother, or whatever older or younger kinsmen were born immediately before or after him. Chagga men usually cannot tell you the ages of their kinsmen in years, but every man can recite to you the forty to eighty names of his living local kinsmen, eldest to youngest, in order of birth in each sub-branch, as fast as we can say the alphabet.

Over the course of life, men see themselves moving place by place up the seniority ladder of the lineage. It is clear who is *due* to die next and who is to succeed him. When people die out of turn, that is something to be explained. It means that something has gone wrong in the order of things, and there may be witchcraft or curses to reckon with. In fact, even when men die in age sequence, younger siblings are sometimes suspected of hastening their seniors on their way by evil means in order to inherit their land or otherwise to profit from having them out of the way. For Marunda to have eaten the kidari of his father was to take his father's place before his time—i.e., in circumstances that had sinister implications. That is why it constituted a mortal sin which ultimately was fatal to him.

There are consequently two sides of the age-seniority system, the good side which assures a man that as he gets older he will inevitably have precedence over more and more younger men and boys, and the bad side which implies that the more senior a man is, the more he will be resented as much as respected, and envied inasmuch as he enjoys prerogatives or property others would like to have. There is immense visible continuity of persons and place in such a life. Isolation from personal relationships in old age, or in fact at any age, is impossible. That too, has its advantages and its miseries. For those who succeed socially, it means a piling up of cumulative gains. For those who fail, it means living permanently with the dislike of neighbors and kinsmen. Fortunately for most men, they manage to be somewhere in between, with some supporters and some detractors.

Age and aging was a traditional focus of Chagga ideology and organization. Theirs was once an age-graded society, and until this century their political life was organized around the successive initiation of cohorts of young men into young manhood and warrior status. In the Moshi chiefdom, and likely similarly in the others, the chiefs regularly called together all adult men in the chiefdom when there were matters of moment to discuss, and the resulting age-grade assembly sat in age-segregated order, the eldest highest on the mountain. The spirits of the dead were considered to reside in the mountain itself, and the glacier covered peak of Kibo had sacred connotations. Hence the age-grade organization, like the seniority system in the lineage, was structured with the idea of past and future generations very much part of a single system. Life was a procession of generations, made the more visible by the customary barriers that emphasized the distinction between them.

Once a parent had a married child, he or she was not supposed to continue having children. Their procreative period was at an end. It was not that their sexual lives were necessarily over, just their right to have children. What was said was that if parents went on having children, then someone would die. It was as if there were a fixed number of places in the world, all arranged in closed generational sequence, so that if an extra person were born out of order, someone would lose his/her place and die. This notion of a chain of life, extending from the dead of the lineage to the unborn, of supernatural connections between the dead and the living such that they could affect the fate, health, or good fortune of descendants is and was traditionally very much a part of Chagga ideology. The living also are thought to be invisibly and supernaturally connected with each other, able to bless or curse effectively.

The age-grades are gone and have been for all of this century. The prohibition on parents having children after their own children are initiated has been reduced to a folk saying that it is not a good thing to do. Most Chagga are Christians today and have changed many of their customs. But the idea that the dead affect the living, the belief in witchcraft and in the effectiveness of curses (now considered to be effectuated by a Christian God) remain very much a part of everyday discussion. Hence, the position of the elderly, as persons closer to the dead ancestors, persons who will soon die, thus whose curses are particularly effective against their close relatives and descendants, is an ambiguous one. Their visible personae may be weakened and less effective than they once were, but their unseen power is feared. It includes the supernatural effects of anger between fathers and sons and the mundane but horrifying possibility of disinheritance.

Elderly Chagga today are never isolated in the sense of being far from kin. Of 300 households surveyed in 1969, only one elderly man was alone in his own kihamba. All other elderly persons shared the same piece of land with spouses, or with even more kin. The average household size was about seven. That does not mean that old persons necessarily occupied the same hut as others. Most of them had their own hut or room, without being in any sense isolated. The one man who was alone had a son two miles away, and other kinsmen who lived closer. In short, there were *no* elderly Chagga in the area studied who were truly alone in the sense of being without relatives whose responsibility it was to look after them. The one old man who was alone was on bad terms with his son and planned to leave his kihamba to his grandson. He had complained to the ten-cell leader about the fact that his son neglected him, and the son had been officially reprimanded by the cell leader on several occasions. Each time he was reprimanded, he produced a few shillings for his father, and the father complained again as soon as he needed money. The son's behavior was universally regarded as very wrong, whatever the state of his feelings about his father. It was not relevant whether they had quarrelled. His duty was to look after the old man, and it was a duty the political cell leader was willing to enforce. Thus does the socialist state reinforce some of the tribal customs of yesteryear.

SIARA'S LIFE

What follows is Siara's account of his life. He was in his mid-seventies when he told it. He wove in and out of anecdotes, and thus his story is not presented in the order in which he explained things. The account came out in fragments in the course of many conversations, most of them not directly about him. He would use his own experience as an illustration of some point he was making. I asked him questions; he asked me questions. Eventually many pieces fitted together, but in the telling, all was an unassembled mosaic. A genealogy produced much clarifying information. The local branch of his lineage had had, in his lifetime, over eighty males he had known. Their histories were as intricate as his. Here we confine ourselves to his own tale.

It must be assumed that what he told me is a highly selective, self-serving story of his transactions. He is always the hero of his anecdotes, always right, and usually wins the disputes he describes. What he says, then, is not to be taken as "true" in the sense that all parties involved would have agreed to his version. It is "true" in quite a different sense. It is what a Chagga wanted me to believe had happened to him in the situations he describes, and it is plausible in Chagga terms, as it describes many events not unlike those that occur in the life histories of other men. Siara's account of his life is an example of a man's old age among the Chagga, unique in some particulars, but enough like others to make it a good illustration. Evidence from other people confirmed large parts of his account, but some of it was impossible to check. There also are obvious omissions. But the events of his life were not unusual in their general circumstances: being the youngest son, having access to land because of various convenient deaths of male siblings, having serious disputes with lineage brothers and with his own sons, and the like. In the course of field work hundreds of cases not unlike Siara's were collected. Some men were less fortunate, some more, but since the common social context is what is of interest, Siara's tale brings it out as well as any.

My introduction to Siara was through a Chagga Catholic priest. At first Siara came to meet me at the mission because he feared having anything to do with me unless the priest was present. He was a dignified old gentleman who wore a battered and greasy fedora and a pale blue wool coat whose original owner and wearer must have been a European woman. Under his light coat he wore faded, somewhat tattered cotton trousers and shirt. His bare feet were in rubber sandals, and he carried a cane. The first time we spoke he fingered his rosary all the time we were together and crossed himself often. He prayed whenever the church bell struck. Whatever the holy father had told him, clearly he still believed that I was dangerous. And he plainly had secrets he feared I might pry into.

We made an agreement. I would pay him for his time, and we would meet at the mission regularly. We did so for several months, but after a time I began to visit him at home and eventually did so very freely. The visits to his home began because he had a bad leg and found it difficult to walk to the mission. (He found it much less difficult to walk to the beer shop.) And it continued because he got used to it, and on some Sunday or other the Padre must have assured him that it was all right. I continued to pay him for his time, but we began to exchange small gifts. I brought him bread I had bought, a European delicacy, since the Chagga have no ovens of any kind. He gave me coffee which his wife boiled in the morning and placed in a rusty, topless thermos he had been given by someone in the mission years before. I brought small amounts of sugar. He collected and gave me bits of local plants to teach me what they were. He gave me beer. I brought him a book. And so it went. We laughed a great deal. We enjoyed each other's company. We were also mutually useful. I had ceased to be a danger, and he stopped being afraid.

I used his outhouse, but he was never sufficiently encumbered by my presence to go further than the nearest bush. He asked me as many questions as I asked him, and he had particular things he wanted to tell me whether I was interested or not, and I listened politely. "Listen to me. Heed what I say." I was the age of his eldest surviving son, and it was for me to show respect, which came easily.

When we drank his coffee and munched my dry bread, he chuckled and said, "Death is distant if we are able to eat." He was acutely aware of being in the shadow of death. He grumbled a lot about his aching leg, and often speculated on whether it augured the beginning of the end. He had been to four funerals that year, three of persons younger than himself. All were members of his lineage (or their wives), or members of his mother's brother's lineage.

Having survived to the age of seventy-five is a rare thing for a Chagga. It is not surprising on that ground alone that Siara thinks he has been unusually fortunate to be alive. A house-to-house survey conducted on 300 Chagga households in the course of this study indicates the following ages distribution of the population:

Total population (300 households) 2,242

Those over 50 245

Those under 18 1,265

Most Chagga expect to live to about fifty. They may hope for more, but they know few survive to a really old age. Siara *knows* he is unusual in having reached his mid-seventies, and he draws from it a sense of power, of being loved by God.

Siara went to the dispensary at the mission for injections to cure his leg, but they did not make him feel better, and he mistrusted them anyway. He sent someone to get the healing bark of a tree for him, and he boiled it up with water and applied the infusion to his leg with a cloth. A few days later the visible sores on his leg seemed to be healing, but he said it still ached. He assured me that Chagga remedies were far more reliable than European medicines. This one he had learned from his mother.

In the early months of our acquaintance, Siara had two women at home, his wife and a granddaughter of seventeen. Then one day when I went to see him, his eldest son, a fifty-year-old Catholic priest, had come to the house to take the granddaughter away. He had been expected to arrive for this purpose at some time that month, but of course Siara had had no idea just when. It is in the nature of things that, without telephones, and without the habit of writing letters (and somewhat uncertain delivery if you do write them), to say nothing of the cost of stamps, almost all visits are sudden. Once in a while, a word-of-mouth message may be sent via a person who is going from one place to another, but as often as not such messages are not conveyed. The recipient may not be at home. The journey may take longer than the traveller expects, and he may find himself going straight to his destination without stopping off to deliver the message. There is a lot of hit-or-miss about communications at any distance. There is no way to change any arrangements that have been made to meet someone. If, at the last moment, it is impossible to meet, there is usually no way to send word that one is not coming. Public meetings are called by having a town crier walk through the paths between the gardens, up and down, here and there blowing a beautiful convoluted horn of a wild animal, the kudu, and then shouting the time and place of the meeting.

In personal meetings with those who are not close neighbors, neither punctuality nor even arriving at all is truly counted on, even if it is hoped for. Much attention is given to premonitions that particular individuals will arrive, and to any omen that suggests a visitor is coming. The arrival is always something of a surprise nonetheless, and the premonitions are only fully given voice after the person has appeared. So it was with the visit of Siara's son, the priest. He could wait only one day while the granddaughter put her few belongings together and went to find her young friends to say goodbye. The priest had arranged for her to go to school in his district, where she was to be trained as an attendant in a dispensary, a sort of nursing aide. It would be a good thing for her in this modern world, but for Siara and his wife it was bad. She had slept in the room with Siara's wife. Now the old woman would sleep alone.

Chagga men do not sleep in the room with a wife, nor do they eat with them, after there are children. A man has his own room, or hut, and when he wants her with him for a while, he calls her to his bed. But she does not stay. She sleeps in her own hut, or room, with the children. When she is old and her children are grown, she has a right to a grandchild. This particular grandchild had lived with Siara and his wife since she was about ten years old, and she was virtually theirs. Siara said he did not know what they would do to find a substitute for her. I asked about the other grandchildren, and he said that as his son the priest "is dead for the purpose of having children," and he and his other son (the father of the seventeen-year-old) were no longer on speaking terms, there were no other grandchildren of his own lineage he could have at home. Perhaps he could ask for the child of one of his daughters. He had two, and each was blessed with seven children. "But you know how it is with children these days. In the old days they were some use and did work. Now you feed them and buy clothes for them and it is nothing but school, school, school," he grumbled cheerfully. It was otherwise for most children when Siara was a boy, though, in fact, he was one of the early ones to go to the mission school.

When Siara was a young boy, he took care of the goats and cattle. Being the fifth of his mother's six children, he slept in a grass hut with her and the others on cattle skins spread over banana leaves. He lived there, sleeping with his mother and the others until he was about twelve years old, when he started school at the mission. His mother's first child had died in infancy. She subsequently had had two daughters and three sons. Of the boys, the oldest was Lakituri. Then came Siara, and after him a little brother who died very young. Siara told me about his death: "The health of the child is the responsibility of the parents. If the child gets sick, they must have done something."

What the parents had done was to quarrel bitterly and violently. Siara's father had had three wives. Each wife had her own house and her own banana garden around it. Lakituri, Siara, and the little brother were children of the third wife. Most of the time the father lived with the second wife, who was his favorite. This beloved wife had two daughters but no sons. This meant that on her death, her land would go to a son of one of the other women. Sons are the offspring who carry on a Chagga lineage, and who live locked in fraternal competition (as well as cooperation) all their lives. Girls marry and leave home, but sons remain and carry on the lineage, and compete for land and beasts.

The first wife of Siara's father had had several sons, but only one survived to a great age, and that was Ndelamio, who was older than Siara and his brothers. It is Chagga custom that the oldest and youngest sons inherit most from a father, and the middle sons must make their own way. That means that Ndelamio, first son of the first wife, and Siara's little brother, had he survived, would ultimately have been the father's principal heirs. The little brother's death, therefore, made Siara the youngest, and principal heir.

He remembered the death very well. It happened after his father had been to stay with his mother for some days. He visited this way from time to time, to see how his children were, and how his land and his beasts were being cared for. On that occasion, he and Siara's mother had a terrible fight. He beat her and she fought back, hitting and biting him, which violated a deep taboo. For a wife to harm her husband was an act against the natural order of things. Not long afterwards the youngest boy died, "because of the fighting between the parents," said Siara. That made Siara the youngest son and principal heir. Siara himself may have felt some guilt about his younger brother's death. He never said anything of the sort directly, but he was very keen that I understand that it was the parents' responsibility. "When a child dies like this, it is because of the wrong of the father or the wrong of the mother."

There is no doubt that it was one of the tenets of Chagga ideology that parents, having given their children life, have much mystical power over those lives ever after. Siara said, "In the old days, they [children] feared their fathers. A son knew his father's word could make him sick or kill him." And by children, he meant adults as well as young persons. Chagga men in their thirties have told me, "I fear my father. I obey him. I respect him and give him honor, because if I make him angry, he might curse me." That does not mean, of course, that they are as obedient as they say. But that is the stand they feel they should take. And it was the attitude Siara thought sons should have toward their fathers—one they were not sufficiently committed to these days. That did not mean that one's father had to be *liked.* He had to be respected and deferred to. There was no need to do it out of affection. Affection was as it might be. A father might like a particular son. A son might like his father. Some did not, and that was how it went. Liking had nothing to do with respecting and obeying.

These virtues were taught in childhood in Siara's time (and often today as well) with the help of beatings and other bodily assaults on children. Siara said, "If you beat a child hard when he is young, then he will remember later. Or you can use some leaves, *kiwawe,* and rub them on the child's body. It burns and burns terribly and itches, like fire. You rub it anywhere, everywhere until the child urinates with pain and fright. I will show you the leaf. I will bring you some." He chuckled at the thought.

"In the old days, when they grew up, the sons had to obey. They were under their fathers, under the law of their fathers. Even if the father was cruel, they had to obey and respect him. And when he became old and sick, he was not to take care of himself. The son was to do it. Even if there were a quarrel with the father or the mother, and they cursed their son or insulted him, he was not to say anything. It was a serious taboo, a complete prohibition. If it was broken, the son had to pay a goat to plead for forgiveness.

"But these days, the sons of today do not have respect. The father curses them and they curse him. It is the law of our tribe that a son should obey his father and mother. Honor your parents. You are under the law of your parents. Anyone who does something that offends the parents must be fined, for something important, a goat, for something less important, a *mtungi* of beer." Siara was, of course, speaking of adult children, not of youngsters, for only adults could pay fines or provide goats. It is Siara's habit to speak of quarrels between parent and offspring as instances of the child being in the wrong. And for reasons in his own life, he is also preoccupied with how much the child ought to pay in fines or gifts of apology.

Some days later, Siara brought me some of the punishing nettle kiwawe wrapped in a bit of old cloth. Very gingerly he opened it and showed it to me. Even more carefully I accepted the package, while he laughed with pleasure at my being wary about touching it. Bringing the kiwawe made him speak more about disciplining children, and about the punishments that were meted out in his childhood.

"Young children stole food. They were beaten if they got caught. Older children stole from younger ones. They were afraid of being beaten and ran away to the house of the mother's brother, or the grandmother. They could not run to the Moshi road, there was none. We were beaten or deprived of food if we did wrong, bad things like stealing food, or not doing work when the parents are not watching, or disobeying. For instance, if you were sent to obtain something and come right back, and you dawdled instead, and did not return when you were supposed to, your father spat on his hand like this and said, "When the spittle is dry, you must be back, or *you shall see.*"

The assertion of a father's authority over his sons in childhood and adulthood, and the rebelliousness of some sons is a major theme is almost every man's life and in the history of any Chagga lineage. Siara was no exception. Quarrels emerging from that relationship are seldom solely matters of personal bad feeling. Serious struggles frequently occur over property and obligation, and in the course of them suspicions about sorcery and supernatural harm.

When Siara was a young man, his father had had very strained relations with Siara's eldest brother, Ndelamio. According to Siara, he, Siara, was the favorite. The first major property issue between the sons concerned their father's cattle. At the time, it was a common practice for people in the province of Vunjo to place their cattle in *agistment* (that is, the cattle were placed in trust; the cattle-keeper had the use of the manure and the milk; in return, he fed and cared for the beast; the original owner could demand the return of the animal when he wished), with men from the better grazing areas of Rombo. The Vunjo men made blood brotherhood pacts with their cattle partners, exchanging blood or bits of food from each other's mouths. These were supernatural precautions to enforce the cattle contracts. The father of Siara and Ndelamio had ten head of cattle placed with people in Rombo in this manner early in the German colonial period. Marealle, a Chagga chief from Marangu in Vunjo, was then master of much of Kilimanjaro. With German help, Marealle had conquered his way through much of Rombo, after which the Rombo people were ordered to pay enormous "reparations" to the people of Vunjo. According to Siara, what they did was to return the cattle that had been placed with them.

"I saw with my own eyes." said Siara, "that Ndelamio argued that these were animals that belonged to his mother. The father was old and ill. It was taboo for a father to haul his son into the Mangi's court and sue him there [Mangi is the Chagga term for chief, and the reference here is to the local area chief in Kilema]. Instead, my father took me with him to go to discuss the matter with the Mangi and ask him what to do. He took me, and not any of my brothers," Siara boasted.

"My father explained to the Mangi that he was ill, and that as his first-born son, Ndelamio, quarrelled with him a great deal, and insulted him, he was no longer to be considered his son. The Mangi said, 'You give me a cow, and when you die, I shall take care of these matters regarding your children.' " Normally the eldest son would be in a favored position with respect to cattle inheritance. As the father was disinheriting his eldest, some official acknowl-edgment of his wishes in the matter was necessary. The father agreed to the Mangi's terms, and thereupon slaughtered a beast for the Mangi to seal the agreement. This was both a way of making his request a matter of record and a way of insuring that it would be carried out by putting the Mangi under an obligation.

The chiefs had numerous ways of collecting levies of beasts from their subjects. In 1913, the chief of Kilema taxed the fathers of all boys being circumcised. Siara and Lakituri were circumcised at that time. In keeping with custom, the Mangi declared it time for all males not yet circumcised to be operated on, because his son was to go through the rite. In the nineteenth century, the timing of the ceremony was a political decision to bring a new age-class of warriors into being. By 1913, because of the colonial regime, it did not have that military implication, but it did bring immense revenues to the Mangi, Kiritta. Siara's father had to pay two goats, one for him and one for Lakituri.

In ordering the mass circumcision, Kiritta was carrying on an old tradition in which the Mangi was not only secular head of the political system, but also was responsible in mystical and religious ways for the well-being and per-petuation of his people. By 1913, a serious erosion of the Mangi's spiritual powers was taking place because of the competition of the mission. However, his political powers, though changed in character because of the German colonial government, were strengthened by its backing. Christianity made many converts. In 1916, Siara, the mission-school youth, was baptized.

Then came World War I and the British not only chased away the Germans, they took Mangi Kiritta away. Siara remembered this very well. Along with a number of other chiefs who were banished from the mountain at that time, Kiritta, accused by informers, was suspected of pro-German sympathies. Joseph Maliti temporarily became Mangi in Kiritta's place from 1917 to 1919. Then Major Charles Dundas, a British political officer, became a significant force on Kilimanjaro. His sympathetic interest in the Chagga led him to return the banished chiefs to their chiefdoms, and thus won him immense local popularity. In Kilema, the British held a large public meeting and asked the senior men whether they wanted Kiritta back. They said, "Yes," and Kiritta was then returned to his Mangiship.

The colonial regimes, German and British, were not merely remote entities to Siara. They reached into his life directly and he was very much aware of the European presence. It is astonishing what a powerful effect a few men had on thousands and thousands of Chagga, and what transformations their activities wrought in the Chagga way of life. Dundas eventually made it his business to encourage coffee-growing among the Chagga, and held public meetings in each chiefdom on the mountain, in which he and the local chief made speeches urging the Chagga to plant their own coffee seedlings in their kihambas. Over time, his efforts were successful to a point of transforming the Chagga economy into one of cash cropping built on a subsistence base. "Dundasi," as Siara called him, was a figure warmly remembered even in the 1970s.

During the war, Lakituri [Siara's elder brother by the same mother] married, and their father gave him a banana grove. Not too long afterward, in 1920, Siara became a teacher. In 1921, he too married. His father then also gave him a kihamba, a grove, and Siara built a Swahili house on it. The rectangular house was made on a frame of interwoven sticks plastered with mud. It had a dirt floor and a thatched roof of banana leaves. It was a very popular modern form, probably first introduced in the late nineteenth century through contact with the caravan trade. Siara said, "I built houses, grass houses, until I married for the first time. Then when I married, I began building Swahili houses, with banana leaves as roof. There was no shortage of anything, so I did it myself. You could just ask and take trees. You did not have to buy anything. Helpers, even skilled men [fundi] were given beer as pay, no money." Siara's generation experienced the shift from exchange labor and free raw materials to the present situation in which much labor is had for cash and raw materials are purchased. For the old people, it means a change from what in retrospect appears to have been a past of great abundance and good will, to a present in which everyone is constrained by the need for money. Money is obtained for coffee, but fluctuations in the price of coffee are utterly beyond local control, and to a great extent the amount of the coffee crop also depends on environmental factors that the farmers cannot affect. That being so, the sense the older men and women have of the past/present is of a loss of independence and autonomy. Actually, their former mode of obtaining services and objects involved them in even more exchange relationships than they now rely on, and even greater dependence on others. But they do not see such relationships as constraining, while they do feel terribly trapped by a dependence on cash. They think of the exchange of services and goods with kin and neighbors as a "natural" by-product of a "natural" relationship. Cash is relatively new, and impersonal dealings are very new, hence unaccustomed and unnatural.

Siara's first wife was a student in the mission school where Siara taught reading, and was the daughter of a brother of his father's mother. "I was returning to the house according to our custom," said Siara. He was, in short, marrying a wife of the same lineage as his paternal grandmother. The next year, 1922, the marriage was blessed with a son.

Meanwhile, Lakituri left to seek his fortune in Zanzibar. He was never to return, and died in Zanzibar in 1954. At the time he left, of course, it was not clear that he would not come back. But his departure triggered disputes about his land. Normally when a man leaves his kihamba, he leaves his wife to look after it. But shortly after Lakituri went to Zanzibar, his childless wife left the kihamba and went back to her own kin—an informal equivalent of a divorce. The question then arose of who would look after (and profit from) the banana grove in Lakituri's absence. It is Chagga custom that an absent kinsman never loses his rights to his land. If it is empty in his absence, it is tended by a brother or other relative. There is always an implied chance that if the owner does not return, whoever took care of the land in trust over the years would ultimately inherit it. Siara wanted Lakituri's kihamba. So did Ndelamio, their eldest half-brother (son of their father's first wife).

There was a hearing before the lineage about Lakituri's land. The decision was made in Siara's favor, and the lineage was strongly on his side. Ndelamio had been fighting with their father, and now he was fighting with Siara. Having been rejected by his kinsmen, Ndelamio complained to the local headman. Siara then went over the headman to the Mangi to remind him of his pledge to their father, and to ask him to come to the house to resolve the dispute. "Brew beer," said the chief, "a mtungi of beer for the Mangi, two *debe* for the house." Through the headman, he sent a message that he would arrive on a particular day. When the day came, the Mangi arrived, inspected the kihamba of Lakituri, and then they all went to another banana grove to settle the case and drink the beer of settlement.

The Mangi asked Ndelamio, "How many children did your father have? And how many banana gardens?" The answer to both questions was, "Three." When he asked whether the three places of land had been given one to each son, he was told, "Yes." The Mangi continued, "And when the kihamba was given to Lakituri, did anyone object?" "No."

"Are you and Lakituri children of one mother?" he asked Ndelamio. "No."

"Who is?"

"Siara."

Then, turning to Siara, the Mangi said, "If Lakituri died, would you be the inheritor of his wife?" In traditional law, he would have been.

"No," he answered, "because of the religion [Christianity], but we are of one mother."

The Mangi then said, "This is the kihamba that the father gave to Lakituri when Lakituri married. Ndelamio was there and did not object, so he cannot object now. Lakituri lives in Zanzibar. He is alive. Thus, this kihamba will stay in the hands of his younger brother by the same mother until he returns. Enough. I have resolved this affair."

Then they all drank beer together, all but Ndelamio, who refused to drink. Siara, when he told about this dispute, added at the end, "And it was God's will that Lakituri died in 1954 without ever returning home, and I kept the kihamba." For him to stress that it was God's will was to say that he, Siara, had not used any occult means to bring about the death, for that would be the inference that any Chagga might make about so profitable a demise.

Thus Siara started out his adult life in the early 1920s with two kihambas and a job teaching in a bush school for the missions. He was a relatively well-to-do young man, and a literate Christian who considered himself thoroughly modern in every way. In 1923, he started to plant coffee in his kihamba and in that of Lakituri. The coffee seedlings were brought to him by a friend from Kibosho. As a boy he had worked in the garden of the mission, had dug holes for the planting of their coffee trees, so he knew how to go about it.

It was some time afterward in the same year that his father died. Just before his death, the father called in the two local headmen and said, "My hour is near. That son who is the youngest, I have nothing to leave him. Therefore, I ask you to go to Ndelamio. He has in his possession my wealth in cattle. I want you to give Siara three head. I leave them to him because he is my youngest son and otherwise he will get nothing from my hands."

These three head of cattle had originally been in the house of the father's second wife. She had died and Ndelamio had taken over their care and had taken them to his own house. When the father died, Ndelamio refused to give Siara the beasts, and chased him away with a stick when he came to collect them. Siara then went to the Mangi.

The Mangi remembered the words of the father and the beast he had slaughtered for him all those years before. He ruled that Siara should get the animals, and that Ndelamio should not have permission to bring a case about the matter in the Mangi's court. The case was heard and the headman ordered Ndelamio to pay. He said, "Give me a bit of time."

They said, "No, right away," and they went to find the beasts in the house of Ndelamio. They asked for the calf.

Ndelamio said, "It is dead."

They answered, "Then you must pay."

When Ndelamio came to compensate for the calf, he brought a male calf to Siara. Siara said, "No, the dead one was a heifer, I must have a heifer." Heifers were more valuable since they produced milk and offspring, while steers were only for slaughtering. Eventually Ndelamio brought the heifer. And he said, "You make beer for the elders, and on that day I shall bring you the remaining beasts." Siara made the beer, including a share for the Mangi, as was the custom.

"Now bring me the cows that are still left," said Siara to Ndelamio. Ndelamio refused, and chased Siara with a *panga,* a large, curved, all-purpose knife. Ndelamio shouted that Siara had come to try to steal his cattle.

One of the elders went to the Mangi and told him about the fight, and then Siara was accused of stealing the cattle. The Mangi said, "It is wrong to bring your brother to my court." Close kinsmen were not supposed to sue each other in the court of the chief. Such dirty linen was supposed to be washed at home. There should have been a hearing of the lineage elders, or at worst, a hearing before the local headman. But the Mangi found a clever way to get around the rule. "You cannot call your brother and summon him to my court. But if I call him, he must come." Ndelamio was summoned to the Mangi, and brought him a goat in the hope of a favorable decision. The Mangi ruled for Siara. He said that Ndelamio would have to hand over the cattle. Not only would he have to give Siara the beasts that should have been his, but also the beasts that would have belonged to Lakituri, had he been there. Of the three beasts, the Mangi ruled that if Lakituri came back, he would have one and Siara two. Otherwise, if he did not return, Siara was to keep all three.

After that dispute, Ndelamio was expelled from the local lineage. He was no longer included in the lineage slaughterings. And from then on, for many years, Siara and Ndelamio were enemies. Meanwhile Ndelamio quarreled with another kinsman and lost. Since matters had turned out badly for Ndelamio, and since he had been expelled from the local lineage, he decided to move to the next chiefdom, that of Kirua. He had three wives. He left one with their son, Fabiani, in the kihamba located in the chiefdom of Kilema where Siara lived, but he took the other two with him to Kirua, and obtained land for them there from the government. There was ample land to be had for the asking at that time.

For years afterward, fortune seemed to smile on Siara. In 1924, Siara's wife bore him a second son, three years later a third, and a few years after that, a daughter. But then misfortune struck. In 1937, after sixteen years of marriage, and five months pregnant, Siara's first wife died. He described her as a good woman. He said he never had to beat her. (One wondered if he did not protest too much.) She did her work. She fed the children. She was faithful to him. Faultless, she had died anyway. "It was God's will." After a year or so, Siara married a second wife and she eventually bore him one daughter.

Around that time, the first son of Ndelamio wanted to get married, and he asked Ndelamio why he had quarrelled with his brother Siara, saying, "It is not right to go on being on bad terms with a brother." Ndelamio and Siara used the occasion of the impending wedding to have a discussion about reconciliation. The implication of this was that Siara, if he were reconciled with Ndelamio, would have to contribute beer and other things to the son's wedding. Ndelamio's son came and invited Siara to come to Kirua to arrange the reconciliation.

Siara said, "Do you know that when I came to Kirua no one knew me. No one knew who I was. They said, 'Who is that man?' They were told, 'He is the brother of Ndelamio.'" He wanted to express the depth of their estrangement and its long duration.

A discussion before the lineage followed. Siara chose one or two men to side with him, and Ndelamio asked a few to come to be on his side. They sat down to talk, to tell the story of the trouble between them and to work out a settlement. The lineage elders heard them out and fined Ndelamio. He was to pay the fine in beer. Later he brewed the beer and they all drank it together. Siara forgave Ndelamio and agreed to go to the wedding.

"I went to the marriage party. I had prepared beer and I brought it. The son was married. Then Ndelamio called his wife and children together and said, 'Come here. Take a calabash of that beer there. When you have brought the beer, serve it to him [pointing to Siara]. You must not give it to me. Give it to him. My younger brother and I have but one father. You know him today. Since our quarrel we have not seen each other. We have now reached an agreement. You shall obey him as you obey me. Now, this beer is his gift. You, Siara, shall distribute it as you like.'" Thus we were completely reconciled and agreed, about fifteen years after the original quarrel.

Then misfortune struck again. Siara's first-born son sickened and died, just when he was of an age to marry. In Chagga tradition, it is a most terrible thing for a person to die before having children, to die without being part of the perpetual chain of ancestors and descendants. It means that after you are dead, no descendants will think of you, and pour libations of beer for you, or offer you meat. The bodies of childless adults used to be flung in a certain place in the forest. They were not buried in the hut as normal persons who had had children were, nor were their bones exhumed and preserved in the banana grove. The earth in which things grow was not to be contaminated with the sterility of the childless.

Christianity has to a large extent done away with exhumation and associated practices, but the feeling remains that to die without offspring is the worst death. It is truly a cutting off of the line, a real end, so untimely that it inevitably arouses suspicion of sorcery. Siara clearly held someone responsible, perhaps his own youngest son (of whom more will be told later). Or perhaps it was Ndelamio.

In any case, an end soon came to Siara's few years of reconciliation with Ndelamio. One of Ndelamio's married sons was in a legal dispute with his father. Siara took the side of the son. This was Fabiani, whose mother was one of Ndelamio's three wives, the one who had remained in the kihamba in the chiefdom of Kilema when Ndelamio moved to Kirua. In Siara's words, "Now that child [Fabiani] began to be hated by his mother who bore him. He was grown up and married and had children. That mother was trying to get the father to take the kihamba of that son and give it to another. But I knew that the kihamba had been given to that young man by the government. The father had no right. I was on the side of the child, to prevent the parents from stealing the kihamba from him. I went to the Mangi Aloisi to tell him that the previous Mangi Josefu had given the youth this land. The father and the son quarreled so much that they had put the son in prison. I told the Mangi Aloisi about this. I then went to ex-Mangi Josefu and I asked him if he would be a witness in the case. He agreed to do it. Fabiani was released from jail, and I took the young man to my house. The ex-Mangi asked for a goat to be a witness. We brought him the goat. The day of the case we went to the court. I explained the case, and the ex-Mangi Josefu was the major witness. Ndelamio and I fought and insulted each other right there in the court. Of course, he lost the case. After that, Ndelamio said of Fabiani, 'The man is not my son. He is no longer my child.' "

Fabiani thus was expelled from Ndelamio's slaughtering group, and disowned. He then attached himself to Siara's, and ate meat with him and his as if he had been a son of Siara.

Eventually a kinsman of Siara and Ndelamio said to both of them, "I shall not eat with either of you unless you make peace together. You shall arrange between you." There was a lineage slaughtering and beer. Siara went, but reported: "I saw the evil. He told me to divide the beer my way. I remained silent. I did not say a word. I was ashamed, embarrassed by the wickedness. Two days later a child was sick, and they slaughtered again. He who had made the mischief slaughtered. I did not go there. I stayed at home. They brought meat to the house. They sent a child to bring me my share. We remained apart, enemies, unreconciled as before." Siara was accusing Ndelamio of sorcery, yet just what Siara saw when he saw the "wickedness" remains unclear.

As for Fabiani, he is in Siara's goat-slaughtering group to this day. His fights with his mother continued for many years, until his sister married in 1968 and moved to Arusha. The mother went with the daughter.

Fission at the lowest level of the lineage, fission of the goat-slaughtering group of brothers has never been unusual, at least not in recent times of which a good deal is known. It is expected that if a man has a number of sons, after his death, as they gradually become elders themselves, each will aspire to become the head of his own goat-slaughtering group, including his own sons and grandsons. It is also common for other individual kinsmen to become attached to the group (as Ndelamio's son did) as a result of the vagaries of dispute, death, and resettlement. What may surprise the outsider is the bitterness of these disputes in Siara's life. But they are not unusual. There are many such bitter quarrels with kinsmen. The fissioning process is often marked by accusations and hostility. Siara is not unusual in having had troubled relations with his half-brother. All Chagga local lineage groups have such controversies in their histories. While some brothers are more intimately involved in disputes than others, none escapes the fallout from them. "There are no people who do not quarrel," was Siara's comment.

What has changed since the turn of the century, in Siara's lifetime, is that the higher levels of lineage, the whole of the local group of kinsmen (not just a living grandfather and his descendants, but a long dead ancestor's descendants), has ceased to be an official political force. They still all get together for the beer drinking parties that celebrate baptisms, weddings, circumcisions, and the wakelike beer-drinking that marks the end of the mourning period of four days after a death. And they watch the land as contingent heirs, always vaguely hoping for some deaths to bring them suddenly and unexpectedly into property, the only source of income for most of them. But the large group, the group of all the kinsmen in the village, seldom meets as a whole except for the life-cycle rituals already mentioned. They used to be taxed as a body, and the lineage had considerable numbers of relations as a corporate body with the chief and with other lineages. Much of that has melted away as change has come about in the nature and structure of the larger corporate groups in the district and in the nation. The chiefdoms, the colonial administration, the coffee cooperative, the current reorganizations and the doing-away with chiefship after independence all have meant major changes at the top, and minor adjustments at the bottom of the organizational system. Thus, the smallest lineage branches go on almost as before, at the bottom of the system, and even the local lineage as a whole (made up of many such sub-branches living in the same ex-chiefdom) has some viability. But the nature of its external relations has changed. Still, it maintains its internal focus on land, on seniority, on fertility, and on continuing the line.

There has also been a great change in economic focus, from cattle to land, and from land used purely for subsistence crops, to land also used for coffee, the cash crop. This has meant fewer slaughterings of cattle, more of goats, because the land shortage occasioned by the coffee-growing and the population explosion makes cattle-feeding difficult. That has meant fewer slaughtering feasts, more slaughtering of goats consumed by very small groups of related men, usually the descendants of one grandfather. The times for the larger local kin group to get together are no longer the slaughtering feasts but the beer parties.

Siara said, "Ah, in the old days we slaughtered together. But these days things have changed. . . . People have died. People have moved away. The children say, 'Give me money. Let us not slaughter. Make beer.' " Yet he still keeps three goats in a pen in his yard, and not to sell them. There are a number of beer parties every year in the local lineage and in the neighborhood to which Siara goes. But lacking sons on the spot, he feels cheated of his own family slaughtering feasts at which he would be the eldest, most respected, and would receive the kidari.

"I keep goats. It is not as easy to take care of a cow as it was in the old days. Most houses used to have a cow or two, usually fewer than three. They did not send the girls to school, only the boys. The girls stayed home and did work. They took care of the little children and the animals. There used to be plenty of grass for fodder. No more. Now you have to buy grass. Goats are enough for me. I cut the banana stems to feed them if I am home. But if I am sick or on safari, the grandchild cuts them for me.

"In the old days there were always people slaughtering, father, father's brothers, brothers, mother's brothers, the others, the neighbors, the friends. Each time they gave me some. They also helped each other with milk in the old days. Meat was always cooked by itself then. Milk and meat we Chagga, we never mix, never in the same meal."

It is probably quite true that there was more food in the old days, as many old people including Siara often assert. If twenty-five meat-exchanging households of kinsmen and neighbors each slaughtered three times a year, there would be plenty of meat for everyone. In the old days, they not only exchanged meat and milk, but did a thousand other services. "There were no matches. If you needed fire, you went to a neighbor. And there were many dangers in the old days for which you shouted to raise the neighbors. Fire, or leopards at night which tried to steal the goats. Hyenas, snakes. There are very few snakes today, but formerly there were many. When a snake appears in the house, people say, 'This snake has been sent by someone.' It is not sent by witchcraft. Witchcraft like that is a thing of today, a new thing. If a snake came, it was sent by someone who was dead, who wanted it known that he was offended. If there had been quarrels or enmity, or something like that and then the person died, then it was he who sent the snake. If you offended with bad words and he was not able to make a case and settle with you, and died before anything was worked out, then it remained, like a difficulty, a complication. If he died after the words, then you will see, something will happen in your house. He who said the words watched carefully, and those who heard, and when something happened, like a snake coming, then they said it was sent by the dead person."

Thus the dead could communicate with the living and indicate their pleasure or displeasure. For the Chagga, there is no end of a relationship between parent and child. Death does not end it. Now that Christianity has pervaded their lives, all the very same ideas can be carried on in a new rhetoric. The immortality of the soul is confirmation of the continuing life of the ancestors. If one man curses another, it is not his words which are effective by themselves, it is God's will that intervenes. When he curses, he says, "You'll see," which translated in today's rhetoric means, "I leave it to God to punish you." Seriously intended to have effect, it is a way of saying "God damn you."

Siara's deep commitment to Christianity thus does not mean he has to forego all Chagga ideas about ancestors, descendants, sorcery, and the effectiveness of curses. Quite the contrary. They all make sense in the new idiom. Sorcery is the work of the devil. Today Siara has the satisfaction of having survived Ndelamio, who died some years ago. That confirms Siara in his assertion that he was right in all of these quarrels. God was clearly on his side, as was his dead father, whose wish it was (according to Siara) that he receive his property. Sheer survival in the face of hatred, outliving your enemy, is a sign of power and rightness.

This strength, this living to an old age itself, reassures Siara in yet another quarrel which is much more recent and more on his mind than his quarrels with Ndelamio: his disputes with his own son, Danieli. As was explained earlier, it was the child of Danieli, the granddaughter of seventeen, who lived with Siara and his wife when I first knew him. But it was by no simple series of events that she came to do so, and her presence in Siara's household was not a sign of warmth toward her father.

Siara refused to disclose the start of the story. It is clear that he disliked this son early in life, but just why he would not tell. It may have been, as suggested earlier, in some connection with the death of Siara's eldest son, just when he was old enough to marry, but it may have been something else. Siara said of the character of children, "You can tell what character a child will have at around the age of seven to ten, maybe up to twelve. Then they do not change any more. After fourteen or fifteen, you cannot teach them to be different."

When Danieli married for the first time, Siara gave him a kihamba. It was not close to his own, however, but some distance away. Danieli, being the youngest son would, in Chagga tradition, have been the son to stay at home. The Chagga form of ultimogeniture is one in which the youngest son and his wife do not acquire their own kihamba at marriage, but build their house somewhere in the father's kihamba. It is the duty of the youngest son to look after his father and mother in their old age, and to care for all their needs. It is in return for his service that the youngest son ultimately is given his parents' land and whatever is attached to it. What Siara did when he gave his son Danieli a kihamba far from his own, was no simple act of paternal generosity, but on the contrary was a clear indication that he did not want this son around. He was very fond of his other surviving son, Johani, who had become a priest, and it was to him he wanted to leave his own house and land. In 1962, seven years after Johani was ordained, Siara spent his coffee money savings on building a new house. He had always lived in a tin-roofed, earth-floored, mud and wattle Swahili house. For his old age, and for the holidays of Johani, he built a completely modern house with a cement floor and walls of cinder block, topped by the inevitable tin roof. The kitchen remained in another wattle and daub building. The inside of the kitchen consisted of three stones on the beaten earth floor which constituted the hearth, some crude shelves on which were kept an oddment of clay pots, old gallon tins for carrying water from the village tap, or beer from the beer shop, a gourd for souring milk, and other such. The modern house at first consisted of two small rooms for sleeping, one for Siara, and one for the granddaughter and his wife. Outside was a small porch. In 1968, two more rooms were added, a bedroom larger than the other two for Johani, the successful son, when he came home on leave, and a sitting room for him, which had a crude table, some stools, and a bed in case there were another visitor. There was also a wood-framed settee with brown plastic cushions. It was a very modern four-room establishment indeed, and Siara was quite proud of it. He told me he would leave it to Johani. When I expressed surprise that a priest could have property, he assured me that there would be no problem. Had there been many other sons who had no land, then it would be different, but in this case, it would go to Johani.

This would effectively and completely cut out Danieli. "I have already given him a kihamba. He cannot say anything. And besides, for fourteen years, he has not been to see me." The story of that break in relations was that some time after Danieli was married and had two children, the granddaughter already mentioned and a little son, he was horrified to learn that his father, Siara, intended to do something no Chagga ever did. He was proposing to give a kihamba outright to a daughter who was getting married. This was in the middle 1950s. Not only did Danieli oppose this, but so did the whole lineage. The lineage sent a representative to the Mangi to complain that Siara was about to give lineage land to a female child in total opposition to customary law. The Mangi called Siara and said, "To do such a thing is very wrong. If you do it, I shall prosecute you."

Siara now says that the difference between him and the Mangi was that he, Siara, was a truly modern man. "Those matters of yesteryear having to do with inheritance have changed. But even in the old days, if a child was bad to his father, he did not get his land. Rosa loved me more than Danieli. The child who loves the parents does what they tell it to do, heeds the law of the parents. Danieli did not obey and Rosa did. In the time of our parents, they said you will die in a hurry if you do not do what your parents say and take care of them."

Since Siara could not give Rosa the kihamba in view of the threat of the Mangi, he got around the ruling by selling the land and giving her the money when she married in 1955. In 1959, Danieli left Kilimanjaro for Arusha, a city about fifty miles away. He sold his kihamba and took his wife and children with him. He was leaving for good. He went to get a job as a laborer in building work.

There in Arusha, Danieli's three-year-old son died. Danieli called his brother Johani, who went to Arusha to see that the child was buried in the government cemetery. Then Danieli and his wife had a third child, a boy. "They began to hate one another. The wife made beer secretly [without a license]. She was arrested. She took the baby to jail with her and it got a fever and died." Since a father is thought to have power over the fertility and well-being of his son, and in turn over the son's offspring, it may be that the deaths of these children were thought by Danieli to have been somehow related to his quarrels with his father.

Danieli was far away. There was much trouble. The granddaughter was taken care of by neighbors. The lineage of Siara feared the mother would flee with Danieli's daughter when she got out of jail. All children belong to the lineage of the father, not to the mother. A member of the lineage went to Arusha and fetched the child, and brought her to Siara to feed and clothe, and pay for schooling, and bring her up, a proper daughter of the lineage, which he did. In return, she worked for the old couple and was a companion to Siara's wife.

Johani saw Danieli from time to time and kept in touch with him, but there was a complete break of direct relations with Siara. Siara obviously thought much about this, as he did about the fact that his whole lineage had opposed him when he sold the kihamba to give his daughter the money. He felt that the ancestors must not have disapproved, that God must be on his side, that whatever had been done against him had not succeeded in harming him. He frequently said with glee, "I am still alive and well since the time I gave my daughter the money, and since Danieli has left." Danieli has since remarried and has two more children, neither of which Siara has ever seen. The thought rankles.

It is an unending source of sorrow to Siara, that he has, so to speak, no sons, and by patrilineal Chagga standards, no grandchildren who count. To be sure, his daughters have given him fourteen grandchildren who visit him, and that gives him some pleasure, but they are not of his lineage. It is not the same. To whatever extent Siara wants to help women gain more rights, and wanted to give his daughters land, despite Chagga custom to the contrary, it is because he has no sons who will carry on the lineage locally. All his fighting for wealth with Ndelamio, and his hard work and thriftiness have made him relatively wealthy, but he worries that he really has no one to give it to, no one to carry on his name. Johani is lost to fathering because he is a priest, and Danieli is lost because he is no longer like a son. Fourteen years without returning home to see his father makes it unlikely he will ever come back. It looks as if Danieli's two children of his second marriage will never see their grandfather. Only his first child, the granddaughter who lived all those years with Siara, is a proper patrilineal grandchild, and she is a girl. Siara sighs over this. But all the same, he considers that he must have been right about it all, because God has seen fit to keep him alive.

He remains anxious, though, that any day his time may come. Much as he loves beer, he had been to only four "wakes" in the past year because, as he says, "The old fear going to too many *mantangas*. The dead people might want to take you with them." He also says that old people greatly fear being made successor/inheritors, because "the dead brother has decided the day of your death. If you get sick, you will not get well again. You will soon die." So he buys his beer each afternoon at the beer shop, and once in a while for holidays and feast time his wife brews some at home, or they go to beer parties given in the courtyard of other houses in the subvillage, and he avoids some mantangas, despite the free beer.

It is of interest, in view of the very much larger number of younger people in the local population, that Siara seeks out the cronies of his own age, and they him, at the beer shop and at all local gatherings. The ranks of the Chagga elderly may be thin, but for ordinary sociability, they prefer their own. Thus, Siara is not without close company in his old age. He is surrounded by members of the same larger lineage, and by neighbors he has either known all his life, or all theirs. When he goes to drink his afternoon calabash of beer, and when he goes to church on Sundays, he sits with the men of his own generation. At home, his wife prepares his food, tends the house and the yard, and cares for him when he is ill. His daughters visit him when they can get away from their many children and their chores. But as his own account indicates, he has reached this moment of longevity, prosperity, and sociability scarred by bitter fights with two men close to him, his half-brother and his son.

Many Chagga lives are threaded through with the disputes between fathers and sons, and brothers and half-brothers. Siara's life is far from unique in this respect, but rather epitomizes the issues. The norms and obligations of filial respect and brotherhood are one side of the coin. The other side is the side of coercion and competition, of accusing and cursing. The question arises how typical or how usual is Siara's experience. The answer provided in this study is that in every localized lineage of twenty-five to fifty households, there are serious disputes at one time or another in every slaughtering group, roughly in every group of five adult men (five households) there is at least one serious bone of contention directly involving at least two of the families, and less directly all the others. The land shortage may have exacerbated the situation, but everything that can be gleaned from accounts of the past suggests that formerly similarly bitter disputes were largely focused on cattle, then the most valuable and scarce possession.

The localized lineage branch is a life-term social arena from which individuals can be expelled, or in which they may be made so miserable they try to leave. But that is a last resort, because it virtually means giving up fighting for one's contingent rights in the property of the others. A few well-timed deaths can reverse positions, and the once unfortunate and shunned may survive and prosper. It happens all the time. How often it must cross a man's mind that he might be rich if only his brother's wife proved sterile or his brother's son died? Apart from guilty feelings about such thoughts, the occult can be actively resorted to, to further one's interests, to protect one's rights, to try to gain through unseen means what seems unobtainable in open dispute. Hence, every illness that lingers, every instance of female infertility, every incident of madness, every death of a domestic animal, may have been sent by someone who has cause for anger or envy. The very persons who are closest in kinship and obligation are also the ones who have most to gain from one's misfortunes. A life in such a setting, from youth to old age, permits no loneliness in the sense of being alone in the world, but clearly engenders other kinds of problems. Looked at from the outside, from the vantage point of our society, where an old age in relative social isolation is possible, old age among the Chagga looks desirable because it precludes isolation. But knowing the story of Siara's life should make it abundantly clear that a life-term social arena exacts a heavy price.

A NEW BABY IS BROUGHT TO VISIT ITS MOTHER'S MOTHER

In 1974, I accompanied Daria when she brought her three-month-old baby son to her mother's house for the first time. Daria, the young mother, also wanted to see her second child, Rosa, a five-year-old who lived with her grandmother. The baby was, in fact, Daria's fifth child, and the grandmother, Aleonica, had already seen it at Daria's house. But the first presentation of a Chagga infant at its maternal grandmother's home has ritual implications, so this was not to be an entirely ordinary visit.

Daria lives some miles from her mother, and she asked me to drive her there. She showed herself to be a very modern woman in being eager to go visiting at that time. In Chagga tradition, there is a period of three months after childbirth when a woman is confined to her house, or rather to the kihamba. Most women observe this to the letter, and it is greatly to their advantage to do so, since it provides them with a vacation-like period during which they cannot do any of their normal work, such as gardening, fetching wood and water, and the like. These three-month confinements (which also occur after circumcision and marriage) are the only vacations a woman ever has in her life. She looks forward to them. Another woman must do the new mother's work for her at this time, and a woman will fight in the courts for repayment for her care and support during this period, if the father of her child fails to provide it, whether he is her husband or not.

Daria was enough of a traditionalist so that she would not set foot in the marketplace until the confinement period was over, and I had to do some errands for her. "To church first," she said, "before going to market. That must be," which shows one of the many ways in which the church has involved itself in traditional ritual occasions and moved their venue to its own house. However, Daria was willing to go to a tailor to be measured for a new dress to wear at the baptism, but not to show her face at the market. The market prohibition is a very old taboo. Clothing and the tailor shop are a new institution.

Daria was about thirty-five. She was the wife of a clerk who had a job elsewhere on Kilimanjaro and only came home on weekends. The fact that he had a salary as well as a kihamba made them relatively well-to-do, much better off than most of their kin, who only had the gardens to support them. For this, her fifth child, her husband had hired a fourteen-year-old girl from a family in Rombo to live in and do the work. In her previous confinements, Daria had had a sister-in-law to help her out, which is also traditional. Most women have one particular sister-in-law (since brothers of the same local lineage live in contiguous gardens), with whom she regularly exchanges babysitting, care when ill, and other personal services. It is normally the wife of the brother with whom the husband also has particularly close relations. However, a fourteen-year-old "ayah," as Daria called her, could be ordered about much more than any sister-in-law, and was available all of the time. Such children are hired from their parents for a specified period of time. The parents receive a small monthly payment for the child's work.

Daria decided to take all of her children with her that day, and the ayah, too. We had arranged between us a few days before that I would come for her early in the morning and we would all set out for her natal home. When I arrived, I found that she had dressed all the children in their Sunday best, as well as herself and the ayah. We walked a half a mile to the place where I had left the car, single file down the narrow path, Daria first, I following, then the ayah carrying the infant, and after that Daria's older children. Behind all of us was a procession of neighborhood children who wanted to see what was going on. We climbed into the car, and Daria told me she would leave the older ones with her only sister who was now pregnant for the first time and who had not seen the whole family for some while. When we arrived at the sister's kihamba, she was out in the garden hoeing. Our arrival was unexpected, but we were warmly welcomed, and she was delighted to receive the older children for the day. We then proceeded to the car again and drove to the foot of the steep hill high up on which was Daria's natal home. We parked at the foot. Roads suitable for cars only take one part of the way anywhere on Kilimanjaro. To visit anyone, one must walk and far, up and down the winding paths between the kihamba gardens.

We set out on foot up the hill, Daria carrying a little package of meat she had bought on the day when we passed a butcher shop. She explained, "On the first visit to the grandmother, we bring meat if it is a boy, beans if it is a girl." Later on, when we were ready to leave, Daria's mother would give her a counter-gift of beans she had grown. Traditionally, the slaughtering of cattle was the concern of the men, the growing of vegetable foods, the occupation of the women. The two foods symbolized the difference between the sexes in the traditional economy, and the symbols remain, though the economy has changed a lot. Today coffee might be a more suitable male symbol than meat. But, as the Chagga say, "No one can eat coffee." It has only one value, to provide cash, and cash is not a source of life, the way food is, but is merely for buying things not usually necessary to life, things introduced in colonial times and not part of the traditional economy. These new purchasable things are highly desirable, but they do not carry the same symbolic significance that attaches to all that was Chagga long ago.

The hill was very steep. It was the first time I had been there, although I had met Daria's mother many times before. The whole hill belonged to Daria's father's lineage. His father before him had married the sister of the local headman. The hill had been empty then. They had settled at the foot of the hill with the headman's blessing, and as their children multiplied, grew up, and married, they were allocated plots further and further up the hill, until it was full. No doubt the reason this hill was unoccupied two generations ago is that it is very steep and has no irrigation channel. Rainwater is evidently sufficient for the gardens, but water for the residents has to be fetched from the foot, a great labor. So steep was the path that I slipped on the red dust trying to climb it. Plainly it served as a runoff gully when it rained, but as it was the dry season, there had been no rain for a long while. As we climbed, Daria pointed out the gardens of her father's brothers, and of their sons, who were her lineage brothers. She had no full brothers. She and her sister were the only children of her parents. "Two children, that is very sad. So few. And no son."

There had been an elder sister who died in childhood. She laughed as we struggled up the hill in our shoes. Better to be barefoot. And she told me how she remembered being sent down every day as a child to fetch water and carry it up. The houses at the bottom of the hill were of cinderblock; those higher up were poorer and of wattle and daub, with beaten earth floors.

More than halfway up, a wife of a father's brother, an old woman, came part of the way down to meet us. She took the baby from the ayah and smiled at it and welcomed us. Soon we reached the garden of Daria's mother, Aleonica, and then passed a dilapidated rectangular, half-collapsing house in which two cows were stalled. They were peacefully chewing banana stems. An adjoining room in the same building was the kitchen–i.e., on the dirt floor there was a hearth place consisting of a few stones. There was a small, crude shelf-like table. In the corner of the kitchen sat a pregnant goat, tethered to a post. The animals were a point of pride, shown me as a sign of affluence.

Nearby was Aleonica's house. Daria told me it was taboo to call "hodi," the Swahili hailing-greeting used when asking to be admitted to a room or house. It was not to be used when one returned to the house where one was born, I presume because it would imply that one had become a stranger, hence by definition hostile. Aleonica came out to greet us. She was a smiling woman wearing a yellow printed cotton dress, very faded from many washings and many dryings in the bleaching sun. She also wore a red printed kerchief on her head, flat, tied in the back, pirate fashion. The most current kerchief-tying style was quite different, and made the headdress into a sort of toque, the tying ends of the scarf wrapped back again to the front, and tied there. To give it height, a fashionable woman usually stuffed another cloth inside her kerchief. Daria did this. But Aleonica stuck to the modes of some years ago. Her husband was a farmer. Though there were no extras for frivolities, even a poor woman might have tied her kerchief in the new way if she had wanted to. It was a matter of age, and the fashion of her generation to use the old style.

Aleonica was barefoot, scrawny, and strong. Old women are all thin; it is only the young who are fat, fattened during their three-month confinements, after circumcision, marriage, and after each pregnancy. Fat is beauty. Fat is youth. Fat is fecundity. To be thin is to be like an old woman. Chagga women thought it hilarious when I told them that American women *want* to be slim.

We sat down in the house, glad to be out of the hot sun. There was one wooden chair which they insisted I sit on. There was a crude low wooden bench leaning against the wall where Daria and the ayah sat down. Aleonica stood and held the baby for a while, then sat on a stool, the only other piece of furniture in the room. In the corner on the beaten earth floor there was a gunny sack full of beans, and next to it a pottery cooking vessel. We talked about the present of meat Daria had brought. She reminisced about her childhood. Much of it had been spent in the house of her maternal grandmother. The second female child and the second male child belong to the maternal side of the family, while the firstborn of each sex belong to the father's side. The grandmother had been widowed early in Daria's life. The inheritor of her grandmother, brother of her grandfather, was a butcher. Since the responsibility of looking after them was his, "Every day he brought some piece of meat," Daria said, "Every day. That is why we are strong, and my mother is strong."

While this conversation was going on dozens of flies walked all over us. There was no slapping them away. Eventually the slight tickle of the walking legs is only bothersome on one's face. The rest one gets used to. People came in and out of the open door, to peer at the baby and to have a look at me. There were old and young women, wives of Daria's father's lineage. They came in and out one or two at a time, about six all together. Then Daria's father appeared. He greeted her by calling her the female name of the lineage. He took the baby and held it up to make it smile and gurgle. It was Daria's second son, hence, the son with an affinity for her side of the family. Her father looked very pleased. He was wearing a tattered, dust-colored shirt and shorts. The fraying, holes, patches are part of the style of a shirt. He had a jaunty moustache, a small chin-beard, and a beautiful smile, which revealed a great gap.

Both he and Aleonica were missing two lower teeth, the incisors. The extraction of these teeth in childhood was a Chagga tradition which is little observed nowadays, but was still fairly widely practised in the generation that is now past sixty. A variety of explanations are given. Most often today, people say it was to permit feeding in case of lockjaw. That sounds implausible, perhaps even designed for European consumption, but it is widely said. Since those are the first teeth to come in, and their advent in the first and second sets was a ritual of significance, their removal must have had some symbolic cultural meaning quite apart from precautions about lockjaw.

When I asked Aleonica whether she was frightened as a child about having to have those teeth out, and whether it hurt much, she said.

"No, it did not hurt. I wanted to have those teeth out. The older girls used to tease the younger girls and say that they were just like pigs, not like human beings, because they had all their teeth." One of the greatest insults that can be hurled at a Chagga is to say he or she is like an animal. Plainly, all prescribed bodily mutilations, whatever their other multiple meanings, do distinguish people from animals. And for Aleonica, as a child, having those teeth pulled meant growing up.

Aleonica's husband was very evidently pleased by the sight of his daughter and new little grandson. He smiled his gap-toothed smile again and again. He asked how our journey had been and by what means we had arrived. Eventually he left. Under foot, among the adults who came and went, there were at least half a dozen children who wanted to see the new baby and the *mzungu,* the European. Most of them left, but one stayed and put her head in Aleonica's lap, and hugged her legs. This was Daria's second daughter, Rosa, who lived with Aleonica. Rosa was about five. She had lived with her grandmother Aleonica from the time of the birth of her younger brother, Daria's third child. Aleonica wanted a child, and Daria thought it would be very difficult to manage two young children. She had even sent her eldest away to stay for six months with friends of her husband when the second child arrived. Many Chagga children grow up having spent considerable time living in other households, almost invariably of kin.

When Daria had a new baby, she gave it very nearly her total attention during the first three months, the months of her confinement to the *kihamba.* After that, it was still very much the most dominant child in her life for two or three years, and the fewer older children she had around, the more efficiently she could manage. It was thus partly for her own sake that Daria gave up Rosa, when she was two, to her mother.

However advantageous this transaction may have been from the point of view of decreasing Daria's work, it was obviously still very painful to her to have given up her child. The child was very much attached to her grandmother, and literally clung to her much of the time that I was there. Rosa did go off to get herself some food. She came back with a bowl of cassava flour and water mixed into a white gluey paste that one of the other women had given her, but once with us, she put her bowl in her granny's lap and leaned on her as she ate. I asked why she was so clinging. She had seen me a number of times before so that I did not think it likely that my presence had much to do with it. Daria laughed and said that she thought it was because Rosa was afraid of being taken away from her grandmother, taken back to her mother's home. "She prefers to stay with her grandmother where she is the only child and gets all the attention. She does not want to go home and sleep in the same bed with three siblings and have to share with the others the scant bit of attention her mother has for such big girls." Daria did take her home from time to time for a day or two "so she would not forget." And the child made a big scene every time. Daria said that normally Rosa slept in the bed with her grandmother, entwined in her arms. Aleonica nodded with a grin. They kept warm that way and neither of them felt lonely. When Rosa went home she tried to cuddle with her older sister, who hated it and pushed her away. The women thought this was very funny. The discomfiture of children is a general subject of laughter. Rosa was now a pet for her grandmother's pleasure. As she grew older, she would become a helper, just at the age when her grandmother might find a young hand useful.

These sleeping arrangements are not at all unusual. As was indicated in the biography of Siara, a husband is not a companion for his wife. Friendships are made with persons of the same sex. A young man may sleep in the house with his wife until there are a few small children. Then he will move out into his own hut or room, and only call his wife to his bed when he wants her sexually. After the earliest days of marriage, a wife does not normally eat with her husband. She prepares his food for him, but he eats alone. When she brings him supper after he comes home at night, she tastes it to show it is not poisoned. Husband and wife are wary partners in an intimate enterprise, rather than friends.

Thus, a child is an important companion for an old woman, a daily companion and a nightly companion, and eventually becomes old enough to share the work. Chagga men are away from the house and away from the kihamba much of the day, unless there is heavy agricultural work to do, or work to do with the coffee. For about six months of the year, men are very free, and have time to go to meet their male friends and talk. In the afternoons, they go to the beer shops, and they come home when it begins to get dark.

The Chagga feel that friendships with persons of the same sex and about the same age are normal and universal. They think it funny to see European men chatting with their wives, taking walks with them, and they have heard that they eat together. They make jokes about their masculinity. Men should be friends with men, women with women. Their separate provinces of work are fairly, though not completely exclusive. A man may not even know on which day the market falls in his own subvillage, because the market is "women's business." A woman is not likely to know anything about local politics unless it directly concerns her kin, because that is "men's business."

The major occupation of a woman, young or old, is to raise the food with which to feed her family. When she is young and has many children, she must grow a lot of food. When she is older, she may grow less, having fewer mouths to feed. But all her life, food is her responsibility. She plants, weeds, cultivates, harvests and prepares the staple vegetable foods which she and her husband eat. She also cuts and cooks bananas from the kihamba of her husband. If there is meat, it is supplied by her husband. Occasionally he may give her a few shillings to buy some meat at the butcher shop to prepare principally for him, or he may bring home a slaughter share from his lineage feasts. From time to time she also may receive a slaughter share from her own lineage. But basically family meals are prepared from the staple vegetable foods, especially beans, maize, cassava, and bananas. Most farmer husbands seldom give their wives any cash. The coffee cash belongs to the husband and he is not expected to give any of it to his wife for her amusement, though he does have an obligation to supply enough to clothe her and the children. When a man does give his wife any cash, it is usually with the direction that she buy a particular thing with it: meat, or grain for beer, or an item of clothing. She does not have any "spending money" from her husband over which she has discretion. Aleonica was only too glad to grumble about how hard it was to get enough cash, and how lucky men were, and how stingy. In fact, it is not difficult to engage most Chagga women in discussions of this kind, and the general tone is invariably the same. It is not merely that the anthropologist is regarded as a possible source of money or presents, as all Europeans are. Such comments represent a much more profound economic reality. It is related to the heavy economic burdens which women bear, and to the particular Chagga configuration of the war between the sexes.

If a wife wants to drink bought beer at the *pombe* shop, she must earn the money herself at the market, selling her surplus produce or the bananas from the kihamba. The markets are women's markets. Traditionally, they were for married women only. Now young girls sometimes come to the market, and there are also some itinerant male merchants who sell manufactured goods, cloth, second-hand clothing, and a few other items not produced on the mountain itself. But essentially the market remains the place of married women. Not only must a wife produce and prepare food, but she must obtain the water and the firewood with which to do so, and in fact must carry all the water for household use to the house each day. If there is a cow, she must cut the grass for it, usually down on the plain. She cultivates some of her vegetables in the kihamba where she can, among the coffee bushes and the banana plants, at the edges, in little patches here and there. She usually also cultivates another field, a shamba, down at the foot of the mountain where she grows more maize and beans and perhaps millet for beer-making. These duties are learned in childhood when female children are expected to help their mothers and are performed during the whole of a woman's life. At a young girl's circumcision party, an old woman of her own lineage gives her a hoe. It must be an old hoe that has produced many beans, so that it will produce many beans for the girl when she is married. It is the small hoe that women use in one hand. The girl then does a dance with it that is a simulation of digging. It is a literal symbol of her married life to come.

Aleonica told me what work she had done each day of the week before my visit. No doubt her account was very selective, and she was telling me what she wanted me to believe. Other material, gathered in observing other women and talking with them, suggests that as far as it went, what she told me of her activities was probably true. The first thing she did every morning was to go down to the foot of the steep hill where she lived. There was a school at the foot and a chapel where she said her morning prayer. "These days," she said,

"I am praying for rain." Next to the school is the subvillage water tap, and she fills her gallon tin and carries it up the hill to her house. That takes care of her usual daily household needs for water. Not much washing is done in that house. When she gets back up to her house, she makes hot water for tea, and drinks. Beyond that, her routine is slightly different each day. On Tuesday she stayed at home to work in the garden and to cut grass for the cows in the immediate environs. She also spread a sack of beans out in the sun to dry. That was around ten o'clock or so (but of course she has no watch, nor clock, nor has anyone in the houses around her). Although she speaks of a precise time, she means, "A few hours later . . . I did so and so." She usually eats some cold food, leftovers from the night before. There are two meals, a morning meal and a night meal, never more. That particular day, because she was staying at home, she cooked some food for the morning meal, bananas and fat, salt, onions, and tomato. When the vegetable stew was cooked, she ate some. After eating, she began the job of shelling the dried beans which she did by putting them in a sack and then beating it with a stick. The shells come off after a vigorous beating.

In the evening she prepared some more food, ate and slept. Rosa was not with her. She had been left at the neighboring house of the wife of Aleonica's cousin, her mother's brother's son, because the next day Aleonica was going to market. When she leaves Rosa with someone for the day, she also leaves food for the person to feed her. When older children are entrusted with the care of younger children, as they frequently are, they often eat the food left for the baby themselves, giving as little as possible to the younger child. Adults are considered more reliable as "babysitters" from the point of view of stealing food. But children are cautioned not to accept food from certain women lest they be poisoned. A mother often has her suspicions about the malevolence of a particular sister-in-law or other neighbor and does not allow her children near her.

On Wednesday morning, after praying, fetching water, and having tea, Aleonica swept the cow stall and cut some banana leaves for the cows. (It was her husband's responsibility to feed the goat, this being the traditional division of labor.) She ate a little cold food left over from the night before and then went to the market. She was going to sell *magaddi*, a kind of soda, which the Chagga used in cooking, rather the way salt is used in our own cookery. Magaddi-selling is her regular "business." She obtains the magaddi by walking to Taveta, in Kenya, twice a month. There she buys half a gunny sack and carries it back to her house. When she goes to market, every fourth day, she carries a small bowlful at a time, gradually selling off her stock. Going to Kenya to buy the soda is no small walk. Taveta is at least twenty miles from where she lives. The Kenyans do not permit Tanzanians to bring in Tanzanian currency, nor to take out any Kenyan currency. The market women thus either must smuggle or go to Taveta with something to sell, like bananas or something else they have grown. If they sell what they have brought, then they can use the Kenya money to buy something to take home again to the Tanzanian side. Sometimes they barter. Taveta is an old market center to which Chagga women have been going for at least a hundred years and probably many more than that. New economic restrictions between Kenya and Tanzania can be an inconvenience but not a complete deterrent to their customary commerce. Aleonica has been going to Taveta to buy mag-addi to resell on the mountain just about all her adult life. Daria remembers going with her as a child, weeping with exhaustion from the long walk and the heavy burdens she carried on her head.

After the market, on Wednesday, Aleonica went to the beer shop to drink with her friends. She had the money from the sales of her soda to spend on herself. She bought a bit of fish, some salt and some milk at the market, but she had enough left for beer. She had had a fine day seeing kin and old friends. It was at the market that day that her daughter Daria had told her we might be coming to visit soon. Since, when they marry, Chagga women move to live on their husband's land, related women and women who were neighborhood friends as young girls are invariably more scattered than men. The major discontinuity in a woman's life is the shift from daughter to wife and mother. Being scattered, kinswomen and friends rely on meeting at the market, on the way to the fields at the foot of the mountain, and on their way to and from church, and at beer parties. Thus, work away from the house, work in the shamba on the plain, or work going to and from market, and even for some women, going to and from the subvillage water spigot, or washing clothes in the river is an occasion for seeing friends. Of these, the market is the most important and regular female social event.

Aleonica's old mother, who must surely be at least eighty, also has a "business." Hers is tobacco. She grows tobacco, dries the leaves, and prepares them to be sold as chewing tobacco. She has done this all her life and continues to keep herself in beer money this way. These are clever and enterprising women. Not all women have such a "business"; some simply sell their surplus produce. But even this may take business acumen. Since bananas do not ripen simultaneously all over the mountain, it is possible simply by walking a distance to bring produce to a market where it will be scarcer item than at the nearest one. There are many ways to raise a few *senti* (cents) and the women know them. Usually it involves long walks, with a heavy head load, for small amounts of money, but it is possible, and it is part of what many women do to finance their own pleasures.

When Aleonica got home from the beer shop, she cooked the evening meal. That day it was cornmeal flavored with the fried fish she had bought at the market. On Thursday, she picked more beans in the morning to put them in the sun to dry. For the morning meal she prepared cornmeal and soured milk. Then she shelled the dried beans, after which she went to the beer shop for the rest of the afternoon. When she returned home, she cooked the evening meal of bananas and beans flavored with salt, soda, and fat. On Friday, for the morning meal she ate leftover food. Then she cut grass to feed the cow, and again shelled dried beans.

In the evening she prepared bananas and meat. She had brought the meat by sending the ayah of Mwali, her mother's brother's son's wife, the same woman with whom she had left Rosa. That time she paid for the meat out of her own pocket. Sometimes she did, sometimes her husband paid for the meat. She had many fights with her husband about money, and told me, "All women and men fight about money." Daria agreed that this was universal. Other women have told me the same, and of course they want to know whether it is the same in America.

On Saturday Aleonica swept the cow stall, and again picked beans to dry. While they were drying, she ate the morning meal of cornmeal and water. Then she shelled the beans, and afterwards sent off to a shop on the main road, where she bought some soda. She told me that she had run out of magaddi for selling, and that she had a friend who ran the shop who sometimes bought soda for her when she did not go to Taveta for one reason or another and did not have enough to sell. She in turn evidently shared the half a gunny sack she brought back from Taveta with the shopkeeper. Then she went home, prepared the evening meal, and went to sleep. On Sunday she swept her own house, cut banana leaves for the cows, got dressed and went to church. After church, she came home for a short while and then went to the beer shop to spend the rest of the afternoon. Sunday is the day everyone on Kilimanjaro who can possibly do so goes to the beer shop in the afternoon. It is the day when the most beer is sold and the most sociability takes place, walking home after church and then later in the beer shops. On Monday, early in the morning, Aleonica went to her shamba, on the plain. It was late February, and she wanted to prepare the earth for the spring rains. She worked alone in the shamba, but on the way there and back met many women she knew, and they walked in both directions together and talked and laughed. When she got back late in the afternoon, she went as usual to the beer shop to relax after the hard work, and then ultimately went home to cook dinner and go to bed.

This is the essence of a woman's week. Because she is old and has only one child to look after, little Rosa, she is free to spend much time at the beer shop and to linger over the more sociable parts of the work days. She reserves no time for Rosa. Rosa is simply there and must amuse herself with the other children. She is usually nominally left in the care of Mwali, or Mwali's ayah, but actually she is out on the path with a flock of other children most of the

time. Chagga mothers, let alone grandmothers, do not consider it their place
to play with children after infancy and toddler ages. In that early period, they
do play with them, but not later. "There is too much work to do," they say.
"They can play with the other children." And so they do, small flocks of tiny
people, seven-year-olds looking after two-year-old siblings, little boys running
around in a gang of little boys of all sizes, kicking a bundle of leaves to each
other for a ball, or fighting with sticks, or sometimes chasing each other,
wrestling together. They return to the house for meals, but otherwise generally stay outside and entertain themselves, except when they are required to
help in the work of the household into which they are inducted as soon as
they are at all competent. Tiny girls can be seen cutting grass for the cows
with the small hooked women's knife, washing clothes, carrying water, and
the like. Very small boys are sent on errands, to get beer, to take a message to
someone, and such.

Aleonica's account of her week is endlessly concerned with food-growing,
food-obtaining, and food preparation. That is her job, and it is the job of all
the farm wives and widows on the mountain. It is a permanent job which no
one wants to take from her, but it is solitary. At home, however, when she
wants her, there is Rosa, and an endless stream of contacts with sisters-in-law
and their children. Her daughters visit her occasionally, and she, them. Her
nonkin friends can always be found at the market, on the road to the
shambas, at Church and at the beer shop. She eats alone or with Rosa, never
with her husband, who always eats alone, like most Chagga men. She does not
see her unrelated friends either at her home or at theirs, unless there is some
special celebration and a beer party. People do not visit for meals unless they
have come a long distance and are staying in the house for some days. Nor do
couples visit other couples. Invited group sociability is at beer parties which
both men and women attend. Hence, a husband and wife may walk to such a
party together, but they usually separate when they arrive, to spend their
time with members of their own sex. A man does not receive his friends at
home any more than a woman does, though certain kin drop in quite freely.
Aleonica is not lonely, nor does she have much problem finding company
when she wants it.

Her complaints about the present are not much related to her age, which
she wears lightly, being in remarkable muscular condition. They have to do
with the general condition of modernity which has brought with it some good
things, but also what she perceives as some very bad ones. "The good thing is
that houses are better than they were," but that, she assured me, was
unimportant compared with the bad things.

One of them which was obviously a matter of concern to her was that in
the old days if a woman were widowed, she could count on being inherited
by one of the kinsmen of her husband, but that these days with the

Protestant Church's insistence on monogamy and its objection to widow inheritance, a widow might find herself very insecure, with a sort of lineage guardian, but no husband. Her access to cash and to sex has been interfered with by these Christian alterations of custom. "A man can marry again, and do as he pleases as always, but a woman has difficulties," she said gloomily. Her husband was still very much alive, but she obviously was worried by the possibility of becoming a widow. Particularly as she had no son, no one in her husband's lineage would be likely to look after her as assiduously as men did in the old days, when women were fully inherited, and did not simply become wards of the heir, but true wives. Asked about how it was that men managed to have more than one wife in the old days, how there were enough women to go around, Aleonica said what most Chagga insist is true, that there are vastly more Chagga women than men. A look at baptismal records in the church seems to indicate that the male-female ratio is fairly balanced at birth in *Uchagga*, as it is in most places unless interfered with. But the generally believed-in myth is that there are far more Chagga women than men and that there always were. And it may be more than myth, since labor migration removes many young men, and old women live longer than their husbands.

Another way in which Aleonica says things were better in the old days is, "In the old days children were the slaves of their parents. They did what they were told. They obeyed. They never did anything without first asking permission. Today, the children no longer obey!" Within a few sentences Aleonica was telling me about the abortifacients cooked up in her youth, and about an old woman who used to abort young girls with a little stick, suggesting that perhaps all was not quite as obedient in the old days as she had asserted, and that she knew it. But she was telling me about the *conventional past.* The truth of her statement lies in the selective recollection of her own childhood, and her irritation with the current behavior of the adolescents in her husband's lineage. Young people do now go very much more their own way than formerly, when far fewer children went to school, and certainly more than she remembers doing herself as a child.

But, without a doubt, the things which come up most often in her conversation about past and present are two: food and witchcraft. She says very often that food used to be more abundant. It was easier to get. There was not so much money, not so much buying things, people shared more, and there was more to eat. That is quite possibly an accurate description of the past, not simply a golden recollection. As the land has been filled with coffee, which is inedible, it has replaced bananas which are edible not only by humans, but also by cattle. The Chagga knew how to dry bananas and preserve them for long periods of time. The population has skyrocketed, so that there is more pressure on the land, and less land is given to food cultivation than ever before, so the pressure of the population is proportionately greater. Since food production and preparation are a woman's life, it is no wonder that that is the most emphatic thing Aleonica has to say about why things used to be better.

Her second preoccupation is with illness and death. That is where witchcraft comes in. She says, "People did not sicken and die the way they do today." In fact, of course, the population is burgeoning and no doubt people died in much greater numbers in the past. But that is not what she is talking about. What she means is that as the trial of witches had been illegal since colonial times, witchcraft and sorcery go almost unchecked. Moreover, good transportation makes it possible to go easily by bus to buy harmful medicine from the Pare, a neighboring people who have a great reputation for witchcraft among the Chagga, or to go to Tanga, a port on the coast where such things are obtainable. The general sense of what she says is also that there is more immorality, more ill will, less respect for the elders and the ancestors which would inhibit such wicked goings-on. Thus, although she prays every day and seldom misses a Sunday morning at Church, Aleonica is not convinced that Christianity has diminished the evil that is about.

This is a woman who wore no clothes as a child except for a string or a chain around her hips, a woman who still urinates and defecates in the banana garden, having no outhouse, and who carefully conceals her body products and hair and nails, lest they be obtained for evil purposes by someone who wishes to harm her. Daria, her elder daughter, has a transistor radio in her house, but has many of the same ideas about sorcery as her mother the magaddi-seller and her grandmother the tobacco-seller. "Many things have changed," says Aleonica, "and many of them are worse than they were. People are worse." This is her comment on the irreversible changes that have permeated the life-term social arena in which she has been permanently enclosed.

CONCLUSIONS

In any society, the fact of childhood implies growth: It clearly denotes the continuing process of getting older, bigger, stronger, more knowledgeable, and more autonomous, more in control of self and others. Whether or not adulthood continues this trajectory of increasing powerfulness, in what form, and for how long, obviously depends on what society one lives in, and what social position one occupies there. Inevitably, physical growth stops at maturity and, as one ages, some physical skills decline. One cannot indefinitely grow bigger and stronger of body. If the momentum of childhood is to increase, the sense of "getting somewhere," of unending achievement, is to be sustained in adulthood and on into maturity, it must involve an accumulation of more than physical growth: skill or knowledge, honor, power, the right to property. It must involve loyalties to kin and friendships. All such accumulations are culturally defined extensions of the self. And many, in the theory at least, could expand almost indefinitely.

Among many nonindustrial peoples, as among the nineteenth-century Chagga, aging (at least ideally) is accompanied by a parallel, lifelong process of social stockpiling that promises rewards for seniority at every stage of life. A successful man in such a society may have more kin, more descendants, more social debtors and social allies, more honor and prestige as he grows older. A woman may have more younger co-wives or sisters-in-law, daughters and daughters-in-law to order about, more grown children and grandchildren to marry off, or to mobilize in times of need, and herself may steadily gain power and honor with age. There is some continuity over the whole course of life for the successful individual in these seniority-oriented societies. Fulsome success requires longevity. The deference a person must give in youth to his or her elders, he or she hopes to receive in maturity and old age from others, if he or she survives to elderhood. There is asymmetry in all the relationships of junior and senior, but they are sequential. Everyone has a turn. That is, everyone has a turn who lives long enough to enjoy it, and also provided the disturbances of social change do not interfere.

There are two prominent dimensions of such an arrangement that sometimes, but by no means always, are different or transformed in our society: social cumulation and continuity. In seniority-oriented societies, in which the social arena is a life-term social arena, old age is potentially the peak of a lifetime of accumulation. And surely the most important of the things accumulated are durable social relationships. Among most if not all non-industrial people (and in many sectors of industrial society as well), it is recognized that access to human beings is the greatest wealth and power there is. This is especially obvious where labor cannot be hired, and most property is not durable but needs to be constantly renewed or newly produced. There social relationships (and the potential assistance they imply) are clearly the most long-lived and reliable riches. That is not to say that property is not also stockpiled where possible, but its very accumulation is often the secondary product of a multiplicity of social relations.

Even under modern conditions, a society like that of the Chagga retains a great many of these characteristics. An outsider passing one of the lush banana gardens might suppose that each household, being potentially nearly self-sufficient in the production of staple foods, is truly independent in ways that no urban American ever experiences. But that would be an illusion, built out of an urban American nostalgia for an imaginary rural life in which each household is a self-contained unit of production and consumption, allied to others, not out of economic necessity, but out of affectionate bonds of kinship, friendship, and neighborliness. It is quite true that in the best of times, and at the right moment in the life cycle, a Chagga household is relatively economically self-sufficient as far as staples are concerned. But the key question is that of time. Over any long run, no Chagga household is economically self-sufficient, let alone socially self-sufficient. If a woman is sick, or bearing a child, or must leave for a day or more to obtain goods at a distant market, her work must be done by someone else. The household must still be provided with water, prepared food, and firewood. The cow must have fodder and have her stall swept. The other animals must be fed. The round of household tasks is relentless, endless, and unremitting. Someone must do them. No one goes through life without illnesses, without absences, without bad luck with crops. Women rely on other women to help them out in looking after the children, in caring for the beasts, in doing the tasks for each other that cannot be done for reasons of illness, or marketing, or absence for whatever cause.

If a man is sick, his wife may look after him, but if his illness lasts a long time, someone must do his work for him, and help out the household. The men sometimes cultivate shambas together, helping each other with the agricultural work, occasionally exchanging labor and sharing work that is more easily and more pleasurably done together. Men also do the house-building and all manner of repairs and heavy work in the kihamba. If a man is temporarily incapacitated, this work must still be done, as it must if he leaves for a while to take a job in the city, or somewhere else. He must take care of the coffee, the pruning and the spraying and the picking and the hulling and drying, and the bagging and hauling the bag to the cooperative for weighing and sale. The work of men is more seasonal than that of women, except, of course, for care of the goats and animals, but men, too, are economically indispensable, and an illness or an absence is seriously dislocating.

The way in which all such crises are coped with by the Chagga is to have reliable established relations of exchange of services with particular local kin. These are also a resource for a loan of cash or beasts in bad times, as well as for every imaginable kind of assistance. But the principal household with which such exchange services are established may itself undergo crises; hence, there are other persons to whom to appeal in that contingency, and still further concentric circles of social relations to which a person may resort if the usual sources are not able to help. One uncle may be able to assist with a loan of cash, while the wife of a brother may help with the child care, and the wife of still another brother may lend a pot, and so it goes. Every family is entangled in dozens, if not hundreds, of such mutualities, all the time. And these forms of mutual assitance are always with persons with whom there are personal relationships. These are not impersonal transactions. They are transactions conducted under the banner of kinship and friendship, acts of obligatory generosity, of mandatory yet seemingly voluntary open-handedness. Usually the exchange is not immediate, but deferred, not an identical exchange, though in the long run it is likely to be an equivalent one. The loan of a pot is not necessarily returned by a loan of a pot, nor need the favor be returned soon, but as the need for it arises. No doubt the ledgers are supposed to balance in the long run, but the time that will elapse before the recipient of a favor can return it is of uncertain length, and the relationship must be characterized by considerable trust for it not to turn into a hostile one. Thus, even under modern conditions, the Chagga are interdependent in a range of relationships that stretches far beyond any individual household. Moreover, those relationships of interdependence are highly personal in content.

Often in a nonindustrial society, the longer the life, the greater the opportunity to assemble such useful, durable relationships and the symbols of obligation that go with them. These obviously are not assembled only for aggrandizement, but out of necessity. No cultivator who is to any extent dependent on himself for food production can *survive* without people who can be called upon in times of disaster, emergency, or danger, let alone to assist in those occasional but inevitable tasks like house-building that are better done by a larger group of people than any household can muster. Between the moments when they are needed, these relationships often are maintained through obligatory ritual exchanges, beer-drinking, conversation, and other apparently noninstrumental forms of interaction. When times are good, these may look quite pointless to an outsider. Yet they clearly give more than pleasure and emotional support. In every life, there are times of illness, of accident, of temporary incapacity. At such times in a subsistence economy, survival depends upon having well-established ongoing relationships with many people in which the obligation to give assistance is recognized. In a full cash economy, such services may be hired, when needed or provided by the state, and the persons who fulfill them may be in contact with their employers or clients only for that purpose and for a very limited time.

In contrast, in nonindustrial societies, in a life-term social arena, a personal reliance on others with whom one has established ongoing relationships is by definition a permanent characteristic of life from childhood to old age. It could not be said from a *social* point of view that individuals in such societies have a dependent childhood, a completely independent young and middle adulthood, followed by a dependent old age. Such a sequence exaggerates the independence of adulthood and does not take into account the exigencies of inevitable emergencies. Only at the best of times are adults or even nuclear families in nonindustrial societies "independent," and they find themselves chronically in need of the relationships of generalized obligation they industriously collect and cultivate throughout life. They are acutely aware that to survive physically over a long period of time in a nonindustrial society it is necessary to be a recognized and active presence in a network of relationships of personal obligation. In contrast, in some modern industrial societies, it is possible to reach old age and have the means of physical survival while having lost any social arena in which one counts as a whole person. In America, it is possible for a kind of social death to precede physical death by many years. Impersonal services may be the only human contact. That is not possible in a society in which physical survival itself depends on personal social relationships accumulated and maintained from the beginning of life to the end.

Margaret Clark has asserted that preindustrial men are much more socioeconomically independent than industrial man. No doubt she has in mind the Durkheimian model in the *Division of Labor in Society*. On the surface, it is a plausible argument. A subsistence cultivator who produces in his garden and in his household all that his family needs to survive looks very independent to a resident of California. But, as has been pointed out, that is to look at the cultivator only at one moment in time, when his family is established and when all is well with him and his wife, children, crops, and domestic animals. It is a seriously distorted way of looking at his long-term situation. Durkheim's notion of mechanical solidarity, of a simple society welded together by its common culture and values, and not by any socioeconomic interdependence, can be exaggerated to a point where it describes no real society that ever existed. In her paper, Clark used the idea of primitive independence only as a contrasting case. Her principal focus is on the actual interdependence of modern American industrial man and his cultural stress on the "value" of independence. This she sees as a psychological denial of his actual socioeconomic interdependence. In her eyes, this is a damaging denial, since it makes the inevitable dependence of old age a stigmatized condition.

The point is interesting, but the analysis involves some basic problems. Psychological and socioeconomic dependence are treated as if they were the same thing. Even more troublesome is the fact that her paper does not take into account the difference between personal and impersonal social relationships when it considers the question of socioeconomic dependence. The ideology of independence Clark is discussing as a "value" may well be connected with the impersonal quality of many social relationships in a cash economy. Certainly she is right that modern industrial societies involve their citizens in a net of extreme socioeconomic interdependence. But this industrial interdependence is characterized by innumerable impersonal relationships. Many services are rendered without face-to-face contact, from the delivery of electric current to the filling of a can of soup. *No* service in a nonindustrial society is impersonal. That is a basic difference, and it means that in nonindustrial societies the recognition of human interdependence is ever-present because the supporting array of relationships *must* be consciously and constantly maintained as a resource. It is only in a society in which it is possible for lone individuals to survive physically without any personal relationships that the kind of idea of "independence" Clark is talking about could be entertained as a "value." In nonindustrial society, the two dimensions of a course of life mentioned earlier, cumulation and continuity, are intimately connected with close social interdependence, which, in turn, in these societies is frequently culturally elaborated into ideas of supernatural interdependence.

These three qualities of the course of life: continuity, cumulation, and close social interdependence are not uniformly absent in industrial society, nor unvarying in their form in nonindustrial societies. There are variations of degree and kind in both situations. Moreover, the greater likelihood of finding all three more prominent in certain nonindustrial societies does not of itself mean that old people necessarily have a thoroughly delightful time of it, as the lives of Siara and Aleonica should indicate. Many of their problems are different from ours, but they have troubles nevertheless. And even within a technologically less complex society, there is tremendous individual variation, just as there is in ours, or in any other society. The culture is a common frame of ideology and custom within which very different individual histories are played out.

Siara's old age, surrounded by familiar faces and spent in familiar places, if taken in terms of those characteristics only, may seem highly preferable to a lonely old age in modern urban isolation, housed among strangers, far from the locale in which one grew up and the people one once knew. But these, of course, are not the only characteristics of his old age. He is not altogether well physically and lacks many comforts. Worse, he must live with his emotional scars and ruminate about the relationships he has broken, first with his half-brother, then with his son. Everyone in his subvillage old enough to care about such matters knows all about his history. His private life is in a large measure a matter of public record. He must contemplate the possible consequences to himself of the dislike he has engendered in these disputes. There also is likely to be a further controversy about his land once he and his wife are dead, since he has no married son on the mountain to be his heir, whatever his hopes are of giving the land to his priest-son Johani. He is aware of the envy and desire for his property to which his longevity and prosperity have given rise. The closeness of the life-term social arena has its companionable pleasures and their twin bitter pressures. These characteristics are bound up with its intimacy and its persistence over time.

In the life-term social arena, one who is neither expelled nor obliged to leave must live constantly with his life history. One cannot avoid having been at one time or another party to taunting and punishing someone. It is not possible to reach maturity without having ill-will toward someone. One cannot avoid taking sides in the disputes of others even if lucky enough not to be directly involved. But if the disputes are one's own, cumulation may be of bad relations as well as good ones.

The continuity of social relations has its price, but there is virtually no being alone and without potential companions. There is no possibility of impersonal presence in the subvillage. And there is always someone whose obligation it is to look after one if help is needed. However, whether such a person is diligent or dilatory in meeting his obligations, whether he pushes one to extremes of want and requires public complaints to prod him into fulfilling his duty, or whether he does what he ought warmly and generously is a matter of individual variation, as it is in any society. The younger obligated person may dislike his older dependent. There is a very wide range of actual behavior subsumed under a common rhetoric or obligation. There are cases of neglect, but there is no possibility of an old person disappearing as a whole social being. It is not possible to become just an impersonal patient or an inmate of an institution with neither a significant social past nor a social present.

The cultural change that the present generation of Chagga has experienced is tremendous. Their fathers were spear-carrying, earring-wearing warriors with shields of leather. In the past seventy-five years, the sons have shifted from an indigenous religion to Christianity. They have moved part of the way into a money economy with their cash crop, coffee. They have built schools, roads, and dispensaries. Their political structure has been repeatedly reorganized. There is almost nothing in the realm of custom that is *exactly* the same as it was when the parents of the present elders were young. But it is distorting to stress these changes and ignore the fact that in the older areas of settlement some men have lived on the same plots of land all their lives and have had their major social relationships with the same people, or their offspring, all their lives. For them, the *cultural discontinuities are no more striking than the social continuities.*

Unlike their urban brothers in multitribal settings, at home their ethnicity has no political significance. The important thing is the subvillage (*mtaa*). It is the geographical social unit to which sentiment attaches. For a man, it is the place of the brothers and the nephews and the in-laws and the neighbors and the sons and grandsons of all of these. For a woman, it is where her children are born, where her sisters-in-law live, and her sons and their children. Often her own kin are in the same subvillage. Of the people who matter, most are there, and the place itself, the gardens and houses, the paths and irrigation ditches, the streams and the rocks are as familiar as the faces.

To properly understand this subvillage and its social continuity, to understand how its pattern works for the elderly, the age-distribution of the population must be considered. Very few of the contemporaries of an old man or an old woman remain. From the age of about fifty onward, the ranks are very thin. What does this do to the continuity of life in Chagga society in which people are strongly involved with companions of their own age as long as they can be, and in which age-cohorts remain very important though no longer formally designated as age-grades? It means that the mature and the elderly must make strong alliances with their juniors to have any continuing influence in the life of the subvillage. Today the strongest "natural" candidates for this within their cultural system are their own children and for men, especially, their lineage grandchildren. For a man, there may be added to these the children of deceased brothers or cousins whose paternal role the surviving inheritor may take over. In the old days, the age-grades were linked in senior and junior pairs.

In no society can social continuity signify going through all of life with the same people, since senior people die off and new junior ones grow up. Social continuity is maintained as a moving chain of connected relationships, linked by kinship and locality and overlapping time. No Chagga can go through all of a long life with a substantial cohort of persons of the same age-group. The contemporary cohort with whom the major contacts and transactions of youth and the early married years takes place is quickly decimated after fifty. The possibility of cumulation over time within particular relationships is often cut off by death. Hence, a socially important old age depends on accumulating strong alliances with the next generation.

Thus does the presence or absence of friendly links with younger brothers, sons, and nephews change the old age of a Chagga man, or amiable contacts with the wives of these men and with her own kin enhance the life of an old woman. In this respect, neither Siara nor Aleonica was alone, nor were they without many ties to other persons living around them, but they still did not consider themselves as fortunate as they might have been. Their situations are relatively good, but they fall short of the ideal Chagga old age. The flaw is that, lacking sons with families nearby, they find themselves surrounded by kin whose interest in them is secondary rather than primary in the Chagga hierarchy of intensity of relationship and obligation.

This Chagga material suggests that the social structure of a life-term social arena has special features. One of them is the heavy social importance of the accidents of kinship. The more fortuitous aspects of the configuration of families loom large. These, like sexual differences are *biologically based features of individual biography.* Analyses of ascribed status do not usually include the social consequences of these accidents, except perhaps for the sons of kings. Yet in the Chagga setting, and in that of many other societies, they are of enormous importance to everyone. It is, for example, evidently important to a Chagga man whether he is the first, the middle, or the last son of his father, and how many sons he has; and to a woman, which of these her husband is, and whether she has brothers and sons. It has been indicated that a structural consequence of the Chagga population pyramid is that since there are few aged, those persons who do survive to old age are likely to become socially dependent on their juniors. This exacerbates the importance of biological accident, not only who is born first, but who dies first and at what point. In old age, it matters very much to a man whether he has juniors in the family close to his own age, or whether his closest juniors are his offspring or those of his contemporaries. And very important, too, as has been indicated by the sketches of Siara and Aleonica, it matters whether he has married sons close by, and many of them, and is on good terms with them. It matters supremely who survives and for how long.

The absence of any real control over most of these accidents of family configuration over time is made the more poignant by the whole complex of beliefs that suggest that deaths and births are no accidents at all, but connected with the activities of living men and women, the dead and the deity. The many norms of obligation of juniors to seniors, and the many ways in which the aged are supposed to have supernatural power over their children may be more indicative of their true structurally weak position and the small number of the truly elderly, than the opposite.

In this century, as individuals have grown older in the more locally focused and closed Chagga subvillages, their options have narrowed, and they have become more and more bound by the facts of their family and neighborhood biographies. This may well be one of the general implications of the life-term social arena in these demographic conditions. It means that old age turns out well for some individuals and miserably for others. Common culture in no way obliterates individual differences of circumstance. The culture itself may intensify them.

The concept of the life-term social arena, generated as it has been here out of the Chagga material, provides a way of taking into account the importance of continuities in relationships over time, even in the presence of vast cultural change. It also implies a double perspective, biographical and collective. In the Chagga case, this double approach brings out the fact that Chagga society shares many features with other small-scale, nonindustrial communities, yet makes it abundantly clear at the same time that the characteristics of any particular social arena are given special meaning by local cultural ideas. It is the special Chagga meaning given to their not unusual demographic facts that gives color and shape to individual biography.

"Life-term social arenas" obviously imply the complementary concept, "limited-term social arenas." Old age reached in a life-term social arena cannot but be quite different from a life and an old age spent in several more temporary milieux. Both concepts stress the time factor in social relationships and postulate perduring arenas of interaction. These frameworks make an analytic connection between the individual and the aggregations of human beings with whom he has contact. But they try to do more, by taking time into consideration. By definition, old people have a past. There is no sound way to analyze their present without taking it into account.

Two old women *sharing a calabash of beer and some gossip at a wedding party.*

Traditional Chagga beehive hut, *modern cinderblock house and prosperous owner of both, standing in his* kihamba, *the banana and coffeegrove and vegetable garden that surround his house.*

Three periods of Chagga history reflected in clothing. *Two old men in costume for a ngoma. They are ready to perform a traditional dance for an American documentary film-maker who paid them to do so. The sweater and slacks are what a prosperous Chagga might wear on a Sunday these days. The white toga-like garment is the kind of costume worn in the late nineteenth century, and the headdresses of colobus-monkey fur are a traditional part of the warriors' ceremonial costume from much earlier in the nineteenth century.*

CHAPTER 3

WINNERS AND LOSERS:

Aging Yugoslavs in a Changing World

Andrei Simić

Kakva mladost, onakva i starost
As is youth so will be old age (Serbian proverb)

Raboti kako za sto godini da živeeš, a misli kako za utre oti Ke umriš
Work as if you would live a hundred years, and plan as if you were
    going to die tomorrow (Macedonian proverb)

Exactly what have modernization and rapid economic development meant
in the lives of aging Yugoslavs? Have loneliness, alienation, and cultural
disorientation become the inevitable results of industrialization, urbanization,
and social mobility? And, in fact, can changing values and customs alone
account for the dissatisfaction of many senior people when clearly disillusion-
ment and anomie were present among the elderly during the traditional
agrarian period?
Yugoslav anthropologist Vera Erlich (1971: 489 [my translation]) quotes
an elderly village informant regarding his unfulfilled expectations in his
declining years:

> This generation of old people is in an unenviable situation. When we were young we strived to please our elders, and now we must please the young. And when are we to live?

In this poignant manner, the author summarizes her impression that many older Yugoslavs now live under extreme stress due to poverty, lack of social services and medical care, the disparagement of traditional values associated with peasant life, and, most significantly, the failure of their children to replicate the kind of relationships they remember having long ago with their own parents. On the other hand, the foreign ethnographer coming from a highly volatile and mobile industrial-urban society cannot help but be struck by the very active and integrated roles played by the aged in the context of kinship and intergenerational relations in both rural and urban Yugoslavia. However, it would be erroneous to imply that these opposing generalizations are somehow mutually exclusive; rather, they simply represent different facets of the same social reality. One possible explanation for this disparity of viewpoints lies in the fact that the native observer enmeshed in the social arena she is investigating tends to assume a longitudinal focus stressing change, while the outsider, experientially lacking this diachronic perspective, is more likely to give weight to those elements that most obviously contrast with his own cultural environment.

Professor Erlich has undoubtedly captured the mood of many older Yugoslavs, but at the same time she has perhaps inadvertently called attention to certain human universals typical of the entire life cycle—the difficulty of coping with change, and the penchant for evaluation with its resultant dissatisfaction based on the inevitable disparity that occurs in all societies between the ideal and the actual. Furthermore, these traits assume new forms and functions in old age in relation to a growing sense of irrevocable finality.

Aging can be conceived of as a kind of career in which some succeed and others fail. Few, however, are the total winners they would like to be, nor are many the absolute losers they fear they might become. Most must resign themselves to somehow rationalizing their disappointments and defeats in light of limited victories and satisfactions, to content themselves with some middle ground between their direst apprehensions and their fondest desires. In this respect, old age is, above all else, a time for criticism, reflection, and retrospection; a time for summing up the debits and credits accrued over a lifetime of aspiration and struggle; a time for bringing about order from the seemingly chaotic chain of events and relationships that constitute a life history. Thus, this analytic process takes on a very special significance with advancing years. As life lies increasingly behind one, the opportunity for corrective and strategic action becomes more and more restricted and tenuous, and to a greater extent the vital sense of self-esteem and honor must be constructed and maintained out of the fabric of the past. In this respect, one measure of success in aging is the ability to conceptualize the present and future as meaningful on the basis of their antecedents, to be able to explain and take pleasure in what *is* and *will be* within the framework of what *was*. In so doing, it is possible to create a sense of continuity and connectedness with those people, places, happenings, and ideas that have now come to constitute the bulk of life's experience and essence. To sever these supportive links, or to fail to attribute meaning to them, is to deprive the present of its symbolic potential, to be alienated and adrift, isolated in the moment. In some cases, misfortune or the fraud of others have rendered the task difficult or even impossible; in others, imprudence, miscalculation, and lack of insight have at one point or another closed the avenues to significant past ties and experience. Clearly, however, old age is not universally a detached and passive state, but rather in its optimal form constitutes a creative period when the paradoxes of both individual and cultural experience are resolved.

For the aged, culture assumes a very special evaluative meaning, providing the measure by which gains and losses accrued over a lifetime may be appraised and interpreted. In highly complex, heterogeneous, large-scale societies such as our own, these standards are various, involuted, and frequently contradictory. Similarly, in periods of rapid change, the criteria for judging men and their products tend to be ephemeral, inconclusive, and even paradoxical. In contrast, in more isolated, stable, and homogeneous social arenas, values appear to be fewer and more integrated. Nevertheless, success and failure occur in all settings though the pitfalls may vary and the cultural guidelines differ in their specificity and pervasiveness. In other words, no social system can offer all of its members a single plan that will guarantee them equally a final reward of absolute honor and satisfaction; rather, those things held in the greatest esteem are always distributed differentially, be they wealth, power, affection, sexuality, or respect. In a sense, culture is a tempter, holding its ideals just out of reach and unobtainable in their entirety, setting a stage whose very ambiguity and redundancy makes conflict, manipulation, and competition inevitable, with the greatest rewards going to the clever and the lucky.

In this chapter, I have chosen to give these viewpoints substance in terms of the recent histories of two Serbian families whose fates are personified in a vitally optimistic seventy-six-year-old peasant visiting his grandchildren for the first time in California, and a depressed octogenerian passing his last years in a home for the aged in a provincial Yugoslav town. Their biographies suggest the possible range of experience in aging within a single cultural matrix, and recall Max Weber's view (cf. Bendix 1966: 260-267) of society as an equilibrium between opposing forces, an entity that can only be interpreted in terms of the understandable behavior of individuals whose most ordinary actions involve and make reference to primary beliefs and assumptions without which they could not function. Stated in another way, these case histories reveal individuals attempting to resolve with varying degrees of success the oppositions inherent in society and culture through everyday choices. In this sense, aging can be seen as a career constructed like any other, with one advantage or value weighed and traded off against another, building upon the present and past for future payoffs.

There are those rare moments when cultural ideals and personal aspirations seem to be realized in some tangible and easily grasped form, when life really appears to be exactly as it should be. During such brief interludes, normal activity and time are suspended, and the values that underlie and generate so much of ordinary and commonsense behavior become overt. However, such occasions not only reaffirm idealized and desired social forms, but also act as a kind of historical marker for the individual, a time to pause and summarize what has gone before, to reappraise one's place in the world, and to speculate as to the direction the future is likely to take.

Mirko's *slava* was such an event. It was the first time he had commemorated the Lazić family patron, St. George, since coming to California over nine years before, by way of West Germany from an impoverished village in the rugged hills of central Serbia.

Somehow until now he had felt vaguely out of place, not really at home in the tree-lined Sacramento suburb with its two-car garages, broad lawns, and cavernous family rooms. For Mirko, "home" had always meant the whitewashed adobe house perched on a rocky bluff overlooking the family's three and one-half hectares of eroded field and pasture, the house in which he, his father, and his grandfather had been born. Until this year, he could not imagine the Lazić slava being held anywhere else. He remembered hearing in the village, "one estate, one slava," and indeed he had never given up his rightful share of the patrimony but had simply turned it over to his father and brothers to work in his absence. In spite of the distance that separated them, they had remained in spirit a single household.

Every year since they had arrived in America, Mirko's wife, Lepa, had prepared a festive supper on May 6 as a recognition of the slava, but there had been no guests or ritual—just a better than ordinary meal of Serbian delicacies for the couple and their three preschool children. The "real" commemoration was taking place in the village where "the old man," Mirko's father Mitar, was celebrating "for them all." On St. George's Day, each of the twelve related Lazić households in Slatina would be receiving guests: neighbors, in-laws, and godparents (*kumovi*). People were not invited in any formal sense to the festivities, they simply knew when it was proper, and indeed obligatory, to

AUTHOR'S NOTE: *The names of informants and places have been changed wherever necessary to protect anonymity.*

appear at the slava. Good friends who exchanged labor, loaned each other oxen for plowing, and extended mutual aid in times of sickness and death recognized the importance of such ritual events. During his first years in America among a foreign and at times "peculiar" people, Mirko had no such neighbors or obligations. All his sentiments remained tied to that isolated Balkan village where he had spent more than thirty years planting, plowing, and reaping like generations before him.

Recently, Mirko's self-image and view of the world had changed, and this year he felt exhilarated and more fulfilled than ever before. He had come a long way, and alone through hard work and cunning had pulled himself and his entire family from the depths of poverty. He remembered Slatina with its more than one hundred red-tiled roofs punctuating the green flanks that rose steeply from the marshy pasture below the village. He recalled the good things: the copses of oak and poplar, spring water gushing ice cold from the rocks, the smell of *rakija* distilling from the fall's harvest of fermented apples and plums, three-day weddings with their gypsy musicians and drunken revelry, and, most of all, how his father would get up at dawn on the day of their slava to start roasting a spitted lamb in the courtyard. Other memories gave him less pleasure: their primitive house with eight of them sleeping on prickly straw mattresses thrown on the floor of a single dank room, his ninety-three-year-old grandmother lying on a cot in the kitchen dying slowly day by day, the constant struggle to extract a living from their "fourth-class" land, and the seemingly endless meals of beans, cornmeal mush, and peppers.

For Mirko, 1958 had been the turning point in his life. For a long time before that he had been troubled regarding what the future might hold for them all. His oldest brother, Kosta, had married, bringing his bride home, and soon there would be children. This meant more mouths to feed, but on the other hand his mother was less robust than before, and soon his three sisters would be marrying into other village homes, so at least a new daughter-in-law would be a welcome help for the "old lady." Nevertheless, the situation could go only from bad to worse. However, Mirko's induction into the Yugoslav army that sultry July day, an event that bore no particular promise of good fortune, was to totally alter the family's fate.

He found it difficult to leave home, and even felt a tinge of guilt that his share of the work would fall to others. Most of all, he worried about his mother. His father was a just and even gentle man by village standards, but stern and aloof with his children and wife. He had always addressed Mirko's mother simply as "you" or "old woman," without any sign of endearment or affection. Mirko did not find this strange, since it was the same in almost all Slatina households. In fact, for it to have been otherwise would have seemed almost indecent. Nevertheless, he was pleased to note that his father was mellowing and becoming more communicative with age, sometimes even openly seeking advice from his wife. Mirko was pleased because he knew how much his mother had constantly sacrificed for them all, giving up what few small pleasures and luxuries she might have kept for herself for the benefit of the rest. He recalled what the village schoolmaster, an outsider living with his crotchety widowed mother in a single room adjoining the four-year Slatina school, had once said: "Our fathers are devils, and our mothers, angels."

Mirko had left for the army like every other village youth, bedecked with flowers and dead drunk in the back of a horse-drawn peasant cart. His family and friends had lifted him barely conscious onto the bus in Soko Banja after a dusty ride over rutted village roads. He had never been further from Slatina than the eighteen kilometers to Aleksinac, where he sometimes helped his mother or sisters sell produce on the *pijaca*, the open marketplace where peasants from more than a dozen villages converted a portion of their crops into ready cash to pay taxes and satisfy their growing desire for consumer goods. Now he was headed for Sombor, some 300 kilometers away near the Hungarian border on the vast Vojvodina Plain with its rich villages as big as market towns. In Slatina there were only Orthodox Serbs, but in Sombor Mirko would rub shoulders with all manner of "foreigners": Catholics and Protestants, Hungarians, Romanians, Slovaks, Ruthenians, and even a few remaining Germans who had not been killed or chased out after the war.

During his eighteen months in the army, Mirko discovered a new way of life. He not only saw Sombor, but also Belgrade, where he perceived a more affluent, comfortable, and stimulating existence than he had known in the village. People lived with electricity and running water, and by 1958 even a few privately owned cars had begun to appear on the capital's streets. Here life was a struggle, but not in the same hopeless way as in Slatina.

Mirko was a good soldier, and was promoted with a small raise in pay to *desetar*, a squad leader. However, most important was the training he received in the motor pool, where he became skilled in repairing the trucks that transported them from their dreary barracks to maneuvers in the countryside. Moreover, arriving in the army barely literate, he had become proficient at deciphering the multitude of technical manuals related to his newly acquired trade.

Mirko was almost sorry to see his army life come to an end, but at the same time he was anxious to return home to be near those places and people he loved most. When he had left Slatina he was still a boy, a *momak*, but now having completed his military service he had become, according to local custom, a man ready to marry. While he had been away his brother Ilija had been formally engaged, and his oldest brother's wife had given birth to a son. His paternal grandmother had died during the past winter when an unusually bitter cold accompanied by a ferocious storm had buried their fields in snow higher than a man's waist. He had returned home on a special furlough for her funeral, and this was the first time he had ever seen his father cry. Grandmother had been infirm and senile for almost as long as he could remember, but nevertheless his father had always treated her as if she were in total possession of her faculties. Frequently, Mitar would stop and kiss his mother's arthritic, brown-splotched hand before leaving at dawn to attend to the stock. At other times, he would ask her advice in a rhetorical manner, knowing full well there would be no reply. She was buried in the same widow's black she had worn since the day her husband died of cholera on the Salonika front during World War I. She now lay buried among the Lazići in the cemetary below the small stone Byzantine church that dominated Slatina's landscape from a grassy promontory above the village.

When he was a young boy, Mirko had often played in the cemetery, climbing over the stone monuments with their enamelized photographs of the deceased, or chasing pigs through the tall grass that grew wild and unattended there. He had felt no fear or dread, and, as was the case with the other villagers, the cemetery was a familiar and even comforting place, a place where three times a year on the Days of the Dead (*zadušnice*) they would feast on the graves of their ancestors, leaving food and drink in memory of the departed. Once, he remembered, after the women had gone home, some men had remained late into the night drinking rakija and singing songs. A terrible drunken fight had erupted, and the priest had run half naked from his house behind the church to restore decorum. Mirko had always accepted without awe or apprehension the fact that he too one day would join the other Lazići in this usually tranquil part of the village, to be visited by his own sons and grandsons whose wives would prepare the ritual boiled wheat with sugar and nuts, the *žito*, to be eaten in his memory.

When Mirko returned from the army, at first he was filled with enthusiasm, but soon he began to feel vaguely depressed and disappointed by life in the village. He still enjoyed its simple pleasures, but what bothered him was the discomfort and poverty. His family was perhaps a little worse off than most. If they all stayed on the land and multiplied, they would surely starve to death. There was no way he could even dream of taking a wife and placing an additional burden on the household. Nevertheless, he tried to make the most of it, working tirelessly with his father and brothers. He stuck it out through the first months of 1961, and then approached his father asking permission to try his luck in Belgrade. He knew that the "old man" had confidence in him and there was no doubt the answer would be affirmative, but it was out of "respect" that he sought his father's blessing. In fact, Mitar himself had been troubled as to how they could all survive, and Mirko's decision gave him hope that their luck might change for the better.

Life had always moved slowly in the village, one season with its specific chores merging into the next. The days flowed by imperceptibly, and new generations displaced the old almost without notice. However, for Mirko, since that day he had set off for Sombor, the months seemed to rush by, and he experienced a new sensation of too little time to accomplish what needed to be done. He will always remember that cold morning in early March when he left for Belgrade in his baggy country pants buttoned tightly down his calves like riding breeches, and the mud sloshing under his peasant moccasins fashioned from a discarded rubber inner tube. Even now, years later, it seemed like yesterday.

He arrived in Belgrade "as poor as one can be without friends or relatives in the city." However, in those days, as badly as they paid, jobs were plentiful. Within a week, Mirko was hired as a laborer with a construction company, and after two weeks had also found extra employment in the evenings as a mechanic working for a former peasant whose "garage" consisted of little more than an enclosed courtyard with a small makeshift shack constructed of salvaged materials. The shack which served as an office and storage room also became Mirko's bedroom. In the mornings he shaved from a cold-water tap that emptied into a pit in the courtyard, and during cold nights he heated his hands over a charcoal brazier upon which he also prepared his evening meals in a single aluminum pan. He lived frugally, satisfying himself for the most part with "bread, cucumbers and yogurt." Nevertheless, in spite of all the hardships, he felt satisfied, since his skills as a mechanic were rapidly increasing, and somehow his small savings, which he kept in a box under his cot, were growing.

Never once did Mirko forget the needs of those at home. In each letter to his parents, there was at least one red thousand-dinar note, enough in those days to buy two liters of cooking oil. By St. George's Day, Mirko was able to greet his father with a wad of blue five-thousand-dinar bills to help pay the taxes and bring electricity into the house. It was difficult to return to Belgrade after that year's slava, back to the city with its dirt, confusion, and loneliness. When he left Slatina, his mother handed him a parcel wrapped in white linen and tied securely with a string. Inside was enough food to last for over a month: white sheep cheese, dried beans, peppers, home-distilled brandy, and dried smoked lamb ribs. Life in his family, as in most, was a matter of giving and receiving, and never once did he question his obligation to contribute differentially in accord with his growing economic capacity. This was tacitly understood, and the recipient of a gift simply took what was proffered as part of the "natural order," and as such not worthy of mention.

It was during the fall of 1962 that Mirko met Lepa quite by chance in a way that would have been impossible in the village where unmarried girls spoke publicly with young men only with the utmost reserve and reticence for fear of parental punishment and a potentially disastrous loss of reputation. When Mirko's oldest brother had married Kosa, they had barely spoken to each other though they had lived all their lives as neighbors and passed each other almost daily on the village paths. In the city, things were different. One's every move was not public property, and a person could move freely without worry about the opinions of others. Though Mirko found this surprisingly exhilarating, it also made him uneasy, especially in regard to marriage, since one could never be sure about a city girl's past. For this reason, he was surprised how quickly he decided to marry Lepa. One evening during the *korzo,* the promenade along Prince Mihailo Street just after dusk when thousands of Belgradians stroll casually up and down the five or so blocks closed to vehicular traffic, he saw her looking at a display of shoes in a department store window. For some reason, almost as if she sensed his eyes upon her, she turned around and smiled briefly in a spontaneous and unguarded moment. Even in the city such an open smile on the part of a young woman was rare, and perhaps it was the very uniqueness of the occurrence that prompted him to timidly approach her. To his surprise he spoke to her easily and without embarrassment. She reminded him of his oldest sister, Jasmina, with her deep-set black eyes, aquiline features, and lack of any hint of urban sophistication. This reassured him.

Lepa was from a village in Bosnia. The family had migrated with other settlers from the barren western mountains to Vojvodina, where after the war they had been allotted a plot of level, fertile land seized from its former German proprietors. After she had finished eight grades in a village school, her parents had sent her to Belgrade to live with an older brother so she could study textile technology. She and her brother shared a two-room apartment with an unrelated family, six strangers. Crowding did not bother her, since she had never known privacy; it was simply that such intimacy with "outsiders" was distasteful. Arguments were common even over the smallest trifles, such as who would replace the burned-out light bulb in the tiny curtained alcove that served them all as a kitchen. However, it was not to escape from her surroundings that she decided to marry Mirko, but rather because his resemblance to the peasant boys in her own village reassured her. Their courtship was not atypical of the Balkans. Hardly knowing her at all, almost on the basis of his first glance, Mirko was seized by some desperate compulsion to marry her. She, in turn, passively accepted his ardent attentions, and after a month agreed to marry him if her parents and brothers approved of the match. Mirko had already made an ally of her brother in Belgrade, and the three of them traveled to Vojvodina to obtain parental blessings.

Lepa and Mirko were married in a simple civil ceremony, and though they protested, both sets of parents were secretly relieved that at least for the moment they were freed from the obligation to finance a costly traditional wedding. Following the ceremony, they traveled to Slatina so Lepa could become acquainted with her new kin, and during the first few days in the village they visited from dawn to dusk until she had met every member of the twelve Lazić households. Mirko had experienced this same ritual in Lepa's village before their marriage, though her extended family had been reduced to a few households during the fierce interethnic warfare that had pitted Orthodox against Catholics and Moslems in western Bosnia during World War II. Thus, Lepa was happy to become part of such a large kinship group. Mirko's mother and sisters immediately took her over, and with boundless enthusiasm began indoctrinating her into the ways of the household and village. Mirko was pleased because the single most important thing for him was that his mother be satisfied with Lepa, and he remembered the words of a currently popular folk song:

> It is my wedding day.
> Everyone is happy!
> Music plays and wine flows.
> Happiest of all is my mother;
> Today a bride enters our house.

There was absolutely no possibility of finding adequate housing in Belgrade, and rather than take Lepa to a dank basement room or his shack at the mechanic's yard, Mirko decided to leave her with his family. Indeed, she seemed happy there, and, in fact, during their week's stay she had spent far more time with his mother and sisters than with Mirko. He did not take offense at this, but rather accepted it as an omen for the success of the marriage. Many migrants to Belgrade left their wives and children behind in the villages. Mirko had worked on the construction job with a Moslem from Macedonia, Gaši, who kept a wife and nine children with his parents near Tetovo, travelling home once a year during his summer vacation to "make another son." For centuries, this had been the custom in much of southern Yugoslavia, and though Mirko felt a strong "sympathy" for Lepa, he had no expectation that she would be a companion for him.

Shortly after returning to Belgrade, Mirko quit both his jobs, rented a small garage, and opened his own auto repair business. He was soon successful enough that he was able to hire an eighteen-year-old Gypsy boy to help him with the simpler and more distasteful chores. He traveled home to Slatina at least once a month, always bringing money or presents of manufactured goods not only to his own household but to a lesser extent to his more distant relatives as well. Lepa seemed satisfied, though she gently encouraged Mirko to find a place for them both in Belgrade. Also, Mirko was mildly disturbed by Lepa's failure to conceive a child and by his mother's fretting about it. Nevertheless, he decided to put off bringing his wife to Belgrade until he was better established.

What money he did not invest in his business or spend on his own maintenance, Mirko sent in one form or another to the village. He did not regret this, though from time to time he felt that perhaps some of the demands placed on him were not entirely fair. For instance, it was at some sacrifice that he financed a cataract operation for his father's brother, Milan, whose land adjoined theirs and had been part of a common estate until 1948 when the two brothers agreed to a formal division because of the squabbling of their wives. This expenditure had depleted the reserve of cash with which Mirko had been planning to buy additional tools and equipment. Nevertheless, in spite of such small setbacks, he was becoming affluent by Yugoslav standards.

The Yugoslav government's attitude toward private enterprise was inconsistent, and at best only one of toleration. There were constantly new regulations, taxes, and restrictions. It was hard to know from day to day what problems would be heaped upon the small entrepreneur in a socialist country. Mirko was worried as to what the future might hold, and he was unwilling to relinquish his newly acquired prosperity. In June of 1964, he travelled to West Germany ostensibly to buy tools, but once there remained to work in a Volkswagen repair shop at wages he could hardly believe. By Christmas, he had brought Lepa to Germany and had managed to send his father enough money to buy another hectare of land, good pasture in the valley less than a kilometer from their home. Mirko would have aided Lepa's family, too, had they been in need, but with almost ten hectares of fertile land devoted to cash crops of sunflowers and sugar beets, such was not the case. Nevertheless, as a token of his obligation to his wife's parents, he would send them small presents from time to time, and when Lepa visited them for a month during her first summer away from Yugoslavia, she took them a radio and ten meters of imitation fur cloth.

Mirko had now become a skilled mechanic even by rigorous German standards, and he was giving increasing thought as to how he could parlay this skill into even greater success. Periodically the family had corresponded with a cousin, Djordje, a man now in his late sixties who had left Yugoslavia for America before World War II. In spite of the years of separation, he had maintained contact with the village, and immediately after the war had sent numerous packages of food and clothing at a time when they were all in desperate need. Djordje was now a successful restaurateur in California, and with a "nothing-ventured, nothing-gained" attitude, Mirko wrote him asking for help to emigrate to America. Much to his surprise, the response was immediate and enthusiastic, and with Djordje's financial aid, sponsorship, and the promise of a job in a "foreign-car garage," Mirko and Lepa secured immigrant visas to the United States. What a few years ago would have seemed like an impossibly dangerous adventure Mirko now undertook with an almost casual ease and confidence. They arrived in Sacramento in mid-winter and were immediately taken under the almost suffocating tutelage of Cousin Djordje, who had remained a bachelor living modestly in a small apartment over his restaurant and bar. That had been over nine years ago, and Djordje was now dead, having succumbed to cancer seven months after their arrival. It was not long after this that Mirko opened his own repair shop with the modest bequest his cousin had left him. Mirko worked incessantly, and the business was now flourishing, with five employees.

Three and a half years after settling in Sacramento, Lepa had given birth to a son, followed at yearly intervals by two daughters. Mirko's mother was delighted, and it was to a great degree her desire to see the grandchildren that prompted Mirko to bring his parents to the United States at this time. In a sense, the trip was a way for Mirko to demonstrate publicly both his personal success and his dedication to family duty.

This St. George's Day was not only Mirko's first slava as a *domaćin* (head of a household), but also a kind of culmination of a decade's struggle. It was also a moment of great pride for both of his parents, a moment they would relive over and over again upon their return to Slatina.

It was hard for Mirko's father to imagine himself so far from home when he had never even seen their own Adriatic Coast. In fact, Mitar had never had any real desire to visit distant places, and in his imagination he had always evaluated foreign countries according to how much he thought they resembled Serbia. However, what he cared about was being near his son and grandchildren. He felt a sense of fulfillment, and regarded his son's success as his own as well. They had all cooperated as a family group, each giving what he could, and now life was better for them all. It was important to be near his grandchildren, particularly his grandson, whose mischievous energy and occasional bouts of temper gave him reassurance of the vitality of his Lazić line. At first he worried that his grandchildren would not speak Serbian, but to his pleasure he rarely heard a word of English in his son's home. When five-year-old Stanko would address him in English, he would jokingly tell him to speak Serbian "so that God would understand." He was not opposed to his grandchildren becoming Americans, not as long as they remained Serbs, too.

Mitar never tired of the attentions of his grandchildren. He would gently cuff Stanko, calling him his "falcon" or "little hero," and would sweep three-year-old Mila up into his arms, tickling her cheek with his bristling, peasant moustache. He had never been able to express this kind of affection toward his own children; respect and authority had demanded otherwise. He remembered how he and Mirko had formally kissed on each cheek the last time they said goodbye. Of course, with women it was different; his own wife, Desa, had thrown herself on Mirko that same day, hugging him and crying bitterly. But this was "natural," and he remembered his own mother behaving similarly, taking every pain and unhappiness of the entire family on herself. Even after his marriage, it was his mother to whom he always turned for advice and solace. For Mitar, the idea of love assumed several forms that he believed to be the product of the "God-given order of life": Children loved their fathers because of "respect" (*poštovanje*); their mothers, because they were the recipients of maternal "devotion" (*odanost*), "tenderness" (*než-nost*), and "sacrifice" (*žrtvovanje*); and the love between husbands and wives based on mutual concern for the family, and cooperation.

Actually, Mitar was not so sure what feelings linked a man to his wife. Certainly things were different now than when he was a young man. For instance, though Mirko was clearly the head of the household, his relationship to Lepa was an easygoing one. The young couple joked with each other almost like equals, and even argued in front of others. Mitar didn't mind this, he even saw some merit in it. Nevertheless, such behavior would have been impossible in his day. Only in recent years did his own wife begin to assert herself, and since his mother was now dead, Desa more and more filled this void in his life. He was increasingly depending on her, even seeking her advice as he once had done from his mother. As a young woman, Desa had always adhered to village custom, staying in the background when her husband entertained guests, waiting on the men, and placating her mother-in-law. She had never provoked gossip or discredited the family, and now with her lined, weather-beaten face framed by a black kerchief worn from the moment she awoke until she lay down exhausted to sleep after the day's work, she was the epitome of the village grandmother. Such women were repositories of village mores, and the final arbiters of custom and propriety. They could be powerful allies and dangerous opponents. Mitar remembered with some embarrassment an aphorism he had once heard while eavesdropping on his two old aunts who, believing they were alone, were laughing and making light at the expense of their husbands:

Čovek je dete dok je živ,
drži ga na prsima i uvek će biti zadovoljan.
("A man is a child as long as he lives,
keep him on your breast and he will always
be satisfied.")

For Mitar, the past had always been as real as the present, not only the past he had personally experienced, but what had gone before that over many generations of Lazići. In Slatina, there were reminders everywhere; each tree, rock, or gully had its lore, and this lore was almost always associated with the history of some local lineage. When Lazić men gathered during the frigid winter nights to drink hot brandy, inevitably the conversation would turn to their fathers, grandfathers, and great-grandfathers. There were endless discussions and arguments over the smallest details, going all the way back to the time of the legendary founder of the clan, Lazar, who according to the "official version" fled from Macedonia and the vengeance of the Turks over 200 years ago, after decapitating a tyrannical Moslem landlord. Such conversations served as a kind of "school" for the younger men, inculcating a sense of pride and self-esteem rooted in the heroic deeds of their ancestors. This was an impoverished and brutal land that in the past offered few other rewards.

When Mitar was young, it was a constant struggle to stay alive. His mother had borne twelve children, but only three had lived to adulthood. He remembered when his twelve-year-old sister had died from some unknown malady that had resisted all the herbal teas and poultices, and in spite of his mother's prayers and the candles lit before the household icons, "fate had its way." His mother had lamented by the graveside scratching her face and tearing her hair, but his father had only stoically commented:

Kolju i kravu i tele.

("They slaughter both the cow and the calf.")

Much had changed since those days. Children now lived rather than died. Life was easier, and perhaps people somewhat gentler. When Mitar was a boy, a father's word was law in the household. It was a man's right to command, to beat his wife and children as he pleased, and to demand formal signs of respect. As now, the head of the household was always served first with the other men; then the women and children ate what was left. Nevertheless, these days women followed such customs not so much out of fear as from the weight of tradition. Things were no longer as they used to be when a wife was expected to kneel in front of her husband and wash his feet when he returned from the fields, or even late at night drunk from the coffeehouse, and young people were obliged to kiss the hands of their elders as a sign of submission. Even adult men, who otherwise engaged in all the village vices, did not drink, smoke, or even joke in the presence of their fathers; and young women, married or single, spoke to older males only when addressed directly. However, in spite of all this, just as now, there were also conflicts in those patriarchal times. Some fathers used their power wisely and with sympathy for the members of their households, while others through abuse and excess brought about their own ruin. Mitar had heard of a case long ago of a son who killed his father. However, such events were rare though disputes between kin and family members had always been fairly common in Slatina. In most instances, resolution was sought and achieved through compromise or the intervention of other relatives who viewed such conflicts as a threat to the all-necessary kinship cooperation that was the basis of social and economic life in rural Serbia.

Mitar could not remember a single instance during his long life when conflict between a mother and son had resulted in an open or permanent rift.

Similarly, daughters long after marriage retained strong attachments to both their mothers and brothers. Indeed, the affection brothers held for their sisters frequently acted as a deterrent to husbands whose abuses might otherwise have been excessive. On the other hand, Slatina men occasionally chased out their young brides because the unfortunate girls did not manage to suit their mothers-in-law. A new bride was like another child in the house, and when Mitar was a young man, husbands were often as much as twenty-five years older than their wives. When he had married Desa, even though she was only a few years younger than he, his mother had advised him that "a husband should be like a father to his wife."

Mitar was thankful that he had never been in serious conflict with his children. Though he had been stern, the welfare and desires of his sons and daughters were never far from his mind. Until recently, the entire responsibility for the management of the family's limited resources had fallen upon him, and if he had allowed his family to be rebellious, lazy or disrespectful, disaster would long ago have overtaken them. Though their household had been, until recently, somewhat poorer than average, Mitar had earned the respect of his fellow villagers, and had been chosen to serve as a member of the governing council of the village church. He had limited wealth to pass on to his children, but his reputation would be left to generations to come.

Not all village parents were as satisfied with their children as he. Mitar was perplexed by the way some sons would go off to work in Kragujevac, Belgrade, or even Germany and forget about the people at home. On the other hand, many villagers were greedy, making impossible demands for luxury items and even gold for their daughters' dowries, not for the girls' sake but to show off and enhance their own reputations. It had not been that way in Mirko's case; they had asked nothing of him, but he had unfailingly known what was "right and proper." For Mitar to be with Mirko and his grandchildren on this most Serbian of all celebrations, the family slava, was a crystallization of all his aspirations.

The very nature and history of the slava embodies those ideas and images that Mitar most revered. The slava is a very old custom in the Balkans, and it may have even sprung from pre-Christian forms of ancestor worship or cults of household gods. However, its first historical mention was in 1018 A.D., when a Byzantine chronicler described its celebration among the Serbs (Filipović, 1964). Although the slava is also practiced by some neighboring peoples, the Serbs think of it as an exclusively Serbian institution, and indeed among no other ethnic group is it so universally observed. (The possible exception is that of the Gypsies in Serbia and the United States, the majority of whom are by origin from southeastern Europe, who have borrowed the custom from the Serbs, and practice it with great dedication.)

The slava is a kinship and household festival, and just as each Orthodox church is consecrated in the name of a saint who becomes its supernatural patron and protector, in the same way each patriline is associated with a saint whose Name Day is celebrated in each independent household of the clan. Popular belief holds that the slava commemorates the day on which each lineage head accepted the Christian religion on behalf of his clan. This particular idea has assumed special significance for a people whose ethnic identity during centuries of Moslem domination was defined essentially by their Orthodox faith. As is ideally the case with the celebration of the slava, Mirko's evoked what are for the Serbs prime transcendental values, those associated with family, kinship, and nationality.

Mirko and Lepa had taken great pains to assure that the realization of the slava conformed to the expectations of his parents, and that no important ritual element be omitted. At the same time, they were anxious to impress their forty-four guests (all of whom, with the exception of two "American" wives, were Serbian-Americans or recent immigrants from Yugoslavia) with their boundless, open-handed hospitality and affluence. Mirko had never staged a slava before, and in spite of the many he had attended, he was vague as to the exact content and order of events. With the aid of the Serbian priest, Father Obren, he planned each detail. Lepa concerned herself entirely with the decoration and arrangement of the house, and with the all-important preparation of an abundance of food. Only "too much" would be "enough." With the help of two women friends and under the eager direction of her mother-in-law, Lepa devoted an entire week to assembling a feast of staggering proportions. Everything except the lamb, which Mirko would roast over an open fire in the backyard on the morning of the slava, was prepared in advance: roast beef; goat-cheese *pita* (a type of pie); *ajvar* (eggplant relish); *musaka* (a spicy and layered casserole of ground meat, cheese, eggs, eggplant, and potatoes); *sarme* (meat-stuffed cabbage rolls); *tarator* (cucumber and yogurt salad); Russian salad; several kinds of tortes; *baklava*; and the all important sweetened boiled wheat with ground nuts, the *žito*. Mirko had already laid in a case of bourbon, a large quantity of beer and wine, as well as several bottles of Yugoslav plum brandy (*šljivovica*). On the day of the slava, he would buy a dozen loaves of the French-style bread that most resembled their own crusty Serbian variety, without which no Yugoslav would consider a meal worthy of the name.

Several days before the slava, Father Obren came to the home for the "blessing of the water." For some reason, Mirko had always felt ill at ease in the presence of priests. This time, his discomfort was difficult to hide, and as the chanting monk blessed the home and family members with sprinkles of holy water, Mirko shifted his weight from foot to foot hoping the visit would not be unduly prolonged. Perhaps it was the proximity of his parents that heightened the anxiety, since these were matters that had always been negotiated by his father. After the ceremony had been completed, Lepa took the remaining blessed water to the kitchen to use in preparing the slava *kolač*, a round bread-like cake that Father Obren had told them stood for "a sacrifice of gratitude to God for all His goodness." However, such explanations were of little concern to Mirko and Lepa, and even Mitar laughed after Father Obren had left, commenting that "priests were paid to keep such matters straight."

In spite of all of Mirko's efforts to remain true to tradition, concessions had to be made to the exigencies of American life. The slava could not last for several days as in the village where work schedules were kept only as the crops and seasons demanded, and May 6, Djurdjevdan (St. George's Day), fell on a Tuesday, which necessitated the postponement of its commemoration until the weekend. Otherwise, the slava was without flaw.

Early Sunday morning, a small table was placed against a wall in the living room, and on it were arranged the slava kolač, the žito, a glass of red wine, and an icon of St. George before which burned a special beeswax candle adorned with a ribbon in red, blue, and white, the Serbian national colors. The guests started to arrive in the late afternoon, and each greeted the host at the door with *"sretna slava"* ("happy slava"), crossing himself in the Orthodox manner from right to left. Then each was offered a spoonful of žito by Lepa, to be eaten "in remembrance of St. George and all of the Lazići who lived in the Orthodox faith and died for it." By seven in the evening, over forty friends crowded the Lazić house. The noise was deafening, since among the Serbs ordinary conversations are frequently conducted at a volume many Anglo-Americans would reserve for angry debates. Children who were not even included in the calculations of those expected but taken as a matter of course scampered wildly among the gesticulating adults, who had segregated themselves into several groups of like interest. The men clustered around Mitar in the family room drinking bourbon or expensive imported šljivovica that did not live up to anyone's remembrance of the quality of plum brandy "back home." The women had formed two cliques, one in the living room, and another helping Lepa in the kitchen. Two younger wives spent full-time serving drinks and snacks to the men who were engaged in their three favorite topics of conversation: Yugoslav politics, soccer, and money. They eagerly sought Mitar's fresh-from-the-old-country observations about life and events in contemporary Yugoslavia. With the exception of one or two American-born Serbs and several grandmothers, the women did not touch alcohol. In short, the slava, with its conviviality and animation, its gargantuan feast, the obligatory singing of Serbian folk songs, and line dancing to the accompaniment of a hi-fi turned up to deafening volume, was typical of almost any South Slav social gathering. However, there was one moment that was somehow extraordinary and set apart, the "turning of the kolač."

Father Obren arrived after the guests were already assembled and before the meal was to be served at nine. The guests and family gathered around the slava table with its ritual objects while the priest censed and blessed them and the home. The pungent smell of burning incense filled the room, and wisps of white smoke drifted lazily in the air. The priest then intoned the Tropar of St. George in his booming bass that during Holy Liturgy on Sunday mornings could clearly be heard on the street beyond the walls of the church:

> As deliverer of captives, and protector of the poor; as physician of the infirm, and champion of kings; triumphant Great Martyr George; intercede with Christ our God for the salvation of our souls.

Father Obren blessed the kolač, žito, and wine, and with a small knife made a cruciform cut on the bottom of the round slava loaf "in remembrance of Christ's Crucifixion." He then poured the wine over the kolač and žito. At this point, Mitar, Mirko, and the somewhat reticent five-year-old Stanko tightly holding his father's hand stepped forward and together with the priest took hold of the kolač, slowly rotating it in their hands as the family members awkwardly followed the priest in his Church Slovanic chanting:

> O holy Martyrs who have fought the good fight and have received your crowns; Entreat ye the Lord that our souls may be saved.

Mirko and Father Obren together broke the kolač in half. The gray-bearded priest kissed the cake and presented it to Mirko saying: "*Hristos posredje nas*" (Christ is among us"), and Mirko in like fashion kissed the cake replying: "*Jest i budet*" ("He is and will be"). The ritual was repeated with Mitar and little Stanko, whose halting attempt to imitate his father and grandfather provided a lighthearted climax to the ceremony, and for old Mitar gave promise of things yet to come.

Eighty-two-year-old Djole still enjoys a few pleasures. He is dedicated to the care of a half-dozen or so pigs that root about in the muddy field that adjoins the Home for the Aged and Pensioners (*Dom za Stare i Penzionere*) in Šabac; and when he receives, along with the other 106 residents, his monthly personal allowance of 200 dinars (about U.S. $1.30) he spends it the first night drinking rakija and listening to the Gypsy singer in a local honkytonk. By Serbian standards, his life is a total failure, and indeed his presence in the dom is testimony to this.

In spite of his age and a lifetime of misfortune and misadventure, Djole has retained a kind of robust, peasant appearance of good health. His already swarthy complexion has been turned brown by years of exposure to the sun, and he still manages to hold his six-foot frame erect. Nevertheless, he is depressed and lonely most of the time except when he is drunk. Then his negative feelings are transformed into boisterous gregariousness. If asked,

Djole will summarize, almost with enthusiasm, his complaints about his present condition: "I have been here for almost four years. Before that I lived in a village near Užice, but I had almost no land, and there was no way I could keep going on my own. I have children, but no one cares about the aged these days. As for my sons: One is working in Libya; one is in Tuzla; and the other has a job in the cable factory in Užice. They don't come to see me, not at all. I haven't heard from the oldest in over ten years. You see, there were problems; I separated from my wife, and then she died. What's really wrong though is that people no longer have respect. In the old days the young obeyed without question—they didn't dare blink in the presence of their elders. Now that's all gone."

Djole was a long time constructing his unfortunate old age. In part he inherited his misfortune from his father, and bit by bit events led him to this institution some hundred kilometers from his village of Krivi Potok. His maintenance cost of 6700 dinars (about U.S. $45) per month is met by the *opština* (a rough equivalent of the American "county") from which he came. In other words, he is a charity case. Other inmates cover their expenses with government pensions or contributions from their children or other kin. Some have even come to the home by their own choice. Several spend the cold winters there as a kind of "vacation," returning to their villages and children with the first warm days of spring. But Djole arrived under the most disadvantageous circumstances, because he had little other choice. Without children close at hand, with his kin alienated, to remain independent on the land in abject poverty and discomfort would have been an even less desirable alternative. In any case the results would be the same. Djole was to spend his last years without the support and alliance of those people Serbian society deems most significant in a man's life.

When Djole was born, Serbia had been independent of Turkey for barely half a century, and in many ways resembled the Middle East more than Europe. There was that kind of grinding poverty that once typified many parts of the Mediterranean. It was in such an environment that Djole's formative years were spent. His house in the village, the one he had been obliged to turn over to the opština with the rest of his property because he was unable to cover his own expenses at the home, had to this very day remained a remnant of that period. The only real improvements that had been made during the last fifty years were the pouring of a cement floor and the introduction of electricity in 1956. Today it stands abandoned, and with the exception of the Gypsy hovels along the ravine at the north end of the village, it is one of the few remaining structures in Krivi Potok constructed entirely of wattle and daub.

As a child, Djole lived in a small *zadruga*, a joint household consisting of his paternal grandmother, his father and mother, two paternal uncles with their wives and five children, and his two sisters and a brother. The sixteen of them lived entirely from agriculture and herding, working six hectares of marginal land, and occasionally selling firewood from their three hectares of forest on the marketplace at Užice. In those days, their zadruga occupied two houses and a *vajat* (a small sleeping shelter of woven reeds) in a single courtyard enclosed by a tall, tied-stick fence and entered through a single covered gateway, the *kapija*. From his earliest memory Djole had worked under the supervision of the older males, and when he was only four or five years old he was expected to collect twigs for kindling and drive sheep to and from pasture. He was never sent to school and today remains barely literate. What skills in reading and "sums" he has acquired were the product of his service in the Serbian army during the Balkan Wars and two years later in the fight against the Austrians in 1914.

Djole's lineage, the Matići, was a small and relatively weak clan in Krivi Potok, and enjoyed a somewhat unsavory reputation for heavy drinking, brawling, and slovenliness, a reputation that Djole did little to dispel during his lifetime. Though several other lineages had at one time or another agreed to stand as sponsors in baptism and marriage to them, the Matići themselves "owned" only one sponsorship (*kumstvo*) that of an even more impoverished family than themselves, and reputed to be of either Gypsy or Vlah (a Romance-speaking minority of low prestige) descent.

Djole's father, Miloš, was the eldest brother and had a tempestuous and even cruel nature. Like many village men, he spent his evenings in the coffeehouse or at a cheap cabaret run by a Serbian Moslem several kilometers away on the road to Užice. Frequently he would return home at dawn, staggering drunkenly through the kapija, and if the women were up and already at their chores he would sometimes cuff them about and swear, calling them "worthless whores." At other times, if it was still dark when he arrived home he would drag his wife out of bed and beat her, and if his eye lit on Djole, give him the same. He would listen to only one person, his mother, to whom he was apparently sincerely attached. More than once "the old lady" would intervene to protect her daughter-in-law and grandchildren. Nevertheless, in spite of his vile temper and profligacy, Miloš could work as hard as he brawled, and somehow he succeeded in coordinating the efforts of the zadruga so that they eked a living from the rocky soil.

With the death of his mother in 1911, Miloš became even more ill-tempered. He began to quarrel incessantly with his brothers over the smallest trifles. His youngest brother, Vasa, offended by Miloš's vile temper and heavy drinking, demanded his share of the zadruga and promptly sold it to an affluent neighbor. With the money, he migrated with his wife and two small children to Užice, where he opened a small coffeehouse near the marketplace. The two remaining brothers, who did not have the money to buy Vasa's share, were embittered by the sale of the land, and on several occasions publicly boasted that they would kill Vasa if the chance presented itself.

When Djole returned from World War I, he found that things had gone from bad to worse. His mother had tuberculosis and only with the greatest effort was able to continue carrying out the strenuous tasks that were the lot of every peasant woman. Sometimes she was seized by terrible fits of coughing, choking up ugly masses of phlegm and foamy blood. His father was more difficult than ever, and now drank almost continually from the ample supply of home-distilled rakija kept in barrels in a shed in the courtyard.

It was during Djole's first winter at home after the war that Miloš quarreled with his remaining brother, Spasa. Spasa had simply tired of his older brother's tyranny and irrational drunken furies. In a rare calm moment, Miloš and Spasa agreed to divide what remained of the patrimony leaving each with a house (the common courtyard was segmented by a single extension joining the two opposite sides of the existing fence) and approximately two and a half hectares of land. The livestock was apportioned in like fashion, but since their tools and equipment were extremely limited, they decided to continue sharing them. However, even this minimal cooperation proved trying, and eventually the plows, scythes, and rakes were also divided, leaving each with less than the minimal necessary. However, Miloš came out worst, since Spasa's in-laws, who had long encouraged him to seek a division, began almost immediately to intensify their cooperation with him.

Djole was twenty-seven when he returned from the war, and his brother Spiro was twenty-three. Neither had married, and both were well passed the "proper time." Spiro was quiet, mild-mannered, and retiring, traits not particularly esteemed in village men. He stayed clear of his father, spending long hours beside his mother, whom he adored. When Spiro was an adolescent, village gangs who regarded him as effeminate and an easy prey set upon him with some regularity. Nevertheless, he completed his military service with surprising distinction, fighting on the southeastern front against the Bulgarians. As for Djole, he came home a braggart and a heavy drinker like his father.

The following spring, Djole's mother died, and since the two sisters had married during the war, one at the age of thirteen and the other at fifteen, the three men were left alone. It had been difficult to make good matches for the sisters because of the family's reputation, and gossip that the older girl, Mira, had been seen rolling about in a thicket with a village boy. Guilty or not, she had been soundly beaten, first by her father and then her mother, in the family courtyard where her shouts and entreaties could publicly proclaim parental control and propriety. Unfortunate Mira had to settle for a fifty-year-old widower with a bossy and ever-complaining mother, while her younger sister, Branka, married a strong but dull-witted boy from a lineage almost as poor as her own. In spite of the obvious drawbacks of these matches, both were happy to escape the excesses of their father.

In the village, a house without women was unimaginable, almost "unnatural." From time to time, Mira and Branka would come to help their father and brothers when their own husbands and mothers-in-law would allow it. In spite of the indignities and violence their father had heaped upon them, the two sisters steadfastly maintained that though they did not respect him "as a man," they honored him "as a father." Once a week or so, Djole's widowed maternal aunt would arrive to work all day cooking and washing for them. Over the open hearth she would prepare enormous pots of white beans laced with garlic, dried hot peppers, and lamb fat, and bring loaves of fresh-baked bread, enough to last for days. However, none of these measures compensated for the lack of a *domaćica* ("a mistress of the house"). In the judgment of their fellow villagers, the three men, regardless of their faults, were simply "orphans" to be pitied. They were held as examples of how man was in constant danger of a capricious and unpredictable fate (*sudbina*).

Much to everyone's surprise, Spiro was the first to marry, taking as a wife a slightly crippled though amiable girl from a relatively prosperous family. Her parents were impressed by Spiro's gentle disposition and found him a perfect mate for a girl who otherwise would have difficulty marrying. There were no sons in the family, and Spiro readily agreed to become part of his father-in-law's household. His new status as a *miraščija* (a man living on his wife's dowry of land, occurring generally only when the bride has no inheriting brothers) was not a prestigious one in the village, and few young men were eager to enter into marriage under such conditions, especially with a cripple. However, for both concerned this was an advantageous compromise, though in reality it only made the situation for Djole and his father more difficult.

That next winter, Miloš went on a drinking bout that lasted for several days, and when he did not return home, Djole took no particular heed of it. It was almost a week later that two neighbors returning in the early evening from cutting firewood stumbled across his drowned body lying half submerged in the stream after which the village took its name. Djole was now alone and unable to work their holdings without help. It became imperative that he either sell the land or find a wife. Actually, in one respect, his economic situation had turned somewhat for the better, since Spiro had relinquished his claim to a share of the inheritance upon marriage. Djole's choices were limited, since most families would not consider promising their daughters to a drunk who gave every indication of eventually following in his father's footsteps. Nevertheless, Djole finally persuaded the impoverished and landless parents of a frail and unattractive girl of eighteen to betrothe their daughter to him. They, for their part, were glad to have one less mouth to feed, and Djole obtained the household help he so badly needed.

In quick succession, his new wife, Zora, bore him three sons. In most ways, life continued as it had been when Miloš was alive, except Djole was even less provident than his father. His greatest pleasures in life were his drunken carousings in the coffeehouses and honkytonks, and at the summer animal fairs (vašari). He was also a gambler, who enjoyed flashing what money he could assemble to impress his cronies. Bit by bit, he sold the land to finance his vices and bolster his male image in the cafes. Once, in a drunken fight, he had a knife driven into his thigh up to the hilt, and he lay for days at home with a fever from the ensuing blood poisoning. It was a miracle that without medical aid he somehow recovered. His sons attributed this to the constant ministrations of their mother, who nevertheless did not receive a single kind word for her trouble.

Life continued in this chaotic fashion for over a quarter of a century, with Djole constantly reducing the family's pitiful resources. Had it not been for World War II and the German occupation, surely his final reckoning would have occurred long before. During the war years, Djole's three sons went off to the mountains to fight with the partisans, and it was only a miracle that they all survived the hostilities to return home. The two oldest sons stayed only a few months and then went off to the city with the stream of peasant migrants who poured into Yugoslavia's urban centers from every corner of the country. Only Nestor remained on the land, not out of affection for his father and village life, but to care for his mother.

One night Djole, in a drunken rage, set upon his wife while Nestor was away at the home of a friend. He beat her unmercifully and chased her out of the house into the snow where she would have surely frozen to death had she not been found by a neighbor, who took her into her own house. When Nestor returned the following day, the entire story unfolded, and that very evening he, with the aid of two maternal cousins, ambushed his father staggering drunkenly along a village trail, giving him such a beating that he was confined to his cot for almost a week. Village opinion supported the wife, and even though she came from a small and weak lineage, Djole, who was unable to count on the aid of his own kin, could not afford an open confrontation with his in-laws, who could probably kill him with impunity. In disgust, Nestor abandoned his father's slava as a further insult and, taking his mother, now in her mid-fifties, went to live with his brother, Jovan, in Užice. Djole travelled several times to the city entreating his wife and son to return, but to no avail. By this time, there was little left of the Matić estate but the house, the plot on which it stood, a small, neglected kitchen garden, and a few head of sheep.

Those whom Djole had alienated, abused, or otherwise offended never forgave him; however, other villagers bore him no ill will because of his actions. Rather, they viewed him simply as the victim of his own predestined and inescapable nature. Thus, he lived on in Krivi Potok alone, working what remained of his land in a desultory fashion, raising needed cash for taxes through day labor for other peasants, and drinking up whatever was left over. Though his kin avoided him, neighbors and the village priest would occasionally take pity on him and provide small services or a hot meal. He was a kind of village fixture, evidence of the evils that could befall a man. Parents would point him out to their children staggering down the village paths in his ragged and dirty clothing, sometimes drunk by noon, and comment:

Mlad delija, star prosjak.

("A young rogue, an old beggar.")

People in Krivi Potok often spoke in such proverbs and could evoke them for almost any social situation. It was almost as if Djole's presence among them served the positive function of providing a negative example against which they could weigh their own virtue.

On his seventy-third birthday, after a particularly heavy bout of drinking, Djole took to his bed, and by the next morning was consumed by fever and barely able to breathe. Nothing escaped the notice of his fellow villagers, and when the priest and the president of the local organization of the Communist Party were informed of his condition, they quickly arranged for his admission into a Užice hospital. Though he eventually recovered, that was the last time Djole saw his home and village, and he left nothing behind but his collapsing house and weed-choked garden.

To understand the values against which Mitar and Djole lived out their lives, it is necessary to know something of traditional South Slav social structure. Clearly now, as in the past, kinship is a central preoccupation for many, probably the majority of Yugoslavs. Not only have archaic forms of household organization persisted in many rural areas, but also in the urban centers the ideology of kinship solidarity has survived today almost intact. In fact, it has even been suggested by a Yugoslav sociologist that kinship constitutes a "national vice" so significant as to inhibit the development of "rational," modern economic and bureaucratic systems (Olivera Burić, personal communication).

Before World War II, Yugoslavia was overwhelmingly rural, and the corporate extended family provided the basic unit of production and social identity. In much of the central Balkans, the primary family type was the zadruga, a patrilocally extended household holding land, stock, agricultural equipment, and other material and ritual property as a single entity. Even today, there are families reported in western Serbia with over 100 co-resident members. However, in regions characterized by the zadruga, since the beginning of the twentieth century, there has been a gradual decline in the size and economic significance of such extended households. This change has been less one of function than form, with a tendency toward lineal rather than lateral extension (Halpern and Anderson, 1970).

In spite of the tremendous social and demographic dislocations following World War II (the socialist revolution, industrialization, and the massive peasant migration from the countryside), South Slav traditional culture has evidenced tremendous vitality. Thus, while kinship has generally been viewed by social scientists as more important in primitive than in contemporary societies, the Yugoslav experience does not indicate that urbanization and modernization necessarily result in the erosion of familial values.

In a study of aging among a largely white middle-class sample from Kansas City, Cumming and Henry (1961) propose a correlation between aging and decreased interaction within a social system, a concept they label *disengagement*. In another American study, Anderson (1972) suggests the idea of *deculturation*, a process by which the aged gradually assume a "cultureless" position outside the body of tradition that constitutes the daily pattern of younger persons. Clearly, disengagement and deculturation are the product of a segment of American experience, and as such should not be attributed universality. Even a cursory perusal of worldwide ethnographic literature reveals that aging assumes a variety of forms depending upon the contexts in which it occurs. For example, though Djole had clearly become alienated from what should have been significant social ties in his later years, it was not because of some inevitable process associated with aging, but rather because of his unfortunate background and his own improvident choices.

The greatest risk in the study of exotic social systems is a natural tendency to interpret them in light on one's own matrix of values and assumptions— that is, on the basis of the observer's commonplace understandings. Certainly many Americans would have difficulty viewing Mitar's almost total dependence on his children in his declining years as a sign of success. In this respect, old age must be studied not in isolation but as the product of the total life cycle, and as a state for which the individual is prepared and socialized from the very moment of his birth. In the Yugoslav case, now as in the past, the training of children accentuates the reciprocal roles they will play throughout their lives with other family members and kin. For instance, the concept of "privacy" in the Western sense is notably lacking, and the need to be alone and to control personal space is not culturally recognized in the context of the family group. Such tendencies are in fact regarded as anti-social or as signs of emotional imbalance. For example, when Mirko brought his young bride home to live with his family in Slatina, she was initially pleased that she would be living in close and continual contact with her affines, and had she found the crowding distasteful or oppressing, this probably would have heralded the end of the marriage.

The strong attachment between the elder Lazići and their children can also be explained by the fact that lines of affect and authority in the Yugoslav family differ markedly from its American middle-class counterpart. In the Lazić household, the strongest affectual links were between generations and centered in the person of the *mother*, while there was a concomitant deemphasis on the communicative aspects of conjugal relationships. Marriage was a union that was principally economic and procreative, and neither Mitar and Desa nor Mirko and Lepa looked to each other as a source of companionship. Rather, they were tied together by an overwhelming concern for their children. With advancing age, Mitar's authority decreased somewhat, and that of his wife became greater, but as was the case with all relationships in the family, the roles constantly readjusted vis-à-vis each other so that they always remained complementary and symbiotic.

The Lazićs provide an example of the manner in which many South Slav families pass from generation to generation without any total cleavages in composition, and even the deceased continue to exert their aura in the context of the living. It is difficult to place temporal boundaries on such a family, as one generation flows almost imperceptibly into the roles occupied by the previous one. Replication takes place not so much within the framework of newly formed and totally independent family units, but rather through the gradual replacement of personnel within the same social entity. For example, postmarital neolocality is not in tune with South Slav values, and for the bride marriage does not necessarily signify newly acquired adulthood, but rather the assumption of the position of apprentice to her mother-in-law. For both men and women, full authority and emotional adulthood is achieved usually late in life, with the death of their own parents.

As was the case with Mirko, even physical separation of household members does not necessarily signify the diminishment of family ties and obligations. For instance, in contemporary Yugoslavia dual or even multiple residence on the part of the elderly is not uncommon. Older people frequently spend the pleasant spring and summer months in their village homes, and winters in the relative comfort of their children's urban apartments. In other cases, older women will divide their time between the homes of several children helping with household chores and the rearing of grandchildren. Another indicator of the psychological ties binding recently separated households is behavior surrounding the celebration of the slava. Similar to Mirko, many adult males hesitate to hold an official commemoration as long as their fathers are still alive even though they may reside separately from them.

Economic behavior also reflects continuing family corporacy though members may be scattered as distant as West Germany or the United States. Mirko's contributions to the extended family suggest an underlying rule of solidarity rooted in the dynamics of exchange. Those having more ideally share with family members and kin in less fortunate positions. Nevertheless, the givers usually feel that they are being levelled excessively, while the recipients suspect that they are not quite "getting enough." Thus, some conflict is inevitable, but, under control, it is the motivative force underlying the system. It is not so important to be satisfied as to be actively engaged in the give and take of kinship exchange, and the most vital exchange is that which links generations. Probably relatively few families achieve the cultural ideal with the same success as the Lazići. However, most Yugoslavs would undoubtedly consider that in the normal course of events children will care for their elderly parents as a moral imperative and that parents in turn will view this relationship not as one of demeaning dependency but rather as an opportunity to further engage in the exchanges which have typified their entire life cycle. In this light, the life story of Djole becomes all the more tragic, since in such a homogeneous cultural milieu, having irreparably damaged the very essence of his familial relationships, there were no alternatives other than to seek satisfaction and honor in the arena of excessive machismo actuated without reference to the more all-encompassing ideology of kinship reciprocity. Djole's behavior would have probably relegated him to failure in any society, but in the context of South Slav values, his defeat assumes a particularly stinging finality; no one will visit his grave and partake of žito on the Days of the Dead.

AUTHOR'S NOTE: *I would like to express my thanks to the Yugoslav scholars, institutions, and willing informants who made possible my most recent field investigation in Serbia during the fall and winter of 1973. Among many others, I am especially grateful to Dr. Olivera Burić, Dr. Iv Nedeljković, and Vitomir Stojaković of the Institute for Social Policy (Institut za Socijalnu Politiku) in Belgrade; and to the staffs of the Home for the Aged and Pensioneers (Dom za Stare i Pensionere) in Kragujevac, of the Home for the Aged and Pensioneers in Šabac, and of the Home for Pensioneers on Kaćarska Street in Belgrade. It is also my great pleasure to thank Professor Vera Stein Erlich of Zagreb and Fr. Dušan Bunjević of St. John's Serbian Orthodox Church in San Francisco for their many pleasurable and insightful conversations regarding South Slav culture and national character. Finally, I owe a great deal to my wife Jacquelene and daughter Saveta who aided me in the collection and recording of field data during 1973 and 1974.*

Extended peasant household—*village of Žitomislići, Hercegovina.*

The final validation of adult status, *grandparenthood—grandmother and grandchildren— village of Žitomislići, Hercegovina.*

A graveyard feast *(daća)* in memory of the dead–village of Topolovnik, East Serbia

In the home for the aged *in Šabac, Serbia*

CHAPTER 4

YOUTH AND AGING IN CENTRAL MEXICO:

One Day in the Life of Four Families of Migrants

Carlos G. Velez

A most remarkable recent worldwide event has been the massive migration of populations from rural hinterlands to cities. The migration has one significant cross-cultural characteristic; it is largely the migration of youth. So what remains in the rural hinterlands are depopulated villages, dying social networks, the elderly living out their lives as best they can with the stimulation of occasional letters and visits from their children. But there are also older people who follow their children into the urban areas, sometimes to find roles within the extended kin network that are more or less continuous with those that they fulfilled when they were "down home." These, however, are the exception, especially for men. In fact, it is largely women who fulfill in their later lives old familiar roles having to do with household, grandchildren, and husband.

To select the elderly out from the social and cultural systems and arenas in which they operate, however, is to skew and distort their participation. The aim here is not to present a "study" of the elderly but to consider the social, cultural, and psychological systems in which "aging" takes place at a particular time in history, in a particular manner. In essence, therefore, this is a study of youth and aging.

The analysis of my material gathered in Ciudad Netzahualcoyotl, Izcalli, (from the Nahuatl: "The place where hungry coyote resides") in the state of

Mexico between 1971-1974 clearly demonstrates that in the daily living of Mexicans the elderly first, are not present in any significant number (889 persons between the ages of 80 and 84 in a population of one million plus); second, do not form a group in any sense and are merely a convenient analytical division for the social scientist; and third, given the median age of 38.5 for fathers and 36.5 for mothers with 77 percent of the total population of over a million under thirty years of age, the aged population by whatever criteria utilized, whether functional or chronological, is merely a fraction of the larger population. To have focused upon the aged therefore, would have misshapen the social, economic, demographic, cultural, and political reality of the field.

Instead here selected randomly from the massive population of Ciudad Netzahualcoyotl are four families, as they live within the scope of one day. In so doing the daily activities, the roles which unfold, the importance of various relations for the young, the adolescent, the mature, the middle-aged, and the elderly reveal themselves within their naturalistic social, economic, cultural, and psychological contexts. This method provides insights into the very processes of aging—continuous, unadorned. The importance of various members within these families arises not from analytical interests but from existing living conditions. In a very real sense, it is from the interaction of the various family members as described here that the crucial insights into the social processes of aging will emerge.

It may seem paradoxical that two of the families described have no aged members within their household. Whatever ties once existed with the previous generation are no longer, in either thought or action. These two families in a very real sense are "ahistoric" in regard to their previous generational relationships. They offer for the careful observer *portents* of things to come. One of the remaining families has a semi-permanent member from the previous generation within the household, and the other includes a nonresident but highly prestigious and influential member of the previous generation. These latter two families offer excellent insights into "historic" families, whose traditions offer continuous but partial referent models to younger members.

These two sets of contrasting families then are the social universes that will be described and from which will be presented the implications for the future of their members. Both types offer comparative universes from which to contrast varying cultural strategies, responses to the pressures of urban migration, economic exploitation, social dependence, and political coercion. The implications for the aging process are such that these pressures determine an impoverished, one-generation legacy of crass materialism for parents and offspring or an equally impoverished one-generation legacy of feeble attempts to grasp "the good life." In contrast, the families which I describe as "historic" have adopted cultural strategies whose contents offer continuity for three generations, supportive values to meet the exigencies of a hostile environment, and ideals to counter the coercion of exploitive political relations.

Both ahistoric and historic families, however, share the same basic migratory experiences and history. In fact, they are all age cohorts, have moved to the area of Cd. Netzahualcoyotl for basically the same reasons, and face the same economic, political, and environmental pressures. The crucial variables for differential adoption of strategies which lead to different kinds of families are the presence or near presence of prestigious, self-resourceful, other-reinforced, older generational members.

THE FAMILIES: 1971-1974

A popular impression both in the Mexican press and in most of the communication media in central Mexico is that Cd. Netzahualcoyotl is inhabited by the poverty-stricken and emotionally arrested—hence, it represents a "culture of poverty." Thus, if a television news program wishes to make a point about the evils of urbanization, ecological conditions, or moral turpitude, Cd. Netzahualcoyotl is used as an example. Even formal studies prepared by governmental institutions about this million plus populated city point out the primitive surroundings of the city, and one study[1] suggested that the area's propensity toward "promiscuity" was bred by overcrowded living conditions.[2]

Such descriptions, including those in government reports, however, are describing only one slice of reality in the lives of some of the people in this sixty square-kilometer area. The "whole" truth is an unfinished and inconsistent mosaic of persons and events, of differences and similarities, of tension and occasional relaxation, and of core principles that are representative not only of people in this urban area but, typically, of those in much of central urbanizing Mexico.

The Garcias

If one were to ask Roberto García[3] why he lives in Netzahualcoyotl, he would probably answer, "Why not?" And it would be obvious even to the most casual observer why he would answer in such a way, because for the García family little in their middle-class home and living style in Netzahualcoyotl differs appreciably from that found in middle-class families in middle-class *colonias* (neighborhoods) outside Netzahualcoyotl. What does differ is that this middle-class home and living style is in the midst of a lower-class colonia in a largely lower-class city. Yet even this difference is not as great as it may seem, for in many parts of urban and suburban Mexico, middle- and upper-middle class families and homes are situated side by side with lower-class *jacales*. So the home of forty-four-year-old Roberto García, his thirty-eight-year-old wife Dolorosa, his two sons, Miguel (17) and Roberto (15)—together with their cars—is found amid the open sewer works, the street hawkers, the roving gangs, and the crying children sick with hacking coughs and with patches of skin eruptions.

In the early morning hours between six and eight, men, women, adolescents, and some school-age children begin to troop from their homes along Calle Suiza to catch buses and *peseros* (cooperative taxis) at Chimalhuacan Street. (Calle Suiza is not a fictitious street—it is located only a few blocks away from the Garcías' real street and is ethnographically the same.) Except for some of the fifteen automobile owners and an adventurous few who brave the morning traffic on bicycles, everyone walks.

For Roberto, the day's schedule is similar to that of others who leave their homes early in the morning, but Roberto and his sons are the only ones in their area who consistently use their cars to get to work and to school.

Backing his black Ford Matador out every morning at seven from behind the six-foot-high iron gates that normally bar the drive of his home, Roberto conveys a certain disdain for the people walking by as he leaves for his *tlapalera* (hardware and plumbing business). Those passing just manage to glimpse what lies behind the eight-foot-high concrete block walls. Inside the gates, one would see that the house is a two-story contemporary building constructed of white, plastered concrete block, with blue-iron sash windows and with two twenty-five-gallon concrete water-tanks on wooden supports on the roof. In front of the house and just beyond the wall which surrounds it is the Mexican-tiled open patio. To the side stands a two-automobile carport. There is little here that is haphazard or unplanned; all workmanship seems to have been carefully done. In fact, all the details are signs of wealth and social standing. For the adults of the household, they are the fruits of hard work, sacrifice, connections, and, more important, outside ties of friendship (*amistad*), all competitively won and accumulated over time.

The real treasures of the household, however, are inside. With two exceptions, nothing is distinctly Mexican. One exception is the use of color: Pastel pinks, blues, greens, and yellows decorate the walls of the interior hallway, the living and dining rooms, the kitchen, the three upstairs bedrooms, and the upstairs and downstairs bathrooms. The other exception is seen inside the front doorway, in the hallway leading to the living room; it is a small grotto for the Virgin of Guadalupe, in front of which sits a candle in a red bottle.

The living room, twenty by twenty feet, is crowded with two large, brocade-covered sofas positioned across from each other, one in a deep maroon and the other in a metallic green, a glass-topped coffee table of imitation woodgrain, two matching loveseats, a twenty-three-inch black-and-white Magnavox television set, and glass-covered end tables. Above the television set are twenty-year-old photographs of Roberto wearing a rented tuxedo, and Dolorosa in a white, short-trained wedding dress with appropriate veil and bouquet, their expressions somber. Next to them are pictures of Miguel and Roberto at ages thirteen and fifteen, also somber and unsmiling, dressed in their Sunday best.

It is the twelve by twelve dining room which accentuates the materialistic living style of this family in comparison to most others in Netzahualcoyotl. For this room, Roberto recently (1974) purchased a new dining table and chairs with a matching glass-covered cabinet for dishes. But it is not just the content of the room that is important; it is its function that differentiates it from the others in the house; and it is here that the majority of the interaction among the various family members takes place. It is significant, both on economic and cultural levels, that the family eats in a room other than a kitchen. On the one hand, few families in Netzahualcoyotl can afford a dining room table much less a dining room, so that this fact alone sets the García family apart from their neighbors and from the vast majority of Netzahualcoyotlians.

In the rest of the home, privilege and prestige are also developed. The kitchen, for example, unlike most kitchens in Netzahualcoyotl, is spacious and equipped with many modern conveniences, including a Kelvinator refrigerator, a large four-burner stove with an oven, and electric mixer, can-opener, and griddle. In addition, the house has indoor plumbing with hot and cold water.

The most distinctive appliance, however, is the Garcías' washing machine; few families in middle-class homes in Mexico City have one, much less in the population of Netzahualcoyotl. In fact, most middle-class Mexicans rely on a household maid to hand wash clothes. Nevertheless, the Garcías' automatic Bendix is probably one of two or three in this sixty square-kilometer area—a particularly conspicuous accomplishment in light of the endemic water conditions, especially in the dry season, when the water table is so dangerously low throughout Netzahualcoyotl.

The house and its many artifacts, however, have not been accumulated easily. As Roberto often comments privately, his home is the culmination of his dreams of "*éxito en una chinga*" (having success in a struggle). *La chinga* (life's struggle) has never been easy for Roberto. Like most conservative males in Mexico, he holds to a rather masculine point of view that life has to be difficult in order for it to be worthwhile. He has stated that "*el que no se chinga, no aprecia ser hombre*" ("the one that does not struggle in life cannot appreciate being a man"). Certainly his expectations of having to struggle have been generally realized throughout much of his lifetime.

As the son of one of thirty impoverished mestizo farmers living in the State of Tlaxcala, in a small rural *ejido*[4], Roberto had an early introduction into the chinga. Growing maize and squash, and clearing land in the traditional slash-and-burn method barely left enough income for the following year's seed. For the most part, he was raised on a basic diet of corn tortillas, black beans, and chile—a diet that was insufficient to feed an alcoholic father, a dying mother, and five brothers and sisters. In between harvesting and planting, however, Roberto claims to have received a fourth-grade education.

This accomplishment was achieved despite the disapproval of his father, his father's *compadres* in the village ejido, and what he calls, "*la brujería del pueblo*" (the witches of the town). By the age of twelve, he had set off for Mexico City to escape "*la chinga del campo*" (the struggle of the land).

For many other rural migrants of that era, as well as of present times, Mexico City was a transitory station on the way to the northern borders. Most of the men Roberto traveled with to the north were from the States of Guanajuato, Michoacán, and Jalisco, but his ability to read put him in good stead with his traveling companions. He was often asked to judge the veracity of news stories which announced the need for farm labor in the United States and the rich wages that were paid. He came to be, in time, unofficial guide for much older men who in turn protected him from the daily dangers of the road.

For three years, Roberto worked in the United States, traveling through the states of Texas, Arizona, California, and Washington, picking berries, cotton, oranges, melons, and the dreaded celery that permanently scarred his hands with dark blotches. These years were difficult, but compared to Mexico, the pay was better, even though the chinga was socially worse. He was discriminated against not only by the *gringos,* but also by the *pochos* who looked like him. (Pocho is a derogatory term used by Mexicans to describe persons of Mexican ancestry born in the United States. "Chicano" is a word preferred by younger U.S.-born persons of Mexican ancestry.)

As he said: "*Los pochos no nos querían en sus bailes, y menos en sus casas*" ("The pochos did not want us at their dances and even less in their homes.") The "boss" (pronounced "bos"), although a gringo, did not mistreat him as badly as the pocho contractors who took 10 percent of his wages.

In spite of both social and physical chingas, the money he made in the fields was, by 1940 standards, a considerable amount.[5] He saved almost half of his total wages over a three-year period ($7,000) and, by 1945, at the age of sixteen, he returned to Mexico City with $3,000 in a gunny sack. With skills learned in the United States, he opened a generator shop in one of the working-class districts in Mexico City. Because of war-created shortages of electrical replacements on prewar automobiles, this business soon became quite successful.

For the likes of Roberto, both adventurous and an entrepreneur, who "*se pone bien*" (positions himself), operating "across the counter" as well as through *arreglos* (business arrangements) and amistad (friends), success came quickly. Ten years after opening his first generator shop, he had expanded his interests to scrap iron and junk. He purchased as much scrap machinery and automobile parts as he could, and then hired apprentice mechanics at little or no pay to repair what he had bought. Over a ten-year period, Roberto accumulated sufficient capital to invest in the tlapalera in Cd. Netzahualcoyotl. This became his sole holding after 1965, when he sold his original generator business.

In the interim, however, Roberto had met, briefly courted, and married Dolorosa Borboa, a maid in a house in an upper-middle-class neighborhood in Mexico City. Dolorosa was the daughter of a mariachi player and a cleaning woman. Like Roberto, she had sought other avenues for success, deciding, "*No quería vivir como mis padres*" ("I did not want to live as my parents"). In the family home, her three sisters called her a "*pretenciosa*" (pretentious person). They chided her for appearing to dress above their class and for using what they termed "movie star" makeup. Nevertheless, in spite of the family criticism, she continued to behave as if she were "*de otra clase*" (from another class) by emulating the behavior of the family for whom she worked.

Dolorosa had been particularly attracted by Roberto's appearance when she first met him in Chapultapec Park. She judged him to be not only "*un hombre honrado*" (an honest man), but also an established one.

When she was twenty-one, in 1957, Dolorosa and Roberto were married, and exactly seven months after their marriage, Miguel was born in one of the local social security hospitals three blocks from their lower-class *vecindad* (neighborhood) in Mexico City. Seven years later, the family, now with two sons, Miguel and Robertito, moved away from the Mexico City vecindad to Netzahualcoyotl and to their new two-story house on Calle Suiza, not very far from Roberto's tlapalera.

It was in Netzahualcoyotl, between 1965 and 1974, that, according to Roberto, his family began to live "*como se debe*" (as one should—in the midst of plenty). That others cannot do the same, from both Roberto's and Dolorosa's point of view, is due to lack of initiative, hard work, and education. During interviews, both pointed to the artifacts in the living room and said, "*Miranos a nosotros*" ("Look at us").

Indeed, Roberto's and Dolorosa's marriage relationship is much like the deals described—similar in that each is to the other *amistoso* (friendly) and respectful as is Roberto to the contractor for whom he finally supplied material, or to the councilman with whom he eventually reinforced old deals. It is not that the content of the relation between Roberto and Dolorosa does not contain warmth and even love. But as each perceives the other and their most meaningful activities, an inescapable observation follows: For each of them there is the fear that the relation is a temporary convenience for the other, even though they have remained together for seventeen years.

The first day in the park, when Roberto met Dolorosa, he assumed that she was "de otra clase" and probably "una pretenciosa," one who would snub him if he approached; in his words: "*Qué quería con un indio*" ("What did she want with an Indian")? But his expectations, surprisingly, were incorrect. A few months after they met, she told him that they were expecting their first child.

Up to that point in their relationship, she had not permitted him to meet her parents, and he had thought that they would disapprove of him when they did meet. She, on the other hand, had not wanted Roberto to meet them since they would chide her for having been a pretenciosa, and now she had "*un pobre*" just like them even though he owned his own business. They would learn that Roberto had even worked in the fields.

As Dolorosa stated to Merced, her cook-helper: "*Con la envidia que me tenia la familia, cualquier cosa o defecto que tuviera Roberto lo hubieran explotado para avergonzarme*" ("with the envy my family had for me, any defect that Roberto had would have been exploited to embarrass me"). However, she never mentioned to Roberto that her father was a mariachi, for she was afraid that Roberto would leave her, especially once she became pregnant. She said she had not told Roberto much of anything about her family, only that they generally disagreed on most matters, resulting in a great deal of discord between herself, her parents, and sisters. It was only shortly after she became pregnant that Roberto insisted that he meet her parents, for he did not want them to think him a *vago* (a vagabond).

Roberto stated that Dolorosa had been afraid to tell him that her parents were basically "*gente humilde*" (poor persons) and that when he found out, she thought that he would leave her. However, he said that by then, "*Estaba muy enculado*" ("I was too passionately in love to care"). For Roberto, Dolorosa has fulfilled his expectations of what he conceives as middle-class order. In few homes were plastic doilies as prevalent as in theirs, the clear glass ashtrays and purple-glass swans so obvious, and the ming-style lamps in dragon colors so ostentatious. She "fits" his image of what the proper middle-class woman in Mexico should be.

However, there are two sources of conflict between Dolorosa and himself that have never been resolved. First, she berates him for having made their home in Netzahualcoyotl, although there is little she could do about where they live especially when he points out that, "*Es mejor que la vida de mariachi y de gata*" ("It is better than living the life of a mariachi and a servant" as her parents did). The second source of conflict is his occasional peccadillos with other women, which he explains as necessary for maintaining his business "*conecciones.*" This rationalization of his extramarital affairs is not accepted by Dolorosa. Roberto, however, has often stated that Dolorosa merely wants a man who is tied and dependent on her. But he will have none of it: "*El hombre no tiene que andar con esplicaciones como el jefe de su casa y menos cuando él la sostiene con su sudor*" ("The man as the head of the household does not have to offer explanations for his behavior, even less when he supports that household with his sweat").

Dolorosa perceives her relation with Roberto as unequal. She feels that she has sacrificed herself rewarding Roberto with two stout sons; bringing order into a disorderly man's life; teaching him not to blow his nose without a handkerchief and even which trousers to wear with which coat. In fact, she has taught him how to speak without the introductory sing-song accent used by lower-class Mexican males of the Capitol. He has repaid her with infidelity; worse yet, he thinks her to have acquiesced to the unequal relation. Nevertheless, she has other resources with which to equalize the relationship. She strives to make herself attractive by tinting her hair, wearing heavy makeup and tight clothing to show off her heavy breasts and wide thighs. She does this so that Roberto will not lose interest and to remind him that other men look, too. She would tell Roberto that young men whistled at her and that she thought it disgraceful, and this information would infuriate him.

Dolorosa has payoffs that can be inferred from observation. She has succeeded in meeting her basic "pretenciosa" goal of middle-class status; she is her own mistress in what can be considered an elaborate setting in Netzahualcoyotl; she has a "gata" (alley-cat maid) over whom she exercises authority; she is able to spend her monthly allowance of 2000 pesos as she pleases as long as the household expenses are met; and, significantly, she does not have to communicate with neighbors whom she considers "comunes" (common). In addition, she has two sons: one very much like her, and the other very much like his father.

According to Dolorosa, Miguel has been an "easy" child to raise. He was an undemanding infant, an intelligent child with the vocabulary of a six-year-old at the age of two, a child who never needed to be spanked and who showed unusual maturity by the age of six. He not only washed and dressed himself, but he was orderly and responsible for his own actions. According to Dolorosa, Miguel was "un hombrecito" (a little man) by the age of ten.

He even sided with her when she and his father argued about Roberto's indiscretions. She said that at times Roberto would strike Miguel when her son "protected her," and then she would fly at Roberto with such vehemence that he finally gave up trying "to correct" Miguel's discourtesy. Significantly to Dolorosa, Miguel had been her protector and her son—the one male figure, unlike most males, who was faithful to her expectations. But six months before his seventeenth birthday, she learned that Miguel, studious, intelligent, faithful Miguel, had been whoring with the shoe-seller's daughter who lived on a corner near their house. Dolorosa thereafter refused to speak to her son, and described his action as a "traición" (betrayal).

On the other hand, Robertito was just like his father. Dolorosa, referring to him, said, "Siempre espero lo peor" ("I always expect the worst"). When the worst occurred on the night the police notified them (as a favor to "Don Roberto") that Robertito was in jail for assaulting a fourteen-year-old girl, Dolorosa was shocked, but not unprepared. After her husband had paid the bribe and talked to his connecciones, and the boy was released, Dolorosa hugged and kissed him while her husband wept in anger.

Dolorosa's activities during the day appear quite routine and seemingly without tension. She is the first to arise when their new electric clock buzzes at 5:30. She then nudges Roberto awake, and he staggers, sleepy-eyed to the upstairs bathroom, while she trudges downstairs. By 5:45, Merced has begun to bang on the outside iron gate. Dolorosa goes out and each greets the other: Dolorosa calls Merced by her first name and uses the second-person familiar *"tu"*; Merced responds with the deferrent term *"Señora"* and with the second person formal "usted."

Dolorosa begins the morning breakfast for Roberto. It usually consists of eggs, scrambled or sunnyside up, bacon or ham, freshly baked bread (*bolillos*), fruit, and coffee and milk (instant Nescafé and Carnation). While Roberto eats, relatively little conversation passes between them, since she usually shuttles back and forth between dining room and kitchen serving his breakfast. By 7:00 a.m., Roberto is ready to leave.

Dolorosa next checks to see if the boys are awake. Miguel is a sound sleeper and, up to the break between them, Dolorosa usually caressed his forehead until he awakened. Roberto, on the other hand, usually awakens early and is listening to his hi-fi while sitting cross-legged on his bed. By the time Dolorosa serves them breakfast, each has showered and dressed. Miguel usually wears bell-bottomed trousers, striped T-shirt or sports shirt, and platform shoes. Roberto dresses in Levis, untucked long-sleeve denim shirt, and dirty tennis shoes.

While they eat breakfast, their mother gives each lunch money, and, if necessary, gasoline money for the 1968 Volkswagen which belongs to both boys. It is also then that Dolorosa questions both young men as to their day's activities.

Questions directed to Miguel include when he expects to arrive at school, the state of his school preparation, and whether he will be seeing a current girlfriend. His answers are soft "yeses" or "nos", or unemotional explanations. Before the break in their relationship, Miguel used to joke with his mother about her inquisitiveness.

Roberto, on the other hand, eats his breakfast sullenly, suffering through his mother's interrogation until sometimes he suddenly explodes in anger, knocking his chair back, dropping his fork and knife, and exiting by way of the front door and gate. Miguel then rises, gathers his school materials as well as Roberto's, and picks up Roberto in their red "bug." Roberto usually waits for him by Calle Chimalhuacán.

Once in the car, Miguel admonishes Roberto for stupidly letting his anger get in the way of common sense. He explains that he too has been bothered by their mother's incessant questions but that he has stopped listening to her long ago. As Miguel explains it:

¿Para qué enojarse? ¿Para qué? No me ves a mi actuando como tonto simple para complacerme. ¿Cuanto tiempo tenemos que pasar por lo mismo? Hace mucho, desde chico, hice una decición: de no oirla. Yo no le pongo atención y ni sé si me habla a mi o no. [Why become angry? What for? You do not see me acting as a simpleton merely for self-gratification. For how long do we have to continue the same thing? Long ago, since I was small, I made a decision not to hear her. I do not pay attention to her and I do not even know whether she speaks to me or not.]

While Roberto continues to be questioned in the mornings by his mother, such is not the case with Miguel. After their rift, although his breakfast is still served by his mother, the two do not speak to each other. One ramification of this break in relations is that Miguel no longer serves as a broker between his brother and his mother. In a very real sense, Miguel had served as an intermediary in the arrangement between the two. However, this intermediary role was only one part of a larger status, as were the expectations of deference and respect toward his mother. The overriding role expectation, as categorized by Dolorosa, was that of the "faithful man" which defines all other roles within his status as son. With his "betrayal," whatever other roles operated within his status have been unravelled and made inoperative. For the most part both boys effectively boycot their mother.

Most mornings, Dolorosa retires to the bathroom, and for the next two to three hours, prepares herself for the day's events. Beginning with a twenty-minute shower, a forty-five-minute facial and makeup session, a twenty-minute manicure, and a twenty-five-minute hairdressing session which leaves her hair in a towering bubble, Dolorosa spends the major part of the morning grooming herself.

Since Roberto's schedule includes the afternoon *comida* (meal) and the hour *siesta* (rest period), Dolorosa must make sure that the necessary food is on hand, and that there is sufficient time allotted to purchase any needed items. Since the family owns a refrigerator, food is generally purchased for the whole week by Dolorosa and Merced at the Cali-Max on Saturday mornings. Dolorosa prefers not to use the *mercado,* or local market. Vegetables previously purchased there, she feels, caused the typhoid attacks she and the boys have suffered in Netzahualcoyotl. In addition, she has long suspected that Merced pockets some of the money for food she buys locally. Dolorosa even suspects that Merced has exaggerated the cost of the water for the *tinaco* (water tank), but she says, *"No puedo yo enterarme de algo así"* ("I cannot inform myself of something like that"). The inference is that she considers such an inquiry too base for her sensibilities.

Whatever the situation, between eleven o'clock and two in the afternoon most of Dolorosa's attention is focused on the preparation of a three-course meal. With Merced's assistance, the first course consists of a soup (*fideo,* chicken, corn tortilla, or butter squash); the main course consists of meat (beef or pork), usually roasted or in thinly sliced strips, and vegetables (corn, cucumbers, tomatoes, or black beans); and the third course is a dessert (*flan*, pudding, or a bakery pastry).

For the most part, Roberto and Dolorosa have little to say to each other except for Dolorosa's questions of who Roberto saw that morning and early afternoon. Roberto's usual answer is "*gente con negocios*" (people with business). If Robertito has exhibited anger that morning, Dolorosa will complain to Roberto. He will usually mumble that "*es hombre*" (he is a man).

On two occasions when I was present, Roberto commented on Dolorosa's physical appearance. On both occasions, they were laudatory remarks about the way her clothing clung to her. Shortly thereafter, Roberto excused himself from the table and retired to their bedroom for his siesta. Dolorosa followed Roberto fifteen minutes later on both occasions and remained for the next hour. One can surmise that his comments concerning her dress were cues for his wanting sexual relations, and joining him upstairs for the next hour was her response.

According to Roberto, a woman's reciprocation should be neither too active nor too passive. In an interview, Roberto stated that there are differences between how women in general should reciprocate and how a wife should reciprocate. If a wife reciprocates too actively during intercourse then she is "*perdiendo el control*" (losing control of herself). On the other hand, a woman to whom a man is not married should be aggressively reciprocal during intercourse. She should be passionate with total "*abandono.*" A wife who would exhibit such behavior would be suspect because then she would "*andar caliente*" (be passionate), and therefore potentially unfaithful. She would be easy prey, according to Roberto, to the *tiburones* (sharks) who are always *buscando culo* ("on the make").

After both occasions when I surmised that Dolorosa and Roberto had had sexual relations, Roberto, upon returning to his office, arranged with *cuates* (pals) who passed by his office to have a "boys' night out." In interviews, Roberto explained that it is important that the husband not become "*enculado*" (infatuated) with his wife for sooner or later she will find a way to "chingar" the man. Each time a male has intercourse with a woman, there is the possibility that the male will become "enculado" so that he becomes the female's slave. A husband who is faithful only to the wife is enculado. Therefore, to avoid becoming enculado a man must seek other women or abstain completely. To abstain, however, is the mark of the *joto* (homosexual).

After the siesta, Roberto returns to work by four o'clock in the afternoon. Dolorosa reserves the late afternoon for television-watching—her favorites are soap operas and variety shows, and she is joined by Merced in watching the soap operas. Both comment on the infidelity of the female lead and the cowardice of the male character. It is during these TV sessions that Dolorosa reveals the way she feels about her world.

Besides revealing Dolorosa's viewpoints on a variety of subjects, including her husband, television-watching has other significance. Dolorosa has tried to maintain social distance between herself, her neighbors, and Merced. She considers the women who live on the same street where she lives as *"mujeres comunes"* (common women), and she avoids communicating with them by ignoring their greetings when she goes on her buying trips to the Cali-Max. She considers Merced a "gata," and she looks upon herself as a *"Señora de la Casa"* (lady of the house). All of this is an imitation of the relations Dolorosa observed at the home of her ex-employer. But, ironically, in allowing Merced to sit with her and to comment on personal subjects, she erodes the subordinate-superior relation of the gata/Señora de la Casa.

Yet it is significant that their conversations are of the same sort as those carried on by the *comadres* in the street. As will be seen in the following section on the Valenzuelas, las mujeres comunes from whom Dolorosa seeks to maintain social distance discuss the same basic problem areas with each other as she does via the television set with Merced. It is as if Dolorosa has replaced the networks of relations with women in the street with a mechanical device that allows her to communicate her feelings and concerns to Merced without the expectation of Merced having to respond or reciprocate in kind. On those rare occasions when Merced has responded nonsupportively, Dolorosa has quickly sent her out of the room to finish other chores.

By seven some evenings, Dolorosa must prepare supper for Miguel and Robertito, but generally she does not expect either sons or husband until nine o'clock in the evening or later. Television becomes her companion in the interim. When they do arrive, she serves them supper, rinses the dishes, then retires to the bathroom to wash off the day's cosmetics before going to bed.

The Valenzuelas

For Julieta Valenzuela there is little time for television. From early morning until late in the evening, strangers, friends, relatives, and family members including her husband and children troop in and out of the house on Calle Cucaracha next to the municipal palace in the central section. As one of thirty-four brothers, sisters, half-brothers, and half-sisters, and others who claim to be *hermanos and hermanas*,[6] Julieta is seldom alone. She is the wife of Arturo Valenzuela Cisneros—one of the *"joven líders"* (young political leaders), and she is expected to attend to the many persons who come seeking her husband's help, intervention, counseling, and even money. In his absence, which is usual during the day, Julieta must keep track of those who enter her home and the nature of their problem. She must also "cover" for her husband when he has missed an appointment with someone at their home.

Surrounded by people for most of the day and much of the evening seven days a week, Julieta has wondered what it would be like to have privacy.

Nevertheless, she recognizes that without the many comadres and amigas, it would be very difficult to deal with the suffering of many kinds which she experiences: the lack of water, the illnesses of her children, the physical dangers her husband generates, and the great pains in her abdomen which confine her occasionally to bed. Without her comrades, friends, and relatives, Julieta probably could not have survived Netzahualcoyotl.

Eleven years before, in 1963 when they had all moved to Netzahualcoyotl from Mexico City, the area was barren, dusty, and lifeless in the dry season, and equally barren, though muddy, wet, and smelly in the rainy season. She, Arturo, and their children—Arturito then three years old, Teófilo, age two, and Marco, soon to be born—Arturo's father, Don Teófilo; his mother, Doña Margarita; Arturo's eldest brother, Jaime and his wife, Lucinda, all moved into this house on Calle Cucaracha to face together what Julieta has described as *"un horror."* And it was a horror—without water, electricity, or sanitary facilities—and with a great many dangers to all of them, especially the children. The two eldest children have both been in the hospital three times with pneumonia and typhoid, and the eldest is suspected of having tuberculosis—all this within the first two years of their having moved to Netzahualcoyotl. What was worse in many ways, Julieta said, was that all of the family had been *"arrimados"* (bunched up) in the small three-room *jacal* in which Julieta and Arturo now live.

For three years, they all lived together, until Arturo and his brother, Jaime, one day agreed that this could not continue, especially with Don Teofiló's *"borracheras"* (drinking episodes). Jaime, his wife, their child who had been born a year after their arrival in Netzahualcoyotl, and the *viejos* (old people—parents) then moved to another jacal a few blocks away.

Arturo and Julieta both agree that their house in Netzahualcoyotl is not much to look at; however, they also agree that it does serve their needs. Neither spouse is "pretencioso" (pretentious); neither is much concerned with how and where they live, although Julieta has expressed her discomfort when a visiting dignitary enters. She has seen the way such persons turn up their noses (especially if their wives are with them) at the chicken offal on the floor and at the furniture in the living room. But both Julieta and Arturo have stated that for his work, the home is ideal since it is a very short walk to the *Plaza de Coyotes.*

A person walking by their home will find the jacal little different from most. By community standards of who has made it and who has not, this home falls in the latter category, with only a few exceptions: Two seven-foot poles stand parallel to each other at the very front of the lot. From them hangs a faded sign reading, *Colonos Organizadores del Valle de México* (Organizing Colonials of the Valley of Mexico). Next to the two poles and parallel to the sidewalk[7] is a two-foot-high rock wall built ten years earlier by Don Teófilo and crumbling from inattention. Beyond the wall a two-foot-deep hole into which a water pipe extends from the main in the street is partially covered by two loose one-by-twos. It is from this source during the wet season that water is taken. When the main is stopped up or the water level is too low, the *pipero* is contacted and drums are filled.

The rest of the lot, set between a two-story building to the north and a *lonchería* (lunch counter) to the south, is cluttered with leftover lumber, brick, a chicken coop, clods of burnt rubbish or piles of ashes (depending on the season), two empty oil drums for water in the dry season, and a concrete washbasin for dishes and clothes. Behind the washbasin and drums is the outside bathroom: a four-foot-square concrete-block structure with laminated cardboard roof. A dirty, flowered curtain serves as a door.

Behind the outside bathroom, in the rearmost part of the lot, is the Valenzuela's pastel-blue, three-room concrete-block house with its corrugated cardboard roof covered with debris. The distinguishing feature of this house is its open accessibility.

Most homes, in contrast, regardless of their location in the city or on the lot, are closed from a front and side view. The Valenzuela home, on the other hand, is clearly seen by all who pass by, and access is unencumbered except for the crumbling rock wall. Not even a gate hinders a person wishing entry, and the wall is in such a state that small children can step over it. It is this willingness on the Valenzuelas' part to be "open" to the view of the passers-by—to provide unlimited accessibility to anyone, children or adults— that differentiates the occupants and their home from the great majority of persons and homes in Netzahualcoyotl.

This external "openess" extends to the inside of the home as well. Upon entering, one sees that the first room is not just the ordinary living room of an average Netzahualcoyotlian. Upon passing the overhanging outside light bulb (the main source of light for the night meetings in the yard) and entering the living room, one sees a large glass-framed photograph of Arturo and a past Mexican president. Although little natural light enters the room through the entry or the one window in the room to the right of the entry, only the most unobservant can fail to notice this photograph.

Clearly, the room is not arranged for family privacy. Except for one small shelf with a small mirror above it which is located in the extreme upper corner of the west wall, no private family utilitarian artifacts can be seen in the room. But the room is cluttered. Next to the west wall leans a roughly made, white wooden desk, its paint badly chipped. On top of the desk is a 1940 Corona portable typewriter and seven bundles of yellowing newspapers. Next to the newspapers is a microphone amplifier and loudspeaker. The eight-foot south wall, like all the walls in the house, is unpainted, but its greyness is relieved by three tacked-on posters, one of which pictures Benito Juárez in somber centennial pose. Underneath these posters and along the width of the wall, three shelves house the legal codes for national, state, and municipal government.

The room is bare of decorative objects such as curtains, flowers, or ashtrays, but two unmatched couches are positioned against the west and north walls. One couch has a large hole down to the springs and the brown color of the fabric is largely worn away. A wooden chair, and a bench on top of two concrete blocks complete the furniture of this room except for the naked light bulb hanging down from the open-beamed ceiling.

In the bedroom is a fourteen-inch black-and-white television encased in a dirty white plastic cabinet and topped by half a rabbit-ear antenna. On the other corner are photographs of Arturo in *charro* (for festive days) suit and Julieta wearing a provincial wedding dress from the state of Oaxaca, and recent school pictures of their children—Arturo, fourteen; Teófilo, twelve; Marco, eleven; Julieta, nine; and a snapshot of Arturo's favorite, Felipe, two. Between the television set and the photographs hangs a one-foot by two feet reproduction of a translucent Christ in flowing robes with arms open and beckoning.

On the other side of the open doorway to the kitchen is a bed shared by the four eldest children and propped up at each corner by concrete blocks which raise it against flooding. The bed is covered by a clean, well-worn, lime-green chenille bedspread.

The users of the beds vary. In the past, each child has slept with his parents until replaced by a younger child, and each time this has caused considerable jealousy. If one or more of the older children sleep at their grandparents' home, Felipe, the youngest, will sleep in the bed with the other children. When Felipe sleeps with his grandparents, none of the other children sleep with Arturo and Julieta. Neither Julieta nor Arturo want any of the older children to become reaccustomed to doing so.

Except for light from the window in the east wall, the light from the 60-watt bulb hanging from the ceiling, and the bit of light that may shine through the doorway from the kitchen window, little light enters the bedroom. The one steel-sashed paneless window in the room is usually kept covered by an old door to keep out rain or dust. However, when the front door of the house is closed, the window covering is usually removed so that the rooster and three chickens may enter the house. Nevertheless, the bedroom is quite dark unless, of course, family members or close friends visit. Then the sixty-watt bulb is replaced by one with a higher wattage.

The kitchen is where much of the significant social interaction takes place between females—not just kitchen activities but much of the private and public political worlds of Arturo become intermixed through Julieta and her comadres. In the kitchen semi-ritual and ritual relationships are reinforced by the women, and these have far-reaching consequences since they are part of Arturo's political resources. This area of the house is both private and public—private within a circle of comadres, but public in their consequences for Arturo.

The kitchen contrasts sharply with the Garcías'. Measuring eight feet square, it has unpainted concrete block walls, one steel-sashed window with three of the four glass panes missing, an open-beamed corrugated cardboard roof, and a rough concrete floor.

Like 84 percent of the households in Netzahualcoyotl, the Valenzuelas' house is not equipped with a refrigerator. Therefore, fresh vegetables, meat, or dairy products must be purchased daily in quantities appropriate to family size and income. However, because of the large number of persons entering the house in addition to the nuclear family, larger quantities of canned goods, cereals, and black beans are kept here than in homes of comparable income and size. These goods are stored under a table directly across from the stove.

In this household, as in most, pails are indispensable. Equally indispensable are two four-gallon containers of Electropura drinking water, which are held in metal tipping frames next to the pails. Since this household, like many, has neither interior plumbing nor a source of uncontaminated drinking water, water for drinking purposes must be purchased from companies specializing in "pure" water. Not many people in this city, however, including Julieta and Arturo, trust the water supply company, suggesting that such companies utilize Netzahualcoyotl sources for water.

For Julieta, the day begins at about the same time as for Dolorosa. But Julieta cannot be positive if the day's activities will unfold routinely. Like Roberto, Arturo is the focus of attention in this household. The difference is that Arturo's schedule is not set. The morning's activity depends on Arturo's schedule for the day, or the previous night's meetings held in the living room or in the front part of the lot. Julieta said: *"Muchas veces no sé si voy o vengo en la mañana con tantas diferentes respuestas que tengo que hacer"* ("Many times I do not know whether I am coming or going in the morning with so many different responses that I have to make").

Although Arturo is neither an elected nor an appointed official, he does act as a consultant to a federal-state corporation, and he is one of a number of mini-*caciques* and brokers in Netzahualcoyotl. Like many persons fulfilling such positions, Arturo is sufficiently established to smooth and grease national, state, and local institutions for clients attached to his network of supporters. This "job" without portfolio or salary, however, places great tensions and stresses on interpersonal relationships, even on the mental health of some of the household's members. Because of Arturo's political status, Julieta's household activities are seldom accomplished without some compromise or change, to say nothing about changes resulting from activities of two-year-old Felipe.

Nevertheless, a "typical" day begins with Julieta arising first, at 6:00 a.m., dressing, and then walking outside with two pails in hand. After filling both—one for washing and another one for the toilet (defecation and urine are flushed away by pouring water into the commode), she eliminates, washes, and brushes her teeth. Except for elimination, all activities are carried out on the open lot. Toothbrushing requires that she take a glass of water from the bottled containers in the kitchen. Face and hands are soaped and rinsed at the concrete washbasin and dried with a towel sometimes hung on a nail inside the bathroom.

By 6:20, Julieta has roused the eldest boys, who, after appropriate protests, rise, and then go through the same basic procedure as their mother. While they wash and dress, Julieta warms the previous night's tortillas or bolillos, and heats sufficient water for "*café con leche*" (coffee with milk).

Since both boys take the bus to the western section of the city where they attend school, Arturito and Teófilo must be out of the house by approximately 7:00 a.m. Although the central section has a secondary school, Arturo has decided that the federal *secundaria*[8] in the western section of the city is safer for the boys in light of his various political enemies. Although he feels that the dangers to them in attending the central section high school are remote, nevertheless, in the past political enemies have attacked his home with a hail of pistol bullets and rocks, without regard for the presence of his family. This has prompted him to take some precautions.

For Julieta, there is great stress: First, she must hurry to ensure that the boys are ready on time, and second, each morning the boys argue about who is going to wear what clothes.

By the time Arturito and Teófilo have left for school, Marco and little Julieta have awakened and repeat the washing and dressing routine that their mother and brothers have pursued. By 7:45, while Marco eats his tortilla and drinks his café con leche, Julieta has combed little Julieta's hair, while checking it for lice, tied it into twin braids, and then joined the braids at the top of the child's head with a red or yellow ribbon. By the time Julieta has finished with little Julieta, Felipe has awakened, and it is Marco's responsibility to help him with the water pails, and to wash and dress while little Julieta warms her own tortilla and makes her café con leche. Meanwhile, Julieta awakens Arturo (if he told her the night before that he has an appointment the next morning). If someone calls at that hour to see Arturo with an urgent problem, she also will awaken him; otherwise she lets Arturo sleep and asks the person calling to return.

These morning sequences, however, may all be disrupted by illness, by visits from Arturo's mother or father, by the availability of water during the dry season, by the flooding of the household during the wet, by the stoppage of the sewage line to the bathroom, by the eldest boys returning because they did not catch their bus, by the younger children requesting money for their report cards, by little Felipe awakening his father who in turn will demand breakfast, by comadres who stop by on their way to the mercado, by an early-rising Arturo who demands special attention for a hangover, and last, by the stomach pains and cramps that Julieta says twist and grab her intestines. From Julieta's point of view, there is no sure thing even in the early morning routines. This is the case for most people in Netzahualcoyotl.

Unlike Dolorosa, however, Julieta can, with relative certainty, count on the assistance of her comadres, and through a number of bad times, she has. For example, when she, Arturo, and the children were to be evicted from their home during the height of political activities in 1970, it was the comadres who surrounded the lot, and for two weeks aligned themselves against the police. They supplied the family with food daily, brought clean water, cared for the children in their own homes, and finally, when the battle against the land-developers had stalemated, helped move the Valenzuelas back into their home. All the while, most men stood back in fear of the police, while the comadres faced them down. These women, Julieta has stated are "comadres y hermanas" (comrades and sisters). Yet, as she has suggested, total trust in any one is dangerous: *"El que no se cuida de los cercanos, lejano se queda"* ("He who does not guard against those closest will be left behind").

She expresses trust for Arturo, for his protection and affection for herself and children, and for his nobility in his past struggles against the land-developers. However, as she has said: *"Como todos los hombres no es fiel"* ("Like all men, he is not faithful" [sexually]). She has stated that Arturo is *"luchador, noble en muchos modos, un valiente pero, de ser fiel—eso nunca lo ha sido"* ("a fighter, and noble in many ways, a valiant person, but faithful— that he has never been").

In a conversation with one of her comadres at which I was present, Julieta stated that in Oaxaca when he first started courting her, she had been fairly sure that he was not going to be like her politician-father who had more children than she could count. However, soon after their elaborate wedding had been finished, when elders had gathered together and compadres had spoken for the other's family as they faced each other in lines to tie the families together, Arturo had *"robado"* (stolen) another sixteen-year-old in the next village. But as she wearily has said: *"Lo perdoné entonces y hoy lo perdono. Yo sé que nos quiere"* ("I forgave him then and I now forgive him. I know that he loves us").

In interviews, Arturo has stated that he always wakes up in his own bed even when he has been drunk the night before and is totally confused as to time and place. And since 1973, Arturo, as I have observed him, has been drunk more frequently than in the past—especially since losing a battle for control over the old political network he had been a part of for three years. Recently, however, his *mujer* (woman), as he calls Julieta, has not been sufficient to comfort him. To cure his *"reprimo"* (depression) he has taken up with Gloria—an old girlfriend whose husband Arturo refers to as a *pendejo* (cuckold). The rationale for his re-establishing the affair was *"para olvidar todo lo que traigo en la cabeza*" (to forget all that he worried about in his head). Besides, as he often pointed out: "*Julieta pude saber nada porque siempre esta preparada para servir*" ("Julieta is not aware of anything since she always has been prepared to serve").

Arturo has stated that he loves and respects deeply his mujer for the way she has stood by him when, except for his mother, few others did. When he first started *chingándose* (getting fucked) five years previously (1969), few people, including his older brother and father, took seriously his involvement in the protest activities of the time. When he gave up his work as a machinist to join the Movimiento Restaurador de Colonos political movement, and the family had to rely on monthly contributions from the membership, most people thought him insane. As Arturo has stated: "*Todos hasta mi padre y Jaime y toda la familia y amigos creían que estaba loco. Todos creian que me iba chingar–todos menos mi madre y mi mujer*" ("Even my father and Jaime and all of the family and friends thought me crazy. Everyone thought I would get screwed–everyone except my mother and my woman"). His friends, father, and brother only changed their minds in 1971, "*después que les convenía*" (after it became convenient). He said bitterly in 1974: "If it had not been for my mother and woman, in that time I would have been alone [without friends and family support]. Afterwards, naturally, after we swept the ground with them, after the functionaries paid attention to us, after I became friends of middlemen, after they found out who I was at "Los Pinos" [presidential palace in Mexico City], after it became convenient for them, then they did not pay [joined the rent strike]. That I do not forget."

However, except for Saturday when he reserves the morning for people wishing to see him without an appointment, Arturo usually leaves the house by approximately 10 a.m. for one of his many appointments with people in governmental institutions in the federal district, state capitol, or in Netzahual-coyotl itself. For the rest of the day, depending on whether his 1968 Renault runs, Arturo travels a minimum of 35 kilometers and talks with an average of eight people. Usually such contacts concern his intervention with an official on behalf of a client (or clients), and always they are couched in the language of amistad, even though afterward he may comment on a particular contact's shrewdness, avarice, or dishonesty. Regardless, his contacts are made to initiate or to follow up a favor for a client. Arturo spends much of the day going from agency to agency, from official to official, from cuates to cuates who know officials he has not yet made amistades of–all done in *confianza* (friendly confidence), even though favors are always costly.

While Arturo is in the midst of his "arreglos," Julieta continues her tasks–preparing food for the young children who return home at midday for their comida, and checking to see that Felipe, who plays in the yard, has not fallen in the water hole.

Seldom, however, will Julieta prepare the meal alone. Usually her mother-in-law, Doña Margarita, has walked over from the house she and her husband share with their eldest son, Jaime, his wife, and three children. Although Doña Margarita spends much of her time caring for the grandchildren who live with her and for Don Teófilo, she nevertheless visits Julieta and Felipe daily. Julieta and her mother-in-law have maintained an affectionate, warm, and deferential relationship. Although Julieta addresses her mother-in-law in the second person formal, "*usted*," each greets the other with close embraces and soft, affectionate kisses close to their mouths.

It is quite obvious that they are very fond of each other, but at times Julieta expresses a certain ambivalence. She has stated that her mother-in-law is "*una torre*" (a tower) *pero a veces demasiado cuidadosa* (but at times unnecessarily particular and meticulous). Julieta has stated that Doña Margarita has been her counsel when she needed it in dealing with Arturo. Early in their marriage, Julieta had considered divorcing Arturo, but Doña Margarita dissuaded her. She had taken Arturo aside and scolded him like a child. At the same time, Doña Margarita had also shown Julieta that all men were expected to be unfaithful, and that Arturo, especially, could never really be made "*manso*" (tame). Yet Julieta left Arturo, taking the youngest children with her to "visit" relatives when she could no longer stand Arturo's infidelity. In 1974, through Doña Margarita, she and Arturo maintained a kind of truce: She continued to serve him until the next time she thought it necessary to visit relatives, and he rationalized his extracurricular affairs by refusing to admit that Julieta suspected them. Nevertheless, Julieta suggests that it has been Doña Margarita who has largely been responsible for maintaining their marital relationship.

Such close association also has its other side. Julieta has suggested that Doña Margarita's constant complaints about Don Teófilo's alcoholic excesses have become tiresome, but what bothers her most is that Doña Margarita has constantly maintained a critical attitude toward her housekeeping abilities. In fact, as Julieta says: "*Ella puso y mantiene la loza sobre la pared en esa manera tan exacta*" ("She placed and maintains the pots on the wall in that exact way"). Clearly, Doña Margarita is an exacting woman, and she maintains that disorder drives men away from their wives more than any other reason. Julieta suggests that is an "*excusa*," rather than a reason. Julieta suspects that the unkempt appearance of her home is what Doña Margarita considers the real cause of Arturo's unfaithfulness, in spite of the fact that the extramarital affairs began long before the Valenzuelas moved into the substandard living conditions in Cd. Netzahualcoyotl.

Yet Doña Margarita was the only one of Arturo's family who helped them when they were dispossessed by the land-developers. This single fact Julieta will always remember. In addition, it was with Doña Margarita's help that the comadres had been organized into self-defense groups so that they could not be thrown out of their own homes during the rental strikes between 1970-1974. *"Esta torre y mis comadres nos salvaron la vida"* ("This tower and my comrades saved our lives").

Since then, many of the comadres continue to maintain a ritual relation with both Julieta and Doña Margarita. Although they do not vehemently support Arturo as they once did, they nevertheless do not oppose him, nor have they joined with others.

By eleven o'clock in the morning, at least one of the fourteen comadres will come to Julieta's home for a visit of at least a half-hour, drinking coffee and chatting in the kitchen. Although they range in age from thirty-four to sixty-eight, these women have shared in the same struggle since they arrived in Netzahualcoyotl. The political movement before 1973 initially brought them together only for politics. As time passed, they have become even more bound to each other, often sharing in the ritual activities of baptism and confirmation of their children, and becoming comadres de casa by exchanging saints for the household. Moreover, the fourteen women making up this network of comadres provided support for one another beyond that created by the consanguine ties among them: two sisters-in-law, a mother and daughter, two sisters, and a first cousin to the two sisters.

There was one crucial difference between Julieta and nine of the women. These nine were women who had been abandoned by men and had been left with a brood of children. Three of the nine who had never been married lived with parents or near relatives. Those who were married were, along with their husbands, friends of Arturo—his *compadres de la botella* (bottle comrades) who sought Arturo's companionship just because he would usually pay the tab. The crucial ties, however, were not between men; they were between women and they extended to Arturo through Julieta and Doña Margarita.

By 1 p.m., between twenty and thirty persons have trooped in and out of the Valenzuela home—men and women of all ages—all of them seeking assistance in resolving immediate problems. Meanwhile, with or without her mother-in-law's help, Julieta also has cooked the afternoon meal for herself and Felipe; for a comadre, if present; and for Marco and little Julieta, home from school for lunch. It is at this time that the front door of the house is closed for a momentary respite against the outside. Sometimes, however, people have not learned this cue, and Julieta must interrupt her cooking, serving, and eating to answer the front door. The few times I observed Julieta visibly irritated occurred as a result of such an interruption. The rest of the afternoon, until 7:00 in the evening, Julieta spends balancing demands of visitors and those of her family.

Normally, if he is not sick in bed (which occurred with greater frequency during 1974 than at any other time), Arturo's day goes by quickly. His numerous activities include speaking to functionaries in the Agrarian Department about the status of a land tenure problem for a nearby municipality;

traveling to the state capital to intercede on behalf of a busline blocked from establishing service (by one like himself who has interceded on behalf of an already established busline); or seeing the judge of the municipio, to persuade him to release a pair of clients who are in jail. Whatever the activity, the day is filled with intrigue, chingas, and ploys. From observation and from interviews, one concludes that each meeting, each arrangement, inevitably results in a price to be paid by Arturo. This stress is what is most exhausting for him. He can never be sure from whom the chinga will come, but he can always be certain it will occur.

Arturo summed up neatly the reason he participates in this business during one interview, but without, tragically, realizing the "zero-sum" game he was playing: "The only thing that is important to me is that my children become educated, and it is not important that they do not have much to wear if they have enough to eat. It hurts me to see them where we live. But they have to learn to sacrifice so that they can learn how difficult political life is."

By the time he returns home, depending on the day's activities, it is usually no earlier than 8:00 in the evening. Julieta has already fed the eldest children; all have completed their homework; and someone will usually be waiting to ask him for a favor. But sometimes, and only very rarely, no one is around except for Armando, his *amigo íntimo* (intimate friend), or a close compadre or comadre, or perhaps his mother and father, or perhaps a combination. Then all will sit in the bedroom with the children, watching them fall, scream, jump on the bed, and wrestle. Julieta will strum the guitar and Arturo will sing. All the men, but not the women, will drink brandy, or tequila, or sometimes beer. Then jokes will be told by the men—raucous, ribald, earthy jokes—and each man will take his turn poking fun at another in the room with all men both object and subject of someone's pointed remarks. Everyone participates except the women, who just laugh. Only Doña Carmen, a close comadre, exchanges banter with the men, but she was a "chingona" against whose allusions no man could compete.

These rare times seldom go uninterrupted. Don Teofilo soon gets drunk and he will have to be taken home; Arturo will receive an important visitor late at night; Julieta will have to treat Felipe's injuries caused by falling off the bed; the older boys will fight with each other and cry; or as it often happens, one of the men will joke too hard and insult another. Then someone, usually Arturo, will intervene, and the front door will close again until the next morning.

The Lópezes

In the eastern section of the city on Calle Imploración, stands the newly captured jacal of twenty-six-year-old Anselmo Lopez; his twenty-three-year-old sister, María Reyna López; her twenty-seven-year-old common-law husband, Refugio Reyna; their children—María Reyna, six, José Reyna, five,

Carlos Reyna, three, Enrique, two, and the infant Juanita, six months—and fifty-nine-year-old José María López, father of Anselmo and María Reyna López. Located in the midst of one of the most recently developed areas of the eastern section of the city, this home is similar in appearance to thousands of others. And like many others, the quality of life, especially as it affects human potential, is not promising.

This family's way of life differs drastically from the Garcías' and in many ways from the Valenzuelas'. Yet all three share a common belief: the expectation of chingar or to be chingado. The difference between them is that, for the López family and for families like them, their expectations for being chingado have been fulfilled faster and at greater cost. In varying degrees, each family seeks to fulfill the values of love, justice, and cooperation, but the activities and relationships of the Lopez family are least influenced by amistad—they feel that affection is either a political resource or a detriment, and that no one for any reason can be trusted.

Like many other *jacales* in this and other recently urbanized areas that reflect the "not having made it" look, this house is situated on a street that for most of the year is cut off from vehicular traffic because of deep ruts and ditches. The López house sits far back on the lot, behind a six-foot-high makeshift fence of old boards and unfolded wire crates.

Besides having deep ruts caused by overloaded buses during the rainy season, the street also has six-foot-deep ditches dug in 1973 for a new sewer line; to date that line is unfinished. The old sewer line, although still connected, has consistently been inoperative, causing raw sewage to collect in large black and green pools. As a consequence, the potable water line, running parallel to the sewage line, has been disconnected because of the fear of contamination. This forces residents on the street to walk to Chimalhuacán Street for their supply of water.

The bathroom, situated twelve feet from the jacal, consists of a brown-stained, seatless commode set on a thick concrete slab and surrounded by three walls pieced together from several sections of cardboard.

Since the sewer line in the street is inoperative for most of the time, sewage often backs up into the bathroom and floods the lot with wastes generated not only by people in the household but also from the other households around it. Other homes in the vicinity are similarly affected. Even when the sewage does not back up, officials disconnect the line to allow the sewage flow out, thus flooding the street. In either case, unless the winds are strong, the stench is nauseating.

All the adult members of the López family agree that this three-room concrete house is an improvement over their earlier living conditions. In their previous jacal in the Colonia del Sol, old cardboard, used wooden crate boards, discarded roofing shingles, and pieces of aluminum made up the walls and roof of their two-room shack. The earth floor was damp and cold in the wet season and dusty and hot when the weather was dry. By contrast, the new house has concrete floors in all three rooms and is equipped with a butane gas stove and two mattresses. Moving into this home, however, has been difficult, and if a choice had been possible they would not have moved. In fact, they had not thought of moving out of the Colonia del Sol and had considered themselves fortunate in what they had there. It was only when the state police forced them to vacate, along with twenty other families in other jacales, that they joined with one of the local *caciquitos* of the Colonia Esperanza to acquire this house. According to Anselmo López, the police had demanded a legal deed for their lot in the Colonia del Sol, and the only document they had was a permit for house construction that their compadre from the same home-town in Michoacán had sold them for 500 pesos. Anselmo, María, Refugio, or old José María had not known the difference. As Anselmo said: *"Nos hicieron pero bien pendejos"* ("We were really made fools of").

However, a cuate, with whom Anselmo López and José María worked in the *toreo* (bullfight arena) had told them that he had a close compadre who helped him acquire his lot. Anselmo, Refugio, and José María were introduced by the cuate to his compadre. After three cartons of Superior beer and an unsolicited gift of fifty pesos to the cuate's compadre were offered, an appointment was arranged at the chingón's house.

Anselmo, Refugio, José María, and their cuate then were introduced by the compadre to the *"mero chingón"* (real leader) as very old and intimate friends from the same pueblo in the State of Michoacán. *"El Capitán,"* the title by which the chingón is addressed, agreed to assist them. Anselmo recounted that the "Captain" suggested that they join his organization of followers and pay a *"coperación"* (contribution).

After much negotiation, 500 pesos was agreed on. Even this amount was more than they could afford since they had no savings. Anselmo said that the period was very close between their acquisition of funds for the chingón through one of the local lenders (at 20 percent interest per week), and their ultimate eviction. He said that a week prior to their eviction they had finally scraped together enough from the moneylender to pay the chingón.

The following day the chingón, Anselmo, Refugio, José María, and four of "el capitán's" *changos* (monkeys) walked to Calle Imploración, beat up the two males who had been living in the house, and threw them out along with their clothes and personal belongings. The four men with the captain then stole 200 pesos from the former tenants, who had previously been members of the captain's organization. (According to Anselmo, neither had paid their coperación [contribution].) So it was in this manner that the family moved into Colonia Esperanza on Calle Imploración.

From María's perspective the improvement over the old home was radical. The new home had the convenience of a butane stove and a place to cook.

The old home, by contrast, had had a makeshift dutch oven which Refugio and Anselmo had put together; food was cooked outside beneath a cardboard-and-wood crate covering which had a hole in the roof; during the rainy season, the cooking fire was frequently extinguished and periodically a new cooking shelter would need to be built when the old one was swept away by the rains; moreover, droves of flies and gnats invaded the outside shelter when María attempted to cook. In the new house, she has a solidly built room and a stove with an oven and burners. As María exclaimed one day in a rare display of emotion: *"Es casi como vivir como ricos"* ("It is almost like living as rich persons").

The newly acquired house with its blue-sashed, paneless window covered with cardboard is a very simple structure. Its only entrance is just five feet high. The first room, serving as the sleeping quarters for Anselmo and old José María, differs little in construction from the Valenzuela's house.

Facing the entrance are two beds and box-springs on top of concrete blocks. Religious artifacts are arranged in a semi-circle beginning five inches above José María's bed: a picture and certificate form the top of the arc, and two crosses are placed one on each side. None of the clothing is in a permanent enclosure, but hung about the room instead. The religious artifacts belong to an older man.

The second room is dark and dank and connects to the first by a narrow passage. It serves as the sleeping-quarters for Refugio, María, little María, Carlitos, Enrique, and the infant Juanita. The eldest male child—José—sleeps with his grandfather. Nevertheless, the temporary arrangement noted in the previous room is also exhibited here. Two double beds are arranged at right angles to each other, one for the children and the other for Refugio and María. A small wicker bassinet located between the two beds serves as the infant's sleeping couch. Both beds are covered with heavy gray Mexican blankets, while the infant's is neatly arranged with well-used white sheets. None of the three beds has pillows.

With little natural light reaching this room from the first, and artificial light from the lightbulb in the kitchen the only other source (the light socket in this room is broken), the room remains depressingly dim for much of the day.

Next to this bedroom, and forming the short section of the "L" shape of the house, the four-by-six-foot kitchen with its bare gray walls completes the López-Reyna household. The stove (purchased used in 1968 by the previous owners) is spotless. It is on four concrete blocks immediately inside the kitchen, its white enamel sides clean but chipped and its black four-burner top polished with care. In fact, María cleans the stove not only after use, but almost compulsively when she passes by it to do something else within the kitchen area.

No other part of the kitchen receives such attention, nor does the rest of the home. The peeling white wooden table, against the wall opposite the stove, is dotted with flyspecks and lumps of dry leftover food—egg, jam, and chile. The four chairs, one at each end and two on the same side, appear in the same condition. The Electropura containers and their stands next to the stove are covered with dust and dirt. The floors in the kitchen and in the rest of the home are swept once in the morning and not again until the next day, even though both adults and children track mud, dirt, and offal from the outside into all the rooms.

There is little time for María to put away much of anything in the household, nor are there permanent places for her to place artifacts. In this household there are no bureaus or shelves, only boxes and bags.

If impermanence is focal in this household, lack of routine is equally obvious. While Julieta in the Valenzuela family found it difficult to respond to the many stimuli in her household, María's principal response is one of passivity. Except for cleaning the stove, which she accomplishes daily, she appears apathetic and resigned. Her expectations of being evicted from her second home and the resultant lack of permanent enclosures are her basis for not expending effort on daily tasks.

By 4:00 a.m., Máscara, the dog, has usually awakened most of the household with his barking. Each adult member of the household and the two eldest children can differentiate the dog's bark, and, from observation, all men will rise if the dog has barked at humans—María will rise first if the dog barks at other animals.

Although most gang activity in the neighborhood has subsided by 4:00 a.m., Refugio's former membership in one of the toughest gangs in his old colonia has made him an unwelcome neighbor. Twice since they moved into the neighborhood the house has been subjected to "*pedradas*" (stonings) by one of the local gangs. The dog's bark, therefore, is an important signal. If the dog has barked at humans, Refugio will usually slip quietly off the bed, put on his trousers, and pick up his homemade *nunchakus,* a powerful fighting stick. By the time he has quietly entered the second room, Anselmo and old José María have awakened and each is armed—Anselmo with a 38-calibre "special" and José María with a machete kept hidden underneath the bed. Little José is carried to the other bedroom. All three men then slip out quietly through the iron door, whose hinges have been heavily greased.

During the period January 1974 through March 1974, the time of direct observation, early morning awakenings occurred an average of twice per week. Actual confrontations between either gang members or street drunks occurred on three occasions. On two occasions, Refugio fought off four persons, and once Anselmo fired two rounds over the heads of the intruders. A barrage of rocks was the response to Anselmo's shots. On those occasions when Refugio was first to use his weapons, all three received knife wounds. On the occasion when Anselmo fired his pistol, none was hurt.

If the barking is caused by animals, however, María is the first to rise. Her first task is to feed the infant and she does so whenever Juanita indicates she wants food. Since she carries the child in her *rebozo* (shawl), she can quickly give it her breast.

Since this house does not have a tinaco for water storage as did the Garcías', and since the water mains have been disconnected, María must take two buckets and walk to the public water line on Chimalhuacán. By 5:00 a.m., when she leaves the front door, she will have already eliminated in their outside toilet, and with Máscara will begin the two-block walk to the public water supply. Although the morning is still dark, the streets unlighted, daylight has begun to appear. With Máscara's help, she can see enough to traverse the open ditches, the puddles of collected sewage, the mounds of mud, and the garbage.

This trek must not be regarded as routine. Depending on the previous night's rainfall during the wet season or the *polvaneras* (dust storms) in the dry, the two-block passage may be impossible. In addition, if few persons are out on the same task, María may decide to turn back rather than to risk walking the two blocks accompanied only by Máscara. This task becomes more complicated if one of the children has been ill (which is often the case), and she has to attend to the child's needs early in the morning. At such times she must choose whether to get water, to tend the sick child, or to feed the infant. When she does walk to the public water line, for the most part she must wait behind the ten or so other persons already in line to fill their buckets.

On those days when she stands in line for the water supply, María does not talk to the others who are waiting. For the most part, the other women, like herself, are sleepy-eyed. They are also overweight at an early age and their abdomens bulge from too many childbirths too close together. They dress in shiny gabardine skirts, simple blouses, and worn sweaters—all covered by a large apron that extends almost to their rubber shower shoes (usually two or three sizes too large).

There are also a few males who stand in line, but these are usually bachelors, young boys of approximately twelve, or old men who fill empty, five-gallon lard cans to sell at individual homes. These old males are the object of much derision by those in line since they take much more time than most to fill their containers. Some of the women scream insults at the *"yugos"* (yokes). (These old males are called "yugos" because they carry the five-gallon cans slung at each end of a yoke-like plank. Wrapped around the middle are gunny-sacks for the protection of the bearer's back.)

The procedure to obtain water differs slightly depending on the season. Since the source of water is a pipe connected to the main, the person getting water must stand in a hole two to three feet in circumference and three feet deep and uncap the pipe by removing a stopper—either a rubber or a wooden object one-half inch in circumference. In the rainy season, the person must bail out the water in the hole, unplug the pipe, slide the bucket underneath, and fill it.

The return trip is much more strenuous than the trip to the water line. By the time Maria has bailed and filled buckets, dodged the buses that have begun to travel Chimalhuacán and skipped over the same obstacles she met on her way to the water line, she is already physically tired.

Meanwhile, if the infant Juanita has awakened, little María will rise, go to the bassinet and rock the child back to sleep. Refugio, María's common-law husband, will rise at approximately 5:30, light a cigarette, and then slip outside to the bathroom. The two men in the next room also awaken, begin to smoke and go outside to eliminate. By the time María has returned, little Maria will have filled the water kettle, lit one burner of the gas stove, and begun to heat water for the men's instant coffee.

If María has returned with buckets of water, Refugio, who currently works in Rescate—the emergency first-aid service which is part of the federal police force—and who has to be in the Federal District by 7:30, is first to use the water for washing. Taking one bucket to the wash basin, he pours in part of it, then soaps his face and hands. Afterward he shaves with the same water and leaves it for either Anselmo or José María. The second bucket is for the children. Nevertheless, little of the first bucket is wasted: the wash basin is drained by unplugging a stopper at the bottom, and the last user drains the water to a bucket which is then used to flush the commode.

While the three men wash and shave, María begins to warm the previous night's tortillas and beans for Refugio's lunch. Anselmo and José María do not have a set schedule to follow because, as vendors, they merely pick up merchandise from different Federal District warehouses to sell at their convenience. Sitting at the edge of their beds, the two men drink instant coffee poured by little María into jam jars, smoke their cigarettes, and flick ashes on the floor. Refugio sits in the kitchen and munches on a warm tortilla served to him by little María.

By 6:30 a.m., little José and Carlitos begin to wrestle on the bed. All the while no one speaks. Except for the movement of raised eyebrows between the men, indicating a greeting, and the wrestling of the two children, neither verbal nor kinetic communication is usually exhibited in the morning.

Meanwhile, two-year-old Enrique awakens, usually with a cry. Sickly, thin, and with unhealing sores on his legs and arms, Enrique is avoided by María and is often left to cry for fifteen minutes or more until she goes over, removes his soiled clothing, and takes him outside to wash with the same rag that was used on the infant. The infant usually awakens again when Enrique begins to cry and both children fill the house with shriekings, screamings, and finally exhausted whinings. The infant, meanwhile, is picked up by little María, wrapped in her mother's rebozo, and is carried by little María in the same manner as her mother.

By 7:00 a.m., Refugio, carrying his lunch in an empty quart lard pail, walks out the front door after nodding to the two men who still sit smoking cigarettes and drinking coffee at the edge of their beds. Refugio, like most Netzahualcoyotl men who work in the Federal District or in Mexico City, must rely on the local transportation system to get to the Federal District. There, those going into Mexico City transfer to the subway. Refugio usually walks to Chimalhuacán for the shuttle bus to the metro station (subway) located two miles inside the Federal District. Like most people, he faces the same indeterminate factors of bus breakdowns, weather, and accidents. On days when he successfully catches the shuttle bus to the metro, he must, nevertheless, contend with thousands who compete for the same space and time.

By the time Refugio reaches Metro Station Zaragoza, perspiration has soaked through his shirt and acetate jacket. Watching the bus driver switch lanes to pass another bus only to see an oncoming bus in the same lane causes concern for Refugio and for many others on the bus. Although few people show emotion, Refugio has admitted that he *"gasta los talones"* (wears the heels out) in bracing for possible crashes.

The next problem for Refugio is exiting the bus in time to catch the 7:20 subway for the ten-minute ride to the Insurgentes Metro Station. This is located in the middle of Mexico City, close to his Rescate station. Since many people on the bus seek to leave it as soon as it stops (although some step off while the bus is still in motion), the three doors–front, side, and rear– become packed.

The same frantic pushing and shoving resumes as Refugio, along with hundreds of others, slides already purchased tickets through an automatic ticket-taker, and pushes through the turnstile, running to the already rapidly filling metro-train. For Refugio, the fact that old women stand, that young mothers with infants slung in their rebozos struggle, and that occasionally old men fall is not disturbing. There may even be a loud gaffaw when someone falls, but as he says: "People do not matter. Everyone who has problems has them alone and here [in the metro] it is no different. The guy who gets up from his seat to give it to someone else–a woman–what is gained? Nothing. A monkey is ready to take it. Why be a fool [chump] yourself when others already try to do so–what the fuck, brother. It's one thing to have to give your ass–but to ask for someone to screw you–no way, brother–that is just being a fool [chump] ."

Yet it is not only Refugio who laughs when such things happen, many of the riders do. It seems that such things offer comic relief from the jostling, the smells, the warm proximity of others, and the necessity to squeeze past others to get off the train. For Refugio, all of this ceases at his station, but then a different type of chinga begins as he starts on his day's work picking up the injured and the dead throughout the central section of Mexico

City—people who have been involved in street or home accidents or crimes.

Meanwhile, the two men left behind in Netzahualcoyotl begin discussing the day's activities. José María and Anselmo, both illiterate peasants from Michoacán, migrated to Mexico City after their ten-hectare farm was devastated by drought ten years earlier. Their options were limited indeed; their only real hope was selling what they could at the toreo on weekends or during the week on the dividing island on Highway Zaragoza when cars stopped at the lights. Weekends at the toreo were most profitable—each could earn forty pesos per day. During the week, however, the center divider on the Zaragoza Highway was the only relatively close "free" area where they could sell without having to pay a *mordida* (bribe) to the *tamarindo* who controlled the corner stoplight. If they attempted to sell at the municipal palace in the central section, or along one of the streets in the municipality itself, either a *sindicato* (union) representative would ask them for their union card as vendors or one of the tamarindos, *inspectores* (inspectors), caciquitos of that block area, or some other "chingon coyote" as Anselmo described them, would attempt to charge them with some infraction, or to extract dues or a fee.

The federal tamarindos on the highway, on the other hand, seldom bothered them, for they were too busy collecting daily fees from the taxi drivers who overloaded their collective taxis with more than five riders on the way to the metro.

Before beginning their selling day, however, they must walk to a wholesale store seven city blocks from where they live to purchase the day's merchandise on credit. It is in the morning, sitting at the edge of their beds, smoking cigarettes, listening to the children cry after Refugio has left, that they decide what they will sell for that day. If it is raining or if the windstorms are heavy, they will opt for light merchandise such as Chiclets, spearmint gum, cigarettes, or candy. If the weather is good they will purchase cartons of Kleenex, toilet paper, and paper towels. Whatever the decision, by 9:30 in the morning they, too, are out of the house.

Like Refugio, both Anselmo and José María leave the house without having said goodbye to Maria or to the children. Each carries a long sling made of pieces of leather and old rags, and a tray to which is attached a short sling: the former is used to carry the large tissue boxes on their backs for the four-kilometer journey from the wholesale house to Zaragoza; the latter is used to carry the smaller merchandise.

For the rest of the day, Anselmo and old José María will trudge back and forth between Zaragoza and the wholesale house, picking up new merchandise after paying for that already sold, and slinging the flexible, awkward-to-handle tissue boxes on their backs. In this manner, they traverse the city until late in the evening when neither can see and the danger from street gangs becomes too great. The family earns their entire income of slightly less than 600 pesos per month.

María copes with the care of the five children, purchases the foodstuffs for the day at the local grocery store, and cooks the next meal by the time the men return home—all of this alone, without friends, comadres, or relatives.

At 9:30 in the morning, María goes to the local grocery store to purchase items needed for the day. With little María carrying Enrique on her hip, Carlitos hanging onto his mother's hand, the infant wrapped and carried in her mother's rebozo, little José running ahead independently to wait at the CONASUPO, the state-subsidized store, for fresh milk—they all eventually meet at the corner of Imploración at the store where María has shopped since moving to this colonia.

Because of her limited income, staple products such as sugar, flour, beans, and cereal are bought daily in small amounts and do not include meat. Cooking oil is also purchased in small amounts, the grocer pouring no more than a half pint into an empty vinegar bottle that little María carries in a multicolored, webbed shopping bag. Nescafé, bars of chocolate for *mole, chiplotes* (red chilies) in cans, pepper and salt, small jars of jam, and canned soup make up most of the purchases. Except for meat purchased on Saturdays—those days when Anselmo and José María make the most money— the López-Reyna basic diet is simple but filling. In addition, powdered milk is purchased for the children two times per week; corn tortillas are purchased daily at the tortilla shop; bread is bought twice a week, for Sunday; a few vegetables like onions and celery are bought; and on Saturday, candy by the handful is bought for the children. By 10:15, María returns to her home and begins to clean.

Purchasing these few items is not a simple task, especially when some of the few pesos that Anselmo and José María earn go to Refugio to spend with his *pandilla* (gang).[9] This causes a great deal of conflict between the men since it is Anselmo who gives Maria the *diario* (daily allowance) and María who gives Refugio money from this allowance for his *parrandas* (carousing). Anselmo and José María have accused María of wasting their hard-earned pesos, but in 1972 Refugio beat María for not giving him sufficient money to go out with his friends. When José María and Anselmo learned of it from María, who had been taken to the hospital in the Federal District with two broken ribs and a broken nose, they waited for Refugio to return and almost kicked him to death. Since then, a kind a tenuous truce has existed between the men. María, caught in the middle, must somehow balance the demands for food expenditures, the continuous demands of an unemployed husband for entertainment money, and the risk of lying to her father and brother as to where the money is spent. She knows that if her father and brother learn that she slips money to Refugio, they will confront her and Refugio; she is afraid that if she does not give him money, Refugio will beat her; and if her father and brother learn of it, there will certainly be blood spilled.

Anselmo and José María both admitted that they would *"matar el cabrón"* (kill the bastard) if he spent food money for parrandas; Refugio stated that he would get his cuates to take care of Anselmo and José María if they ever tried to beat him up again.

This conflict, however, did not begin in Netzahualcoyotl, as María indicated. According to José María, the real basis for the conflict is the fact that Refugio *"se la robó"* (stole her). Refugio's father was José María's compadre and first cousin who also lived in the State of Michoacán but not in the same *ranchería* where José María, his wife (now deceased), María, then thirteen, Anselmo, and an aged uncle lived. Three married daughters lived in outlying rancherías when Refugio on a visit became enculado with María. After this "robo," María moved to Refugio's parents' home until the drought in 1964, when they moved to their present location. José María refers bitterly to the lot in Colonia del Sol which his compadre—Refugio's father—sold to him and Anselmo for 500 pesos but from which all were evicted. This last chinga by Refugio's father has strained all relations within the household to their limits.

In the afternoon, things are a little different for María—she must ensure that none of the children slips out the front gate and falls into one of the sewage-filled ditches, or that the children do not strike each other with one of the many rocks in the yard, or that the neighboring children do not throw rocks into the yard—all this besides taking care of sores, the coughs, the fevers, and the intestinal pains that most of the children suffer from.

Teams of young interns frequently visit such homes trying to provide preventive medical assistance. The López-Reyna household has been visited four different times, and the visiting intern and nurse have provided medicines for the children's sores, coughs, intestinal parasites, and ear infections. Each time María has been instructed about the importance of ensuring that the children do not run a fever or have a runny nose since permanent deafness will result from the drainage.

Yet even though María recognizes and understands the importance of such vigilance, she denies that any of the children are ill when they are examined even though it is obvious that each is sick. María does not believe that *"aires"* (airs) are responsible for her children's illness nor is she unconcerned that her children become ill. Instead, she has come to deny her children's illnesses to the point of passivity and despair as a defense. She cannot survive the chinga without this type of denial. Her passivity and despair are analogous to the behavior she exhibits before the men in the household. Her silence with the men, her silence with the children, her avoidance of Enrique, and her denial of their illnesses are the same sort of defense. She is thus able to cope with the various stresses.

And passivity does not stop with María. For José María and Anselmo, passivity takes the form of gifts to the tamarindos on the corner coupled with denial by joking that their gift is just to keep the police from getting rusty. Refugio, on the other hand, assumes an exaggerated form of denial—the assumption of a super-macho identity, complete with bloody job (rescate), gang membership, and martial arts.

While María places the children in their beds and breast-feeds the infant, Anselmo and José María warily walk the darkened streets to their front gate, and Refugio begins the long return by metro and bus.

The Reynosas

"To live, one has to exploit others, and some exploit more than others, but the one who always gets kicked in the face is the poor one. I do it too, but I just do a little to each one so it won't hurt them as much." From the lips of Armando Reynosa-Beltrán, such an observation has merit; not only does the sociological reality of Netzahualcoyotl and of much of Mexico point up the truth, but Armando is a validation of his own observation—not only has he lived it, but he continues to live it.

Armando Reynosa-Beltrán, thirty-four, lives on Calle las Golondrinas (the street of the doves), three blocks west of El Palacio de Coyotes in the heart of the central section. Living with him is his sister Guadalupe ("Lupe") Reynosa-Beltrán, twenty-seven, her son, Davíd Tomás Reynosa-Beltrán, ten, and, intermittently, their eight-year-old niece, Martita Reynosa-Beltrán and their sixty-five-year-old father, Armando Reynosa Mendoza. Between 9:30 in the evening and 6:00 in the morning, the homes on this street are one solid wall of closed iron gates and doors and curtain-covered windows. From appearances, the occupants of these homes are either "making it" or have "made it." Although signs of wealth are not ostentatious, a privately owned bus stands in front of the home across from Armando's, and two Renaults, old but running.

Persons living on this street have easy access to major bus lines, to bakeries, to neighborhood stores, to schools, to bathhouses, to the city's only post office, to one of the few telephone booths, to newspaper vendors, and, in 1974, to the city's only bookstore. Curiously, the sewage lines usually work, the street is in relative good repair—no deep ditches—and only one lot, next to Armando and Lupe's next-door neighbor's house, is covered with refuse. Except for the lack of drainage and the invasion of flies, this particular block on this particular street is a model of comfort—in contrast, that is, to those already described.

Inside Armando's home, the "making it" look persists. Few people in Netzahualcoyotl have built a second home on the front of their lot, but even fewer have begun a second story. Armando is one of the latter, but of course he has not always been so successful.

Like many migrants, Armando is typical in some ways and atypical in others.[10] He was born in a pueblo of 1,500 persons, 84 percent of whom were still (in 1974) involved in primary agricultural labor with the rest employed in a fireworks factory. Armando's life in his pueblo consisted of wage labor in the cornfields when work was available—a miserable existence which he described as *"para 'los desgraciados"* (for the misbegotten). But as the first born of four sons and daughters, he quickly learned deference to authority, respect for the elderly, and hard, back-breaking work.

His father, Don Armando Reynosa Mendoza, had been considered a prestigious individual, the son of a wealthy landowner in the area. Don Armando's father, however, had parcelled out the land in equal shares to twelve brothers and sisters who, in turn, parcelled out their land to their children. The parcels of land were thus so reduced in size that in 1974, Don Armando had only one and one-half hectares—the rest having been sold as unmanageable and unprofitable even for subsistence. Yet Don Armando still retains prestige: He had held elective office in the pueblo, and, later, after he had been a *bracero* during World War II and again during the early 1950s, he was considered to have some wealth in comparison to the rest of the population in that depressed pueblo.

Armando considered his pueblo to be *"típico"* (typical)—one in which young men tipped their hats before authorities and kneeled to *padrinos* (godparents), but also a pueblo in which conflict was endemic, especially during drinking bouts. After the fifth grade, Armando worked in the fields as a wage-laborer and learned from his father the rudiments of bricklaying and house construction. During the nine months in which there was no work in the fields, he worked in the village or in surrounding villages, and it was also during this period that he began to court the leading family's only eligible daughter.

Her family's pride—the pride of the nouveau riche—was pitted against Armando's family's once-prestigious community reputation, which was now without economic foundation. The girl's parents forbade her to see Armando, but as he succinctly put it: *"Entonces me la robé"* ("Then I stole her"). They moved to the city of Puebla and lived together for six months, where he was employed as an unskilled laborer in an electric company, and she was pregnant with what was to be their only child.

Difficult economic problems arose, however, and after writing her parents for assistance she left Armando and returned to them. Three months later, a daughter was born, but Armando's wife died in childbirth. Her death, according to Armando, *"me volvió casi loco"* ("drove me almost crazy"). However, he and his in-laws became reconciled, and over the last fourteen years, Armando's mother-in-law has cared for his daughter, and Armando has become part of that family's affective network.

Following his wife's death, Armando worked three years for the electric company. During this period, his mother died, leaving his father, two sisters, and younger brother. A year later, the two sisters—Magdalena and Guadalupe—

and Pedro, the younger brother, joined Armando in Puebla while Don Armando stayed in the pueblo. This arrangement lasted until Armando was laid off from his job because *"el jefe necesitaba el trabajo para su primo"* ("the boss needed the job for his cousin"). Without a job, Armando decided to send his sisters and brother back to the pueblo, and he moved to Mexico City alone.

Armando's introduction to Mexico City was startlingly difficult. It demanded all of his creative skills to survive. Arriving with another migrant whom he had met on the bus, he slept on park benches, in police stations, and in churches for the first weeks until he and his cuate managed to steal some old clothes from one of the central markets for resale. This first success began his career as a street-clothing salesman—a vocation which he has followed to the present time (1974).

During this four-year period of living in Mexico City, Armando suggests that he came to know the world—the world of hustling or being hustled. Moreover, he was introduced into the world of the historical mestizo. Even though he denied an indigenous background, his father admits that *"nuestros padres todavía hablaban Tarasco y no Cristiano"* ("Our fathers still spoke Tarascan and not Christian [Spanish] when Armando was a child").

Here, in one of the working-class districts, he first began to read extensively the city and federal law codes that spelled out the rights and duties of judicial, administrative, and legislative institutions, and it was here that he began to recognize the disparities between those legal institutions and attempts by individuals like himself to avail themselves of them. He soon learned that the buying of clothing, the application for a seller's license, or the marking off of a specific sales territory were all activities that required *"conecciones"* (connections), and/or *palanca* (leverage). As a result, as Armando suggested, *"Me tuve que hacer muy zorro"* ("I had to become like the fox"). But this new world was not just "chingando otros" (fucking others); in the process of making connections, he also made cuates.

Yet not all relations were with men. Among the networks that he built up in Mexico City, his relations with women were largely sexual in nature and all ended in failure. Although he yearned for a more permanent relationship with women, *"Todas me han salido mal"* ("All have turned out bad for me"). As an example, he cited an emotional arrangement that he established with a young woman by the name of Florencia Martínez Almasán—an eighteen-year-old who Armando described as *"una vieja coqueta, chichona, y nalgona"* (a flirtatious woman, with big tits and ass).

According to Armando, Florencia was attractive, intelligent, and vivacious. The daughter of a security guard whose grandparents had migrated to Mexico City in the twenties and who had established themselves in one of the local working-class neighborhoods, Florencia had attended the local grammar schools and had completed the first year of *preparatoria* (roughly equivalent to North American senior high school), in preparation for a career in nursing. However, her aspirations were cut short by her mother's illness. She was forced to quit in order to care for her mother in the mornings and to work in the afternoons as a clerk in one of the local Mexico City drugstores. This was where she met Armando.

Armando's meeting of Florencia was a *"relámpago* (lightning bolt), and he began to court her seriously. However, he faced a number of obstacles—first, a number of other suitors were also active; second, his economic situation was unstable because, at this time, his sisters and brother had moved in with him; and third, he did not have *"confianza"* (trust) in Florencia's ability to remain faithful because she had already been engaged to another person. Nevertheless, over a period of a year, he sufficiently impressed Florencia so that she terminated her previous relationship—or so he thought.

During this period, two other events took place which played an important part in what was to follow—Magdalena and Guadalupe both bore children out of wedlock. Although Magdalena had since become self-sufficient as a seamstress, Lupe, on the other hand, had no such skills. Armando therefore decided to purchase a small lot in Netzahualcoyotl and to construct a jacal for his sister and a small grocery store by which she could support herself and her child, David.

As a result, two other factors entered into his relationship with Florencia. First, Armando spent considerable time in Netzahualcoyotl constructing the jacal and store, and second, when he had finished the construction, he assisted his sister in the sale and ordering of merchandise. Accordingly, he spent less time courting Florencia, who then resumed seeing her former suitor. He, in turn, learned where Armando was constructing the jacal and one Sunday took Florencia to the house in Netzahualcoyotl which, he said, was to be her home after she and Armando married. According to Armando, Florencia confronted him and said that she could not live her life in Netzahualcoyotl.

Armando explained that the jacal was to be his sister's home and not their love-nest, and that all the time that she had been doubting him and seeing her former suitor, he had been busily preparing home in another colonia of Netzahualcoyotl. Soon he would take her to see a two-story home that was to be theirs. In the meantime, Florencia continued seeing her former suitor, and Armando caught them together in his rival's car. At this point, he put the finishing touches on a plan to chingar Florencia.

Although he had told Florencia that Netzahualcoyotl was not to be their home, he admitted during interviews that he planned to move in with Lupe in order to avoid paying rent in the Federal District after he married. Florencia's rejection of the jacal, her "unfaithfulness," and her willingness to break off their relationship convinced Armando that she would have to be punished both to restore his honor and to satisfy hitherto unfulfilled sexual urges.

Armando therefore contacted a cuate[11] who was in the process of finishing the construction of his home, a partially furnished two-story house. One morning he borrowed an automobile from the same cuate, took Florencia to his friend's almost finished home, and claimed that this was to be their new home. Armando said that Florencia *"armó un mitote de gusto"* (raised joyous shouts) and swore undying love. In addition, he informed her that the furniture was only temporary, since the expenses involved in building the house had been great, and that soon they would have quality furnishings. With this last bit of encouragement, Armando then suggested that they should cement the relationship with sexual intercourse since they were going to marry anyway. According to Armando, after he convinced her of his love and affection as evidenced by the construction of the house, she finally relented. *"Me la troné"* ("I cracked her"), Armando said. This implies that Forencia was a virgin and that he was the first to have sexual intercourse with her.

By late afternoon of that day, Florencia requested that Armando drive her back to her home. He answered that she would have to ride the bus back, since he did not ride with *"putas"* (whores). It finally dawned on Florencia that she had been chingada, and after a brief but violent altercation, Armando drove away.

It is ironic that of the two women Armando selected, both were seeking upward mobility. Yet his first wife, the daughter of the leading citizen of the pueblo could not "bite the bullet" economically and left him, and Florencia's affection was limited by Armando's ability to pay off. The similarities in both cases are striking. In each case, he sought relations with similar persons whose beliefs centered on instrumental payoffs. "To be on the make" is considered a good thing both for Armando and for the females with whom he established relations. Conflict arose when the opposite "half" of those expectations surfaced—values regarding trust on Florencia's part and "biting the bullet" on the part of his ex-wife. A further contradiction, on which the rest is predicated, is that the initial expectation which Armando had for his first wife was that of coercion—"Me la robé." Second, his consistent expectation of Florencia was that of a sexual object even though he knew that she was also the object of similar expectations by other men. In neither case were expectations based on other than coercive support. As a final irony, the payoff for Armando fulfilled his expectations in regard to Florencia, but this very payoff was utilized by the cuate from whom he borrowed the house and car as a coercive threat in order not to pay his share of the tanda. Nevertheless, Armando considers Florencia's "traición" (treason) and his ex-wife's *"debilidad de mujer"* (weakness of women). Thus, his final enculturation into the mestizo world was accomplished.

One of the most difficult processes that Armando must undergo is "making it" in Netzahualcoyotl. Three primary reasons motivated him to live with his sister: first, to escape the high rents in Mexico City; second, to establish his clothing business in Netzahualcoyotl; and third, to utilize profits from his clothing business to keep the profit margin of his store at a low level, so that it is more competitive than surrounding stores. Such actions reflect Armando's desire not to remain a "*fayuquero*" (street salesman), and to establish a "home for my daughter." In addition, Armando wished to be established, an important factor that signifies an easing of the strain of the "chinga" (having to struggle and be screwed).

Although he has undercut four of the five neighborhood stores on Golondrina Street with the 50 percent profit-taking from his door-to-door clothing business, thereby driving two stores out of business, Armando is "making it," but he has not yet fully succeeded. Moreover, he has acquired a prestigious reputation among his circle of multiple and single relationships, but the prospect that such a reputation can be lost quickly and suddenly is always present. Nevertheless, both the outside and the inside of his home suggest that Armando "has made it."

The store which he and Lupe established in 1970 differs little from most others, except that the outside walls are plastered and painted a pastel green. Shelving extending to the roof contains the major part of the store's merchandise. All items are stocked in small quantities, but the variety ranges from cigarettes to bars of chocolate, from religious candles to instant coffee, from macaroni to Carnation milk, from cooking oil to hemp washcloths. Except for fresh meat and vegetables, this store was quite complete. But, from observation, candy and "Twinkies" accounted for a large share of the store's sales.

In 1970, Armando and his father built a three-room jacal on the rear of the lot. Basically, it is much like the jacals so far described—a simple rectangular structure, with the first two rooms serving as bedrooms, and the third serving as a kitchen. Construction is simple: unpainted concrete blocks, rough cement floors, two iron-sashed windows, and corrugated cardboard roof supported by open beams.

As time progressed, however, Armando and his father began constructing on the front of the lot. First the store was built. Over the period of a year, two large rooms were constructed that connected to the rear of the store and a bathroom replaced the one previously used. With the idea that a second story was to be added, the store, rooms and bathroom were built on very high and deep foundations.

Like the outside, the inside of the new additions were plastered, painted, and well finished. The light fixtures were much like those in the jacal. Large windows in each room extended from one side of the wall to the doorway, and each room, in fact, was a separate unit although joined together by a common wall. It was as if the rooms were built with a separate-but-equal intent rather than as part of a household for conjugality.

The furnishings in each room were unlike those in the jacal. While the jacal had double beds in the first two rooms, a few bags attached to the walls, an old wooden table in the second room, and few furnishings except for a wooden chair used by Don Armando during his stays, the new rooms contained two large clothing chests, a large cabinet in Lupe and David's room, two new beds in Armando's room, and a chest of drawers with mirror. In all, the furniture in the new rooms was heavy, sturdy, and much more permanent than any of the furnishings of the older jacal.

In addition to the new bedrooms, a tinaco and a bathroom were added over a two-year period between 1971-1973. Furthermore, in 1974, Don Armando began to place the shaping forms and reinforcing rods on the roof of the store for new rooms on the second story–a task that has not been finished because of inflation, two car accidents, the reneging of a tanda contribution, and the demise of a cooperative clothing store.

In 1971, the process of "making it" was simpler. Armando arose at 6:00 a.m., before Lupe and Davíd, and after washing quickly, he heated water over the butane stove in the kitchen and gulped down a cup of instant coffee. Next, he gathered his merchandise from his storage-bedroom and began to pack for his morning round of clothes selling.

While he was still fresh in the morning, he began his route at extremes of the *municipio,* usually in what was then the corner of Colonia Esperanza, seventy city blocks from Calle Golondrinas where he lived. His low-pressure approach was amiable and friendly. He would knock on the customer's door, usually to the yelping of a scrawny dog, and wait patiently until someone answered. Generally, a pre-school-age child answered, at which time Armando asked for his mother; if an older female answered, he chatted briefly before asking if the household needed anything. If the answer was "no," he mentioned a new item she might be interested in. Usually the person took an interest and he would dig into either his bundle or the basket to present it for inspection.

In addition, Armando established different sorts of relationships with his customers. When conditions were right, he would trade credit and clothing for an amorous episode. Such relations, however, had two drawbacks: first, each street was open to many vendors, and invitations to enter a home during a public event (selling), while other women in the street conversing could overhear the salesman's pitch, were dangerous–according to Armando, word could filter back to unsuspecting husbands.

During 1971-1973, Armando also began to establish a network of cuate, amistad, compadre, and amigo íntimo relations with males whom he met on his seventy-block travels. These contacts proved crucial for the political activities that he became heavily involved in during that time. Moreover, his clothing business established a network of community relations throughout the city without which it would have been impossible for him to have maintained his business and prestige statuses that were built up over that period.

Even when he made his account collections, his approach was mannerly, warm, and affective. He would usually approach a home on Saturday, his collection day, ask for the lady of the house, and chat amicably about the weather, current events, and then gradually lead the client to bring up the subject of her account. Many times the client would suggest that the payment was insufficient, but he would assure her, "*No hay problema*" ("There is no problem"), at which time the client would smile sweetly and indicate that the next time she would have more money for him. Nevertheless, Armando never allowed the client to feel uncomfortable about her inability to pay nor to feel as if her inability to pay interfered with the seller-client relationship.

For Armando, the importance of "*intenciones*" (intentions) to pay was almost as important as the money itself. He would usually ask such a person if she needed any more items that he could help her with, at which time she might answer "yes," but that she did not want to charge any more on credit. He would repeat his favorite phrase: "No hay problema." This is a technique of "saving face" for the client—a process much repeated among Mexicans.

The majority of his networks of buyers came to be composed of such relations over the three-year period. He carried with him both the beliefs of chingado—the belief that the appeal to basic values by politicians is an appeal with a hidden agenda—and the contradictory values that justice and honesty will be carried out by those politicians. Yet it is important that his own participation in protest activities had hidden agendas. One of the reasons he was able to construct his house and bathroom, and could later purchase a car to be used as a taxi, was his joining with others in a massive rent and mortgage strike during this same three-year period. Not only did he not pay the 220 pesos per month that he owed the land-developer, he did not pay electricity, water services, tax assessments, nor permits for home-construction. This provided him the capital for his successes, but also presaged his 1974 failures.

By 1974, Armando hardly "had it made," but within his circle of relations, he was respected for his general abilities, and more importantly, he was regarded as an honest and not a stupid man.

Depending on the day of the week, Armando rises first, washes and dresses and if the taxi-driver has arrived, he discusses whatever automotive problems the car may have. Meanwhile Lupe also rises, washes, and dresses.

While they never directly greet each other, Lupe and Armando still discuss the day's activities. If he goes out to collect on his accounts or to purchase more goods for the store, then it is Lupe who must open the grocery store by 8 a.m. Between 6 and 8, she must awaken her son Davíd, and also Magdalena's daughter, Martita, if she has slept there that night. While the children wash and dress themselves, Lupe will prepare their breakfast in the jacal's kitchen.

Depending on his desire, Lupe will also prepare breakfast for Armando, but usually she prepares only coffee, and she sends Davíd to the corner bakery for hot bread. Lupe will go through the same routine if Armando stays at home, but after he has opened the store and she has sent the children off to school by eight, she will begin to clean the rooms, wash dishes, make up the beds, and mop the built-up foundation outside of the rooms. In the meantime, she is always on call if Armando goes out of the store.

If Armando stays in, few days go by that friends, kin, clients, or persons seeking favors do not appear, and it is Lupe who must drop whatever she is doing to take over for Armando. Armando never orders Lupe to do so. Instead, he will softly say: *"¿Me cuidas la tienda? Tengo que ir"* ("Will you take care of the store? I have to go"). She nods her head, walks into the store, and if there are no customers, sits in the corner on a 100-kilo bean bag and usually reads one of the romance comic books so popular among lower-class females in Mexico.

Since they do not own a refrigerator, daily shopping is required, and the process of preparing a simple breakfast requires a trip to the meat market and the bakery. Meanwhile, Armando will take care of customers, check in arriving merchandise, fill grocery shelves, figure debits and credits, and, most importantly, count his money for expenses for the day—an exercise that he undertakes at least four times daily.

After her return from the market and bakery, Lupe will prepare breakfast and serve it either in the patio-enclosure, if it is not raining or in the small kitchen in the jacal. While Armando eats, she will serve customers. After he finishes, he will continue his tasks in the store while she picks up the dishes, washes them, and finishes her household chores: making beds, sweeping, and washing clothes. By 2 p.m., she will begin to prepare the comida for the children who will have arrived from school.

Since Martita and Davíd always arrive in tandem, Lupe will prepare sufficient food for each of them as well as for Armando and herself. It is during this hour that most of the kinspersons and cuates will arrive and business "amigos" will also occasionally visit. They, too, will be served if Armando eats at that hour, but at no time does Armando eat with the children. Moreover, it is during this period that conflict between Armando and Lupe will arise, since she is required both to eat and to serve customers while the children and Armando eat.

Lupe feels exploited, and she states, succinctly: *"Como la mayoria de las mujeres mexicanas, soy esclava del hombre"* ("Like the majority of Mexican women, I am a slave of the man"). Lupe has stated about all males: *"Se creen muy machotes con la mujer, pero con alguien de su tamaño y medida—no son nada*" ("They think themselves manly with women, but [with] someone their own size and cut—they are nothing").

Nevertheless, Lupe never openly displays her feelings; instead she becomes mute and refuses to speak to Armando who, in turn, avoids her as much as possible. The avoidance is a device which allows the continuation of their relationship, but prevents the verbal surfacing of the conflict between them— i.e., Armando's more prestigious status within the home which is based on the support she provides by fulfilling the role of "esclava." Yet she admits that without Armando, she could not have survived the abandonment by her son's father, particularly since she was without skills to support herself.

On the other hand, her refusal to speak to Armando allows her to express hostility within the "amistad" range, but does not resolve the basis of the conflict either between them or within herself. She loves her brother as a sibling, for the sacrifices he has made, and for his concern for her son. But she resents the exploitation of her labor, of her being on call as a maid, and the fact that her prestige is based on her brother's standing. She is known as "*la hermana de Armando*" (Armando's sister) by the butcher, customers, and even by friends who visit.

Yet, important as the brother-sister relationship is, the relationship between the two is really cemented by the bonds between Armando and David, her son. The two males have a basically deferent and distant relationship. In the three years that I observed them, never once did I note that Armando touched, caressed, or soothed any part of David's body, nor have I observed Armando counseling David directly. Instead, if David's behavior does not meet Armando's expectations, he calls Lupe to correct her son's behavior. If Lupe is absent, and David and Martita misbehave by fighting or by playing with the stacks of empty soda bottle cases in the corner of the patio, then Armando would shake his forefinger in the air but would not say anything to correct them. The children, however, would immediately cease.

Conversation between David and Armando is minimal since the children eat apart in the jacal's kitchen. However, they do greet each other in the morning before David and Martita leave for school and they speak again before David retires for the night. David addresses Armando as *Tío* (Uncle), but the formal usted is never used in their brief conversations except when David asks for permission to eat cookies or candy from the shelves. At no time did I observe Armando raising his voice, and the relationship on the whole appeared markedly egalitarian.

From Armando's point of view: "*David es un hombrecito*," but he is not required to fulfill male roles in the store, sweeping, washing the steps outside, stacking bottles in the empty cases. The only task that I observed him performing was washing the evening's dishes for his mother, but this occurred infrequently. Instead, David is allowed a wide range of personal freedom within the household and, in fact, his only routine task is his homework, which he does without being told. Occasionally he might ask his uncle for assistance, especially in regard to a mathematical problem, but this is more the exception than the norm.

For the most part, the relationship between Armando and Davíd is less affectionate than it is instrumental, although Armando does express concern for Davíd. But this concern is always couched in terms of goals of independence. For Armando, education and school success is the manner in which Davíd will not be "chingado" by others—education is power; it is the learning of the behavioral cues from more educated men than himself that Armando admires.

Yet the relationship between Davíd and Armando is much like the relationship between Armando and his father: distant, respectful, but potentially withdrawable and instrumental. Don Armando is an occasional visitor to the household from his own home town of 1,300 persons. There he lives alone on his one-hectare farm, growing black beans and corn and working at odd jobs within the pueblo. When he runs short of funds, he travels widely in central Mexico seeking employment.

An extremely independent person, Don Armando has worked as a bracero in the United States and as a construction worker in his own home town, in Mexico City, in Puebla, and in Cuernavaca. His visits to Netzahualcoyotl are intended to assist Armando in the continued construction of his house. Although the invitation to visit is by letter, the timing of these visits is determined by two factors: first, Armando's economic condition, and second, Don Armando's "state of mind." One factor is often in conflict with the other even though both may be initially congruent.

The first factor, based on Armando's financial status, reflects his reliance on cheap labor for the construction of a second story to his home. His goal is a home large enough so that it may have private bedrooms for his nephew, sister, daughter, father, and eventually when he marries, for himself and his wife. In addition, he also wants to include within his building space for an office for his future business activities.

The decision to invite his father for a "visit" is greatly influenced by Armando's ability to acquire enough surplus funds. Obviously it is extremely difficult for him to provide long-range predictions concerning when he will have such surplus funds. Therefore, his invitations to his father are usually made when he has immediate access to them. Armando has little choice in this method of operation once he has entered the "feedback" system of meeting his goals. The irony is that he never truly controls his decisions in a long-range sense. He is as coerced economically as he is a coercer of others.

This instrumental variable is of crucial importance in understanding the content of the interaction between Armando and his father. In one sense, Armando determines that the status relation between the two is a coercive one in that his father will expect short-range payoffs, money. However, such a relation is couched in the idiom of *"le ayudo a mi padre"* ("I help my father")—the idiom of amistad—the idiom of friendship, trust, cooperation, and assistance.

On the other hand, the payoff for Don Armando is also short-range, economically and emotionally. If those values of deference, respect, and paternal obedience are the basis for legitimate relations between father and son in Mexico—and they are—then these are undermined by the shifting of son-to-father support based on short-range considerations—and in fact, shifting the content of that support to coercion. This presents an interesting problem: If, in fact, the paternal figure is valued as a source of emotional gratification, these values come into direct contradiction with the belief that the father should be called upon only when surplus monies have been acquired to build a house which will fulfill long-range goals of "having made it." This lack of consistency between value and belief created by economic factors is a most important consideration.

The second factor which determines Don Armando's visits is dictated by his "state of mind." Don Armando lives alone in his pueblo, farms his plot of land, and within his circle of acquaintances is a respected figure; however, as in many small communities, the nuclear family is an important aspect of community-recognized prestige. In his pueblo, Don Armando is regarded as one whose *"familia se le fué"* (family has left him) and he is, at times, seen as being *"solo"* (alone and lonely).

Even though he maintains a circle of amigos íntimos, cuates, compadres, and consanguine and fictive kin, he has fallen victim to a process of discontinuity in terms of valued roles within the network of immediate consanguine relations—his nuclear family. While he has always been an independent person, that independence was expressed only in relation to the contributions it made for the maintenance of the family unit. He tilled the land, worked in the United States, worked in various urban centers, for one purpose—*"para la familia."* But tragically, all the roles of father, protector, provider, and prestige figure have been dissipated by his children's migration. He attempts to reinstitute such roles during his visits; however, such attempts are not congruent with the relations now established between him and Armando.

In a very real sense, Don Armando is a "hired hand." Many of his valued culturally defined roles are continued neither in the urban nor the rural environment. When not active in worker roles within the home in Netzahual-coyotl, he sits in front of the television set in Lupe and David's room or frequents the whorehouses in the city. He goes through cycles of depression, in both the urban and the rural environment, especially in the aftermath of not fulfilling meaningful "uncoercive" roles. A compadre in his pueblo refers to him as "un hombre solo." If he receives Armando's invitation to visit during such periods of depression (expressed in sullen and menacing behavior), then the probability of acceptance is small. Indeed, invitations at such times have prompted Don Armando to leave his pueblo for Veracruz, where he has some cuates. However, if the invitation arrives when he is not depressed, then in all probability he will accept. However, once in Netzahualcoyotl, Don Armando may spend a week irrationally yelling at all present, sullenly cursing his daughter as a "puta," and accusing Armando of "*hablando de él*" (speaking behind his back). Interestingly, when Armando and his brother and sisters are in their father's own pueblo, Don Armando does not behave in this manner.

The day does not pass in this home in Netzahualcoyotl that Armando's brother, Pedro, and his sister Magdalena do not also visit. Pedro, a tailor with his own shop in Netzahualcoyotl, is Armando's constant cross. For Pedro is a dreamer who consistently seeks the short-cut, the easy way to success by utilizing others, their energies, their funds, and their connections. He in fact is the perfect Ishmael. Although Pedro works terribly hard doing piece work in his home for various clothiers in Mexico City, he dreams of the time in which he can be wealthy, own a new car, move to Chapultepec, an expensive suburb, and have scores of young women surrounding him.

Married and the father of four children, Pedro is not "respected" within Armando's household nor by many persons within the circle which frequents it. Having a strong propensity for drink and little stamina, Pedro is known as an undesirable person to have present when alcoholic beverages are served.

Pedro is both an embarrassment and a responsibility for Armando. It is Armando who frequently rescues Pedro from immediate economic problems, and thus Pedro becomes increasingly dependent upon him. The more dependent he becomes, the more Pedro expects Armando to provide short-range assistance. In a political sense, consanguine ties have degenerated by the constant intervention of instrumental requests, and have become even more accentuated in the aftermath of Pedro's sudden and unpredictable parrandas. It is Armando who "patches up" the social damage which ensues in these parrandas.

In contrast to Pedro, Magdalena resembles Armando. She is independent, intelligent, vivacious, well-dressed, and reliable. Next to Armando, she is the most prestigious person within the consanguine relations living in Netzahualcoyotl. Similar to the relationship between Davíd and Armando, the relations between Magdalena and Armando are the most symmetrical within the family. Yet such relations are also modified by Armando's assumption of responsibility for the care, protection, and education of Martita, Magdalena's daughter.

Magdalena, married to a young man from Oaxaca, lives in a two-room jacal with her husband, his brother and wife and two children. Since she, her husband, and her husband's younger brother work in the Federal District during the day, the younger brother's wife cares for their children and the home. However, Magdalena neither likes nor trusts her sister-in-law. Constant friction arises over the proper division of labor when Magdalena returns from work, over the allocation of income to meet expenses, and over who has control of the household. Therefore, Magdalena never permits Martita to be alone with her sister-in-law, fearing, she says, *"que la bruja le haga daño a la niña"* (that the witch hurts the child) as revenge for the friction between them.

She therefore drops Martita off in the morning so that she may eat breakfast with Davíd and attend the local elementary school with him. When she returns from work, she then picks up the child at Armando's house. Martita frequently stays in the Armando's household overnight, perhaps three times during an average week.

From Armando's point of view, he wishes the child would stay permanently for two reasons: First, he sees his sister's in-laws as *"poco primitivos"* (a bit primitive) and therefore not healthy influences for Martita; furthermore, he likes her as a companion for Davíd. In fact, the children do play together frequently and cooperatively with little of the sibling rivalry common to most Mexican households. All ritual activities that concern the child—confirmation, birthday, and *dias de santos* (saint's days)—are celebrated in this household and not in her own, which points to the importance that Guadalupe and Armando give Martita's presence in the household. It is not the case that such rituals are held merely for convenience, but at the insistence of Guadalupe and affirmed by Armando.

By late afternoon, Guadalupe and Armando have completed a full day's work and until nine o'clock in the evening both will chat with the customers passing by; Armando continues stocking the store; Guadalupe will send Davíd and Martita to bed and she will then heat water for coffee. Meanwhile, Armando takes care of customers, friends pass by, neighbors stop to greet Armando on their way home from work, and at 9:30 he will pull the chains on the iron shutters and slide them to the floor. He then retires to the jacal or sits at a table to wait for Lupe to serve him coffee.

Even when Armando has retired for the night, cuates knock on the front gate until he awakes—kidding his propensity for going to bed early. Armando protests loudly, but to no avail. He has to rise, open the front door, enter his store, and bring out two cases of *caguamas* (quart-size beer—literally, turtles). By 3:00 in the morning all of them will be exhausted or drunk. Someone insults another, and a fight begins. Armando goes to sleep against the corner of the store and the first bedroom, and the men curse him and laugh and then leave. And the next morning, with a headache and nauseous, Armando will begin the chinga again.

Guadalupe will scold him in the morning for keeping her awake and for his foolishly supplying beer to his cuates, who never pay their bill. But his response generally is: *"Pasamos por mucho todos nosotros"* ("We have gone through a lot, all of us").

THE IMPLICATIONS

The basic attempt in this study was to decipher the crucial differential adaptations of two sets of families to the same basic environment, to the same basic demographic and urban pressures, and to the same basic economic and political sources of exploitation. The ethnographic descriptions of these families indicated that two of the families: the García and the López-Reyna could be considered as "ahistoric," and the Valenzuela and Reynosa families as "historic." The crucial indicators were the social and cultural presence of previous generational members and the capacities which they fulfilled. I indicated in the introduction that the differential adaptations revealed would suggest portents of things to come for the following generations within those families.

The crucial indicators, however, must be carefully delineated. First, it is not merely the physical presence of an older generational member which will determine the historical character of a family that will provide long-term emotional supports and value-based ideals. It is the prestige content of roles that are fulfilled within the household that will influence the historic family and the continuation of belief systems which buttress individual family members against physical and economic forces of stress.

Second, members of the older generation must have a private domain of resources, either skills highly valued, or personality development such that other members of the family system "listen." This personality development is usually charismatic in character and related to capacities in the immediate past which have been considered either "heroic" or symbolic of valued constructs. These constructs include such series of beliefs in this culture as stoicism, physical strength, success, intelligence, and the ability to confront and solve problems.

Third, such older members must be able to draw reinforcement from other social relations outside the immediate family circle. Such relationships include "down home" consanguine, fictive, or affinal relations even within a "new" urban setting. Such continuity provides the screen against which the socialization of children and the transmittal of values and belief ideals takes place. In effect, the enculturation and socialization of children do not occur in a larger social and cultural vacuum.

These indicators—the presence or absence of prestigious, self-resourceful, and other-reinforced previous generation members—are the crucial variables for the development of "ahistoric" and/or "historic" families in areas of rapid urbanization in developing countries such as Mexico.

The consideration of the ethnographic evidence validates the causal relationship between the presence of generational indicators and the development of family systems in which the legacy transmitted leads to an emphasis of the "historical" or "ahistorical" traditions. In the latter condition, family members will seek nonfamilial sources of gratification and support which encapsulate the individual to relations of short-range support. In so doing the stereotypic urban homo sapien is developed—the "ahistorical" traditions of "discontinuity" introduced into the following generations. Such individuals must seek sources of support outside self and outside face-to-face relations. These relations are basically transactional ones which in their repetition reinforce a tradition of conspicuous consumption or a reliance on strategies devoted solely to the acquisition of consumable goods as symbols of gratification.

Let me consider the ethnographic evidence in the families described by beginning with the "ahistoric" families first, and comparing these to the "historic" families. The first family that was described was the García family and the third was the López-Reyna group. These families present the extreme of the "ahistoric" families; the other families represent different degrees of historicism. The most historic is the Valenzuela family, and less historic is the Reynosa family.

The Ahistoric Cultural Strategy

The ethnographic evidence starkly suggests that both ahistoric families have either eliminated previous generational support, not developed previous generational support, or relied totally on limited intragenerational or external, nonfamilial support of an urban nature. The implications for the socialization of children include the early severance of consanguine ties, and the reliance primarily on outside-familial resources for need-satisfactions, including self-esteem and prestige. For each of the family members, crass consumer ideology is emphasized and conspicuous materialism is sought as a reference to success as postulated by nation-community standards. It is not that this belief and value system is antithetical to the nation state; it is, in fact, the full realization of urban homo sapiens in central urbanizing Mexico.

When Roberto García leaves his home each morning and conveys disdain for those walking by, those walking by also share with Roberto the value system by which they may be looked upon in disdain. Those walking by share with Roberto to one degree or the other the desire to back out from their homes in a black Ford Matador, and also look with disdain upon those who have not yet "made it." The price for Roberto and Dolorosa, however, has been very high. Roberto escaped the leveling mechanisms of his village,[12] the oppression of unsatisfying brutal labor, and an alcoholic father. By the age of twelve, he in fact had begun his trek to sever himself from an unrewarding past and into a foreign country where he could measure the fruits of his labor. Later, with his future in a gunny sack, he gained entry into the urban milieu—a milieu of temporary and coercive deals, and of cuates and short-range relationships. His association with his wife-to-be, also a person running from her past, became consummated as the aftermath of misconceived histories.

For Dolorosa, ex-maid and pretenciosa, her mariachi-father and servant mother were stark contrasts to her employer's cultural milieu. For Dolorosa, her mother, father, and sisters constantly reminded her of whence she "came," and functioned as the *brujería* in Roberto's village: They served as levelers to her vertical aspirations. For her aspirations, Roberto became the avenue for her escape to shared ahistoric expectations. For both Roberto and Dolorosa past relationships were painfully unfruitful, and both replaced them with a high investment in middle-class symbols. What was "new" including home, artifacts, business, and children became the raison d'être for social expectations and personal needs, and became also the sources of gratification.

Yet both Dolorosa and Roberto sought other than immediate gratification in other kinds of relationships. These, however, were largely incomplete, impoverished relationships lacking lasting definition and noncoercive goals. For Dolorosa, with her maid with whom she shared her fears mediated through the television set; with her dolls carefully placed on her bed as idyllic symbols of what never was; and with her fantasy relationships with her sons, such transcendental social goals remained unfulfilled. Roberto, like Dolorosa, also sought gratifying relationships, but like hers got equally impoverished imitations. These are expressed in his ambivalent sexual relations with Dolorosa, and in his nocturnal carousing with his cuates. For neither are there valued referents for gratifying experiences except those of the present. The past is dead.

This "ahistoricism" is a tradition carried on by their sons, and Roberto and Dolorosa can look forward to greater and greater investments in objects and less and less gratification. Future portents lie very much in the present.

Like the Garcías, the adult members of the López-Reyna family have invested their actions, thoughts, and feelings upon equally short-range goals and relationships in the present. What is carried into the present from the past are memories of María's robo by Refugio, José María's seeming forgiveness of him through the intercession of Refugio's father who was also José María's fictive kin, and Refugio's father's perceived treachery in selling an untitled lot from which they were later evicted. The past for López-Reyna adults, like the past for the Garcías, was severed in pain, and the drought which pushed them off their ranchería was the initial shock into the present.

Even though José María López is a previous generation member, he differs little from the other adults in the household in either function or prestige. Like the other two males, José María is part of the same feeble efforts at making a living, warding off intruders in the night, sharing the scarcity of resources of the household, and paying obeisance to power holders such as the police at the highway intersections and to the changos who removed the previous tenants from their jacal. It is their joint effort which barely allows their physical survival and subsistence. There is no reservoir of skills to be called upon, no storage of knowledge to be tapped, and no watershed of wisdom from previous generation-member José María to be utilized as necessary for survival. Survival is based upon who is jointly strongest in the present. The result is that, with physical survival so precarious, survival of human emotional investment in other than exploitive terms becomes a luxury. Survival of the soul is moot.

Such mootness is expressed in Refugio's penchant for violence directed toward María, in his continuing shallow adolescent investment in martial arts and tough-guy posturing, and his emotional callousness as expressed in his world view. In addition, his dependence upon and exploitation of the other members of the household bear the same relation to his exploitation and dependence by his superiors in rescate where he works for nothing. His superiors exploit his free labor and depend upon his labor for their own positions. Refugio exploits and depends upon the free labor of María and the barely compensated labor of Anselmo and José María. Such exploitive relations round out Refugio's present social universe.

For the rest of the members of the household, the same basic exploitive relations persist. All exploitation, however, points in María's direction. It is she who must balance the demands of her unpaid husband with those of her father and brother. It is she who must balance the inevitable future violence and the violent present. The past is partially responsible, and it is she who must try to keep it a dim memory. In addition, she must go through the daily physical and emotional operations which in a very real sense are self-defeating in a defeating environment. From the first movement in the morning to attend to the water pails to the warming of the previous night's tortillas, and from the denial of the screaming of a sick child to the furious scrubbing of the only object that does not give pain, María becomes the object for the full acrimony of husband, father, brother, and children. In defense, she maintains an emotionless silence of seeming passivity.

Like the Garcías the López-Reynas are totally involved in the present with no reference to the future except the activities for the maintenance of a precarious existence. What will occur to José María when he can no longer carry the unwieldly boxes of Kleenex tissue? Certainly his present muted relationships with daughter and son will not provide him assurances in old age: There is no past to which to refer. The interdependence for survival then will be broken, and no system of support is available for him to take advantage of when he can no longer function in the continuing struggle for subsistence.

María, Anselmo, and Refugio face the same inevitable end as José María. Their children, however, may very well seek to break from this painful "ahistorical" tradition, but in so doing create their own but of a different version—perhaps like that of the Garcías. The irony is that ahistorical breaks begin the chain for a cultural system whose tradition includes further breaking of tradition. In essence, such a "feedback" system dissolves its own beginnings. Ahistoricism becomes a traditional cultural system.

The Historic Tradition

In contrast, the Reynosa and Valenzuela families are part of a cultural system in which the "feedback" process is such that an older generational member plays a crucial prestigious role based on historical tradition. Such tradition stabilizes the family as a social group or mitigates against the urban "breakaway" tradition. For example, although the belief system expressed by Armando Reynosa perceives the world as a very limited and exploitive universe, it is balanced by older-generational values that define activities as to be centered in the survival of the extended family system. Like Don Armando his father, who tilled the land, worked as a bracero in the United States, and worked in various urban centers to ensure the survival of his family, young Armando seeks to "make it" in the urban milieu to be able to reestablish that which has been dissipated by urban migration. It is, in fact, young Armando's dream to finish the second story of his home not just as the physical expression of community beliefs but also to provide the household habitat for his father, sister and son, a wife-to-be and children, and his own daughter. He, in fact, seeks to replicate a three-generational system—a system usually particular to a rural environment. In a very real sense, he seeks to provide the basis for that which his own father could never establish in spite of his best intentions. That in part is derived from the sharing of similar values with his father.

Young Armando has effectively replicated his father's ideal—without his father. Young Armando stands as patriarch to the social group consisting of his father, sisters, brother, and their children. He is the exploiter-provider on the one hand, and the nurturent-instrumentalist on the other. He fulfills the many varied roles which his father values but in so doing he creates the conditions that are most responsible for his father's "state of mind." On the one hand, his invitations to his father arise according to the economic circumstances of the time and the goal of building the second story in order for his father to become a permanent resident of the household in his old age. On the other hand, the conditions in which his own father maintained family prestige—that is, his village—are part of the past. While young Armando seeks to replicate the conditions in which his father can once again have full, prestigious membership in the social group, the methods for the fulfillment of that goal are not of the past. Theirs is not an interdependent relationship in the present. In fact, Don Armando need not rely on his son's assistance economically, and emotionally Don Armando maintains a widespread network of blood and friendship ties. Yet, young Armando must depend upon his father to fulfill his own personal and group goals while fulfilling his father's roles within the family group. This conflict between generational past and present and the methods employed to replicate what never was lie at the crux of his father's "state of mind."

This conflict, however, is not a conflict between an older historical tradition and a new historical tradition. What are different are the economic, social, and demographic conditions which have shifted the locale in which such historical traditions can be followed. The roles which young Armando fulfills for his father are of the same kind that his father sought to fulfill but could not because of economic and demographic conditions in the village. In the urban milieu, his father cannot fulfill those either, but still has access to others which are at least rewarding. Young Armando, however, unlike his father, can probably look forward to his own historical tradition taking root in the urban present without discontinuity. His efforts are not to break from the past, but to reconstruct it in the image of his father.

The historical tradition within the Valenzuela system is derived not from replication efforts of any of its members but from the group processes arising within the living cycle of the Valenzuela extended family grouping. Except for the division of the physical household three years after their arrival in Netzahualcoyotl, the three-generational kinship system operates efficiently and supportively. The one exception is Don Teofilo who drinks excessively, but the rest of the family group provide him basic emotional support. It is Doña Margarita, Arturo's mother and Julieta's mother-in-law, who is the fulcrum of stability between the members of the family system and is the ideal role model for her dauthers-in-law, for her sons, grandchildren, and the comadres who aided Julieta and Arturo during political protest activities.

It is Doña Margarita, it must be recalled, who provided Julieta the rationale for not divorcing Arturo, and thus established an effective truce between them. It was Doña Margarita who first supported her son in his political struggles and is one of the key figures in the support provided him by the comadres. As Julieta describes her mother-in-law, she is the "tower" who has held the family system together by the force of her own personality.

This tower image, however, has its reverse side. While Doña Margarita is a positive cementing influence derived from the force of her charismatic character, she is also the cause for resentment on Julieta's part for her mother-in-law's interference in the running of the household. While her assistance is gratefully accepted, Doña Margarita nevertheless imposes her order upon the household, even to the arrangement of the household pottery upon the wall. Such an imposition, however, extends not only to Julieta, but to Arturo, and it could be hypothesized that his constant rebellion against political authorities even when he participates in the same kinds of political activities, may stem in part from his relationship with Doña Margarita. His frequent absences from home, his frequent extramarital affairs, and his participation in zero-sum political games are both punishments and escapes from his "towering" mother. Yet he will serve, as he says, as a model for his children to refer to. This historical tradition will most probably continue to function quite effectively and be transmitted to the succeeding generations.

NOTES

1. *Encuesta Definitiva En Cd. Netzahualcoyotl.* (Dirección) Jorge L. Tamayo. Contratistas Oaxaqueños, S.A. Mexico D.F., 1972:12.

2. "Unemployment is notable, especially among those groups that dedicate themselves to vagrancy, committing robberies, bloody crimes, and who are known as 'rebels without a cause.' The blame is, in part, on the authorities for tolerating centers of vice and prostitution that replace centers of social and cultural activities in the city." Javier Garcia Martinez. "memoria de Trabajo," Direccion de Educación Pública del Estado de Mexico. Escuela Normal del Estado; Netzahualcoyotl, Mexico, 1969:20.

3. Fictitious. All surnames, places, and to some extent, events have been changed to protect the informants after publication of this work.

4. *Ejido* is a communal landholding system which was revived after the 1910 revolution and given great stimulus during the presidency of Lázaro Cárdenas, 1934-1940.

5. Roberto was never a "contract" worker of the bracero class in which a minimum daily wage amount was set and/or piece rate guaranteed, but considered himself and was considered by his peers in the United States as a *mojado* (wetback). The result was that his hourly wages varied according to the personal relations he had accomplished with a contractor, farm foreman, or owner.

6. Thirty-three of the thirty-four persons are those she recognizes as consanguine, full, or half siblings. Her father, a Oaxacan politician, had numerous children said to have totaled about eighty or so. He had been married three times and maintained three *casas chicas* (polyganous arrangements) until his death in 1974.

7. The road and the sidewalk are really the same. Electric light poles along the streets define the area on which cars may travel. Pedestrians use the protection of the space between the light poles and the front of the lots of homes as sidewalks.

8. Mexico has federal, state, and municipal schools so that a city like Netzahualcoyotl may have all three within the same municipality.

9. Pandilla members are age heterogeneous and are centered in the Colonia del Sol. Speaking an "in-group" argot when together, some of the members specialize in extorting money from store-owners in the colonia. Refugio returns to his colonia periodically and goes on parrandas with them, not returning for three or four days.

10. Of the families so far described little has been said of their previous rural experiences nor of periodic visits to their former places of origin. The Garcías do not maintain rural relationships; the Valenzuelas do, but only as Arturo's escape valve and Julieta's intermittent "visits"; except for Jose Maria's reminiscences of hardship, the López-Reynas do not maintain any relationship with a rural environment. On the other hand, as will be seen, this family does.

11. This cuate, who was from Armando's home town, later used this knowledge as a political resource in not paying his contribution to a tanda that Armando was responsible for. Armando eventually was chingado with his own ploy.

12. What Roberto stated was that he escaped "*la brujería*" (the witches) of the town. By this he meant either actual or imagined witches who function as the anthropological literature has shown, as the means by which social upstarts are eliminated or made to conform to community standards. They also point to the source of social tension within a community–in this case, the tension between generations.

Rituals of Comensality: *An age heterogeneous process in a historical family.*

Role Continuation of Females into Late Adulthood

Alone, Resourceless and Dependent: *The aftermath of ahistoricism*

CHAPTER 5

A SYMBOL PERFECTED IN DEATH:

Continuity and Ritual in the Life and Death of an Elderly Jew

Barbara G. Myerhoff

What they had to leave us—a symbol: a symbol perfected in death.

—T. S. Eliot

Jacob Kovitz died in the middle of the public celebration of his ninety-fifth birthday, amid friends and family gathered to honor him at the Aliyah Senior Citizen's Community Center, which had become the focus of life for a small, stable, socially and culturally homogeneous group of elderly Jews, immigrants to America from Eastern Europe. The event was remarkable in

AUTHOR'S NOTE: *The methods used to gather information for writing this chapter included the conventional anthropological techniques: participant-observation, interviews, tape recordings, group discussions, films, and photographs. I taped and photographed the event described, and later had access to 8mm. film footage taken by one of those attending. I interviewed Jacob Kovitz many times before he died, and interviewed members of his family before and after. The final interpretation I developed was discussed with the family, who had no objections to it, though it varied in some points with their own. All names used, including that of the center, have been changed.*

I am much indebted to many people who helped me in various ways, including: Andrew Ehrlich, Laura Geller, Walter Levine, Riv-Ellen Prell-Foldes, Beryl Mintz, Morris Rosen, Chaim Seidler-Feller, and Dyanne Simon. Naturally, no one is responsible for this chapter but myself.

many ways: It dramatized the ubiquitous human passion for continuity. It called attention to several kinds of continuity and the manner in which they overlap. And it pointed up the ways in which ritual provides and presents continuity.

RITUAL, CONTINUITY AND DEATH

Continuity is a fundamental necessity for human life, collectively and individually. It is central to social gatherings of all sorts, when people assemble to experience their interdependence and overcome their human separateness. It is central to culture, the shared life ways of a group which are continued and preserved over time. Continuity is essential for psychological well-being and personal integration, for an individual to experience him/herself as one person, despite change and disruption, throughout the life cycle. And, ultimately, continuity figures largely at the end of life, when the individual devises ways to fend off the possibility of complete extinction. These four kinds of continuity—social, cultural, personal life-historical, and what must be called spiritual—all came into clear focus on the day Jacob died. His ritual death was an assertion that his community would continue, that his way of life would be preserved, that he was a coherent, integrated person throughout his personal history, and that something of him would remain alive after his corporeal departure.

Jacob's birthday is interpreted here as a drama of continuity, in which death was transformed from a potential antagonist into a partner. On this occasion, *malakh-hamoves*, the Angel of Death, cooperated with Jacob to produce a triumphant celebration which defied time, change, mortality, and existential isolation.

It is not surprising that such a drama would center around death. Inevitably, death presents a crisis in continuity and the threat of irrevocable and total discontinuity. In a case like Jacob's, this threat is especially acute. When history has not noted a man's existence, when his peers are also very old and on the edge of mortality, when his way of life has not been taken up by the succeeding generation, when his religion has not assured him that his name will be remembered by God, what is there to expect but oblivion? By making his death a mythic and symbolic drama, Jacob transcended it.

Neither is it surprising that ritual figured so largely in the occasion. Ritual is a prominent element in areas of uncertainty, anxiety, impotence, and disorder. By its repetitive character, ritual provides a message of pattern and predictability. Ritual is an assertion of continuity. Even when dealing with change, ritual connects new events and elements with preceding ones, incorporating them into a stream of precedents so that they are recognized as growing out of tradition and experience. Ritual states enduring and even timeless patterns, thus connects past, present, and future, abrogating history, time, and disruption. Socially, ritual links immediate fellow participants but often goes beyond this to connect a group of celebrants to wider collectivities—absent members, the ancestors, and those as yet unborn. Religious rituals go still farther, connecting mankind to the forces of nature and purposes of the deities. And rituals link the celebrant to his/her very self, making individual history into a unified phenomenological flow.

What happens when ritual is not predictable, when it is interrupted by an unplanned development, and chaos or accident menaces its orderly proceedings? What is done if a death appears out of order, in the middle of a ritual celebrating life? Such an occurrence may be seen as a mistake in ritual procedure, as a warning or message from the deities, or as a devastating sign of human impotence. But there is another possibility. The unexpected may be understood as fulfilling a different, but loftier purpose, and a new, higher order may be detected underneath the original disturbance. A ritual may be altered in midstream to take account of an emergent reality, and fulfill its purposes by establishing a new meaning, made out of older, extant symbols and rites. In order for such a transformation to occur, the celebrants must have at their fingertips sacred, familiar symbols and sentiments with which to build a new interpretation; in this case, fortunately, the celebrants were so endowed. Jacob transformed his party into a celebration of his entire life and culture, and his death, thereby, was "tamed."

The notion of a tamed death, to use Aries' (1974) term, is not common in our times but it is far from new. In the Middle Ages, knights of the *chansons de geste* also tamed death. Forewarned by the spontaneous realization of imminent departure, the dying person prepared himself and his surroundings, often by organizing a ritual and presiding over it. Death was made into a public ceremony, often very simple, including parents, children, friends, and neighbors, gathered around the deathbed. The ceremonial nature of these assemblies was strong though not usually emotional. Death was "both familiar and near, evoking no great fear or awe" (1974: 13).

Such a death among peasants is described by Solzhenitsyn (1969: 96-97). "They didn't puff themselves up or fight against it and brag that they weren't going to die—they took death calmly. . . . And they departed easily, as if they were just moving into a new house." Death was not romanticized or dramatized. It was not banished, denied, or removed from the household and domestic circle. Through the end of the Middle Ages, this kind of ceremonial death persisted; later it took on a more dramatic character. The important part played at the final moment by the dying person lasted well into the seventeenth century. The dying man, actively directing the ceremonies surrounding his own death, remained at the center of the event, "determining the ritual as he saw fit."

As the individual, distinct from social and communal setting, emerges as an important concept, the moment of death comes to be regarded as the opportunity in which one is most able to reach a full awareness of self. Before the fifteenth century, the dying person accepted death "in a public ceremony whose ritual was fixed by custom. The ceremony of death was then at least as important as the ceremony of the funeral" (Aries, 1974: 104).

In reading these historical accounts, the anthropologist is immediately reminded of practices in many preliterate societies. Here is an account of a death ceremony among the Polar Eskimos:

> In some tribes an old man wants his oldest son or favorite daughter to be the one to put the string around his neck and hoist him to his death. This was always done at the height of a party where good things were being eaten, where everyone—including the one who was about to die—felt happy and gay, and which would end with the angakok [shaman] conjuring and dancing to chase out the evil spirits. At the end of his performance, he would give a special rope of seal and walrus skin to the "executioner," who then placed it over the beam on the roof of the house and fastened it around the neck of the old man. Then the two rubbed noses, and the young man pulled the rope [Freuchen, 1961: 194-195].

All the elements of a tamed death are present also in the case of Jacob's birthday party: his foreknowledge of death, its occurrence in a public ceremony which he directed, his attitude of calm acceptance, his use of the occasion to express the meaning of his life, and the presence and participation of those with whom he was intimate.

Jacob's death is certainly not without precedent. It is perhaps most remarkable because Jacob lacked the usual assurances of continuity: the religious beliefs of the medieval knights and the Polar Eskimo which promised them that they would continue in an afterlife, and their knowledge that a stable, ongoing community would preserve their way of life. Jacob created the continuity that was not there before his party began.

ETHNOGRAPHIC SETTING

Before describing the birthday party, some social and historical background is necessary, first about the community and culture, and then about Jacob's life. At the time of this study, the relevant community consisted of about 4,000 people at its broadest extension. These individuals were spread over an area of about six miles around the Aliyah Center; the center membership consisted of 300 people, about 200 of whom were present at the birthday party. Intensive interviews and more casual discussions were held with about 50 people, those most central to Jacob's life and the event. The great majority of people belonging to the Center were between eighty-five and ninety-five years old. Most had been residents in the neighborhood for twenty to thirty years.

Nearly all had lived as children in the little Jewish towns and settlements of Eastern Europe known as *shtetls*. Yiddish was their mother tongue and *Yiddishkeit*, the folk culture built around the language and customs of the shtetl, was a major emotional and historical force in their lives, though their participation in and identification with it varied in intensity throughout the life cycle. In great numbers, these people and others like them had fled their natal homes intent on escaping the extreme anti-semitism, intractable poverty, and political oppression which was growing more intense around the turn of the century.

As adolescents and young adults, they came to the New World and worked as petty merchants, unskilled laborers, craftsmen, and artisans in the Eastern industrial cities of America. On reaching retirement age, with their children educated, married, and socially and geographically remote, they drifted into their present community, drawn to the mild climate, the ocean, and to the intense Yiddishkeit of the area. Now, they were isolated and old, but freed from external pressures to be "American." In this condition, they turned more and more toward each other, revived Yiddish as their preferred language, and elaborated an eclectic subculture which combined elements from their childhood beliefs and customs with modern urban American practices and attitudes, adapting the mixture to their present needs and circumstances.

These circumstances were harsh. Family members were distant or dead. Most of the group were poor, very old and frail, suffering from social and communal neglect, extreme loneliness, and isolation. As a people, they were marginal to the concerns of the larger society around them. Their social, political, physical, and economic impotence was pronounced and except on a very local level, they were nearly invisible.

Added to these afflictions was their realization that the culture of their childhood would die with them. The Holocaust had wiped out the shtetls and nearly all their inhabitants. The center people clearly apprehended the impending complete extinction of themselves as persons and as carriers of a culture. The group was entirely age-homogeneous and, except for ceremonial occasions, no real intergenerational continuity existed. Their own membership was being depleted constantly, and there were no others to replace them. Death and impotence were as real as the weather and as persistent.

Moreover, the social solidarity of the group was weakened by the people's ambivalence toward one another, due in part to enforced association and perhaps, too, to displaced anger. Their cultural traditions inclined them to a certain degree of distrust of non-kin and despite the stability, homogeneity and distinctiveness of past experiences, circumstances, and extensive time spent together, they had less than entirely amiable feelings for each other. Factions, disagreements, and long-standing grudges marred their assemblies, most of which took place in secular and sacred rituals within the center and on benches outside it.

But despite their ideological discord, they were united by their common past. This was expressed as Yiddishkeit, the local customs, language and beliefs that characterized these people's parental homes and early life in the shtetl. Very few were orthodox in religious practices. They had broken with strict religious Judaism before leaving the "old country." A great many were agnostic, even atheistic and anti-religious. But all were passionately Jewish, venerating the historical, ethnic, and cultural aspects of their heritage. Most had liberal and socialist political beliefs and had been active at one time or another in the Russian Revolution, various workers' movements, labor unions, and similar political activities. Since the Holocaust, all were Zionists, despite some ideological reservations concerning nationalism. For them, Israel had become an extension of their family, and its perpetuation and welfare were identified as their own. This constellation of beliefs and experiences— the childhood history of the shtetl, Yiddish language and culture, secular and ethnic Judaism, and Zionism, were the sacred elements which united them.[1]

The subculture which the group had developed was made of several distinct layers of historical experience: that of Eastern Europe in which they spent their childhood, of America at the turn of the century until the 1930s and 1940s where they lived as adults, and of the latter part of their lives in a California urban ghetto of elderly Jews. Though there were many discontinuities and sharp disruptions during these eighty and ninety years, there were some notable cultural and social continuities, particularly between childhood and old age. These continuities seem to have helped them adapt to their contemporary circumstances. Not surprisingly, many of their rituals and symbols emphasized those situational continuities. These are summarized in Table 1, which is a compound of individual life histories, representing a kind of collective profile, emphasizing features most mentioned by the senior citizens themselves.

It is likely that the elders would not have elaborated this subculture had they remained embedded in a context of family and community. Their very isolation gave them much freedom and originality; they improvised and invented, unhampered by restraints of their original traditions and social disapproval of authorities, with only themselves to please. For the first time since coming to America, now in old age, they were able to fully indulge their old love of Yiddish and Yiddishkeit without fear of being ridiculed as "greenhorns" by their sophisticated, assimilated children. Now living again in a small, integrated community, which emphasized learning, where Yiddishkeit flourished, where individual freedom and autonomy were exercised in isolation from mainstream society, they were able to revive their earlier responses to conditions which they had known before. Their present poverty, impotence, physical insecurity, and social marginality recalled shtetl existence.

Such continuity is adaptive, despite its painful contents. People who have always known that life was hard and fate unreliable if not downright treacher-

TABLE 1

Continuities and Discontinuities in Life Circumstances

	Eastern Europe	America (earlier stay)	America (California)
(1) Locale			
(2) Community	*Gemeinschaft of small settlements and villages	Gesellschaft; urban centers and suburbs	*Gemeinschaft of an urban ghetto
(3) Family	extended, patriarchal, stable, cohesive	nuclear, more egalitarian, less stable and cohesive	shallow and narrow; infrequent contacts with family members
(4) Generational continuity	*rejection of their parental traditions; geographical and social separation between generations due to immigration	strained relations with children as assimilation occurs; social separation grows, geographical proximity	*virtually severed relations between generation; strong geographical and social separation between generations
(5) Religion and ideology	*Zionism; growing agnosticism; Yiddishkeit; "Learning" a major form of religious expression; pronounced identity as Jews	*Zionism; agnosticism; Yiddishkeit; "Learning" as a religious expression is superceded by "learning" for assimilation and social success; less pronounced identity as Jews	*Zionism; less pronounced agnosticism, more preference for traditional religious forms; "Learning" a major form of religious expression; pronounced identity as Jews
(6) Language	*Yiddish; some Hebrew for men; Slavic languages for some	English gradually acquired and replaces Yiddish to some extent	*Yiddish assumes more importance; some study of Hebrew; all fluent in English
(7) Age, sex distinctions	sharp division between sexes; males dominant economically and ritually; seniority valued	age and sex roles blurred; women become important economically; seniors largely absent; juniors dominant socially	age and sex roles no longer relevant; females dominant; males largely absent; younger generations absent
(8) Autonomy and nurturance	nurtured by family and community; dependent on others	nurturant of own children, independent	some nurturance by others (health and economic matters); some nurturing of others (Israel); partially dependent on others
(9) Economic circumstances	*poverty; little or no social mobility; insecurity	relative affluence; security and much social mobility	*poverty; no social mobility; pronounced insecurity
(10) Relation to outside, dominant society	*physical danger; religious oppression; social and cultural separation, enforced externally and self-imposed	no physical danger; very little religious oppression; moderate and diminishing social and cultural separation, more enforced than self-imposed	*physical danger; no religious oppression; moderate social separation; pronounced cultural separation, some external enforcement but primarily self-imposed.

*Indicates distinct continuity.

[169]

ous are not surprised to encounter these hazards again. They know how to cope with them and are not discouraged. They never expected life to be easy or happy. "Happiness," said Sarah, "happiness is not having a broken leg." It is not a terrible shock to discover that there is no golden age at the end of life; they never believed in a golden age to begin with.

Aging as a Career

Jacob Kovitz was an expert at making aging his career. In varying degrees, all the Aliyah Center people were engaged in this work. Their very continuing existence was an accomplishment, individually and collectively. In the face of tremendous difficulties, survival becomes a life work. They had outlived all their enemies—Cossacks, Nazis, anti-semites—and successful defiance of those determined to extinguish them was a conspicuous source of pride.

The old people marked each day by calculating the successful completion of many small tasks: making a meal, doing the laundry, visiting friends, finding a bargain, reading the paper, walking to the ocean, discovering that their limbs and minds still obeyed them. Their knowledge about survival was their technological expertise—managing their meager funds, using the human contacts around them to meet their needs, asserting their autonomy and worth dramatically and symbolically by fulfilling their roles as members of the center, exploiting those who came in contact with them and in whom a sense of obligation could be sparked, raising funds for others needier than themselves, celebrating holidays, and the like. Their center provided the arena in which they could enact their worth and dramatize their visibility, if not to the outside world, at least to each other and to themselves.

It may be noted in passing that in making aging a career, the women had many natural advantages over the men. They were experts in establishing and maintaining social relationships, and they had long experience in developing their nurturant roles into full-time, serious work. These tasks were as pertinent in old age as they had been in youth. The men had always been much more tied to external circumstances: in using time, in calculating accomplishments and self-worth, in asserting their autonomy and expressing themselves. The women more than the men were able to parlay earlier roles into serious occupations for later life. And the women more than the men knew how to take care of themselves and their tiny households. For them, cooking, shopping, laundry, and the like were stable accompaniments throughout life; there was no shame in these small tasks—indeed, they were often a source of pride.

Jacob exemplified a career in aging appropriate to a man, but he was unique in this. For the most part, the women worked out this adaptation far more successfully.

For a dozen years, birthdays had been celebrated by the members in their small dilapidated center. These were collective occasions, grouping together all those born within the month—modest, simple affairs. Only Jacob Kovitz had regular birthday parties for him alone, and these parties were great fêtes. This reflected his unusual standing in the group. He was a kind of patriarch, a formal and informal leader of the group. He had served as its president for several years, and even after leaving the community to live in a rest home, he returned frequently and had been named president emeritus. He was one of the oldest people in the group and the most generally venerated. No one else had managed to provide leadership without becoming entangled in factional disputes. He regarded himself, and was generally regarded by others, as an exemplar, for he had fulfilled the deepest wishes of most people and he embodied their loftiest ideals.

JACOB

Jacob's case is an especially useful one in this context, for it illustrates so well two of the issues which concern us here: continuity, and aging as a career. Continuity was a conscious and passionate value for Jacob himself, a consistent force in his life, about which he often spoke and wrote, and which he demonstrated. He was a teacher and a model; like an Exemplary Prophet, he intended his life to be a lesson to his followers. Ultimately, he was himself a symbol of continuity.

Jacob's attitude toward aging might be called professional. To it he brought the same consciousness, intensity, hard work, high standards, and demands for growth and success that he applied to himself through the years preceding his retirement. Indeed, the word "retirement" is misleading in referring to his life between ages sixty-five and ninety-five. There was no leisure there, no relaxing of his commitment to strict, valued, long-range goals, no sense of being irrelevant or useless. Simply, he was no longer paid to do some of the things which he had always done. After sixty-five, he was a professional elder, and one could say the high point of his career in this capacity was realized the day of his death.

Jacob, the Man

How is one to account for such success? In this case, as in all life histories, the explanation is an inextricable combination of personal characteristics, physiology, and a set of cultural and historical circumstances which could be turned to advantage and which suited the man's abilities and desires. And in some measure, success is also a matter of luck. Jacob had good luck, especially in the form of great energy, good health, intelligence, and talent. In addition to his personal endowments, his good luck was manifested in his successful marriage, and the production of four intelligent, healthy sons. Psychologically, his characteristic resourcefulness, independence, and resilience served him well.[2] He seems to have been a remarkably balanced man, always struggling to integrate the often conflicting pulls between family obligation and worldly success. He appears to have been repeatedly able to rebound from blows and losses with added perspective and energy.

Jacob was clearly able to tolerate ambiguity and ideological conflicts, and perhaps this prepared him for a successful career in aging. His writings bring forth his lifelong struggle to reconcile his commitment to socialism and social equality with his achievements and acquisition of power and wealth. He struggled also to bring together his beliefs in and dedication to Zionism and American patriotism on one hand, and internationalism on the other. Finally, he managed to forge a position concerning Judaism which was not a simple one. Jacob was passionately Jewish but agnostic, even anti-religious. As a cultural-ethical Jew, he was completely engrossed in his heritage, but separated it from all aspects of the formal religious establishment, beliefs, and practices.

In these last two conflicts–nationalism/Zionism/patriotism vs. internationalism; religious vs. cultural Judaism–Jacob was not alone. Most members of the center struggled with the same issues, and the handful who had been economically successful also struggled with the conflict between their wealth and their commitment to socialism or communism. Is it possible that dealing with ideological dilemmas may have predisposed these people to a successful career in aging? These conflicts, it must be noted, were not matters of Jacob's individual psychology. They were the collective dilemmas of a whole population, generated by their cultural membership and the historical circumstances they encountered. It may well be the case that active engagement with ideological conflict has given these elderly people the ability to age well. It may have given them experience needed to achieve the complex, even paradoxical attitude toward aging so thoroughly articulated by Jacob, and to some degree practiced by all center members.

What precisely is that attitude which marked Jacob as a professional elder? Jacob's conceptions about and approach to aging were indeed complex and dynamic. He knew how to intensify the present, how to deepen his satisfaction in small rewards and pleasures, how to bring the past into his life for the continuity that gave it intrinsic meaning; yet he never remained fixed on the past nor used it as a negative standard in terms of which to view the present. He knew how to look at the inevitable destiny the future held and accept it without moving toward it with unnecessary speed. Too, Jacob could provide new standards and desires for himself as the old ones became unattainable, generating from within appropriate measures of accomplishment and worth, in a continual process of discarding and creating. This is aging as a career. It requires a dynamic equilibrium, and leads to an integration of internal and external forces. It is hard not to see Jacob's aging work as continuous with his prior experiences in coping with paradox and conflict.

This acceptance of ideological complexity, the understanding, even delight in dialectical argument and multiple, relativistic perspectives, the use of sometimes sardonic, resigned humor about life's inevitable blows has cultural antecedents, both in Talmudic debate (*pilpul*) and in the literature and folklore of the shtetl. The approach is exemplified in the figure of speech, "On the one hand—but on the other hand," so characteristic of Jacob and most center people. There is always another way to look at things; closure, simplicity, certainty in outlook are disappointments, small failures, since everyone knows truth is provisional, and knows, too, that as long as there is debate there is possibility, sociability, and excitement. Jacob's attitude toward aging was rooted in this tradition, exemplified in two Yiddish proverbs he was fond of quoting:

Az men vil nit alt vern, zol men zikh yungerheyt oyfhengen. (He that would avoid old age must hang himself in youth.)

Der mentsh iz voz er iz, ober nit voz er iz geven. (A man is what he is, not what he used to be.)

This intransigent realism tempered by a mocking, undefeated acceptance of life, was woven into a philosophy of aging by Jacob and many of his peers.

Jacob's Writings

A final factor contributing to Jacob's success in aging, and a major one, is attributable to his passion for writing. In this, too, his work was continuous, for he wrote all his life, expanding the quantity, use of different genres, and content of his products greatly after age sixty-five. He was fortunate that literacy was a traditionally valued activity in his culture, and brought him public esteem. In Jewish tradition, old age is regarded as an appropriate period for the study of the Torah and for reflection. That Jacob studied himself and the world around him was his variation on a conventional cultural theme. He used his writings to teach and with the hope of passing on to his descendants an account of his history and philosophy. And he used his writing to clarify his thinking, stave off occasional periods of depression, anxiety, and fear of senility. Above all, in the writings, he organized his conception of himself and the meaning of his life.

Jacob's writings achieve continuity on several levels: vertically, over time, as he weaves his past into the present, and passes it on to the future; laterally, across personal boundaries, as he passes his work on to others in his age group and community. He creates personal continuity when he integrates all the phases of his long life into one narrative account, contemplated by one conscious being, aware of having been other beings at other times. And he establishes social and cultural continuity, as he incorporates into his account worldly events and issues, meshing inner and outer history.

In this work, Jacob constructs a sacred story, a personal myth, which takes up the ultimate eschatological questions, "What has it all meant?" "Why was I here?" In traditional, religious settings, answers to these questions are provided collectively. In our secular world, the individual must provide his/her own, and this Jacob undertakes. For him, the work was obviously urgent, and this is not surprising. When a man is facing death, when he does not believe in God, and has no reason to believe his way of life will be perpetuated, when the world does not consider his wisdom and experience germane, discontinuity is so extreme as to constitute the threat of total nothingness. What Sir Thomas Browne said in 1658 is still true: This threat is "the heaviest stone that melancholy can throw at a man."

The desire for temporal continuity, the wish to be remembered, is only one of the tasks served by Jacob's writing. The struggle to find internal continuity is not less important. The search for the sense and meaning which continuity bestows is fundamental to serious autobiographical work, and in this task no audience is necessary but the writer himself, who becomes subject and object at the same time. Self-reflection then becomes self-creation, expressive of the powerful human impulse to order. Through autobiography, "man creates by the very act of seeking, that order he would have . . . looking for a oneness of self, an integrity or internal harmony that holds together the multiplicity and continual transformations of being" (Olney, 1972: 6).

Throughout his writings, Jacob repeatedly makes bearable his periods of anguish and confusion by finding them "interpretable." And, to paraphrase Langer (1942), one can bear anything of which one is able to *conceive*. Without our conceptions, our sacred symbols, we lack a vision of coherence and continuity, and we become utterly vulnerable and disoriented. When we contemplate and construe our experiences, building up an explanation for self and the universe, we make Cosmos out of Chaos. Eistein refers to this activity as "free conceptual construction," the "only way man has of making the universe stop pounding and washing away at his little light of consciousness" (Olney, 1972: 16).

When his eyesight had failed him, when passivity and defeat were threatened, when his body no longer moved as he wished, Jacob's mind and fingers served him still. He continued through the writing to be the engaged, lucid man of purpose that he had always been.

Jacob's writings consist of two nearly book-length autobiographies, one covering his life up to the age of sixty-five, the other from age sixty-five to ninety-four; a collection of essays, speeches, letters, short stories, a travel diary, and poems in English and Yiddish, amounting to several hundred pieces. From age eighty-nine on, he regularly used his birthdays as occasions to reflect upon his life and revise his interpretation of its sense and worth. He wrote pieces for the rites of passage in the lives of his children, grandchildren, and great-grandchildren, relating their history to his own. Several pieces are reminiscences of his childhood, his parents, and his grandparents. He was also inspired to write by external events—for example, moments in the history of

Israel, developments in Jewish history, especially the Holocaust and the destruction of Eastern European Jewry. Some of his pieces were occasioned by the deaths of friends and family members. Some marked Jewish holidays, and others were written for celebrations held at the center.

Jacob's confrontations with some of the regular difficulties facing the aged are especially interesting: his despondency over illness, his revulsion at the home for the elderly in which he lived for a short time, his dismay at the loss of contact with younger generations. Regularly, he admonished the elderly on the necessary ingredients for a positive response to old age—humor, perspective, the preservation of tradition, the necessity for continual learning and adapting to change.

The attitude is exemplified in one of his pieces, which he called "Ten Commandments for the Elderly." It combines humor, lofty ideals, and homely, realistic advice. The last commandment illustrates this:

> Dress neatly and don't try to save your best clothes, because after you leave this world, you won't need them anymore. Keep your head up, walk straight, and don't act older than your age. Remember one thing: if you don't feel well, there are many people who are feeling worse. Walk carefully, watching for the green light when crossing. If you have to wait a minute or two, it doesn't make any difference at your age. There is no reason to rush.

Jacob's passion for continuity is a leitmotiv, woven throughout the body of his writings. This passion goads him on despite the weariness he feels as he begins his second autobiography at ninety-four. In it, he reminds himself of the reason for fighting apathy—to leave his life story for his children.

"So, Jacob Kovitz," he writes, "pick up your pen, don't be lazy, for time runs too swiftly while we humans fall behind. There is a saying in Hebrew, 'The day is short and the work is long.' So, I will begin my work now, and I hope the Angel of Death will allow me to complete my work before he performs his."

The resultant writings, he concludes, should be read at family and center gatherings after his death. Whenever these readings occur, he states, "I, in my new home, will feel both happy and serene, being with all of you in spirit as I am now in body." By these readings, Jacob is providing his own memorial. His written final words constitute his legacy to the children, when he urges them "to try to draw out the thread of our family, in order that your children and grandchildren will have some understandings of their origins." Here, Jacob goes beyond assuring his own personal continuity. He bequeathes the concept of perpetual continuity, not merely as an individual memorial, but as a permanent process, to those who will follow him.

Jacob's History

Jacob's life was very long and rich and can only be outlined briefly here. He was born in 1880, in a small Ukrainian town, the third child in a family of six. His father was employed by a road construction company and was often away from home. Like all Russian Jewish boys, at age three he was taken to *cheyder*, religious school, to learn Hebrew. He seems to have disliked the rigidity and narrowness of his religious education from the first, and was relieved when, at age nine, he was enrolled in a secular school.

Even as a child, Jacob was aware of and revolted by class inequities. His little town was socially segregated, and he was keenly distressed that because he belonged to the middle class he was not allowed to play with the shoemaker's boy, on pain of punishment by the rabbi. Jacob's mother managed an inn, and his father was eventually made a partner in his road company; between the earnings of both parents, the family was quite comfortable. Jacob's secure, stable family life ended abruptly with his father's death when the boy was twelve. The company camp in which his father worked was sealed off when cholera broke out. Hundreds of men died there and were buried in a mass grave. Jacob's mother was determined to remove her husband's body to a Jewish cemetery, and sold nearly everything the family had to pay for the opening of the workers' grave and the finding of her husband's body. She returned penniless, sold the house, and decided to move to Odessa where she would attempt to earn a living for her children. After all the household belongings were sold, there was only enough money for her to take four children with her. Jacob and an older sister would remain behind until she could send for them.

Jacob managed to eke out a meager living for himself and his sister by teaching Russian to the Jewish children in the town. After several months, he had even saved a small amount toward the fare to Odessa. But he was tricked out of his money by a stranger who offered to buy him a cheap ticket and soon found himself penniless, without a ticket, on a train far from home and Odessa. After many harrowing adventures, during which he was jailed, tried to become a hobo, slept in synagogues of small towns, begged for food, and rode the rails, he eventually made his way to the city and was reunited with his mother and siblings.

In Odessa, he tried many jobs, and for a time was an apprentice to a metal worker in an effort to learn a trade. But he learned nothing in this situation. For four years, he was driven mercilessly, half-starved. He was forced to sleep on the shop floor, without any heat, covered by old rags. But worst of all, when he ran away and found employment in a sheet metal factory, he discovered that after four years of suffering, he had not learned enough to become a sheet-metal craftsman. That position required knowledge of pattern cutting, and of the thirty men employed in the factory, only one had such knowledge, working in secret and jealously guarding his skills from the sight of the others. Young Jacob's responsibilities included cleaning up the shop after the others left. This gave him the opportunity to study the discarded pieces and from these he reconstructed the process of pattern layout, secretly working for several months in the dark shop late into the night. The acquisition of this skill was a turning point in Jacob's life—it was to be the source of his independence and freedom many times in the future. The work suited him, satisfying his aesthetic desires and talents and his respect for manual labor, a respect which soon grew into a fully developed political philosophy.

This was the eve of the Russian revolution, a time of great philosophical and social ferment. Jacob found the working conditions in which he labored intolerable and though at sixteen he was the youngest man in his shop, he organized a strike. It failed, and the men were fired. Undaunted, Jacob managed to acquire some tools and set up a small cooperative, making a sheet metal shop in his mother's kitchen.

Gradually, Jacob was indoctrinated into the principles of socialism and began to attend, then to organize, political meetings. Many times he found himself in demonstrations which were broken up by mounted armed Cossacks. During this time, Jacob's life was completely devoted to work, politics, and avoiding the police. This continued until 1900, when Jacob was drafted into the Russian army and stationed near Warsaw. He resumed his illegal political activities in continual fear of detection, since now, as a soldier, discovery meant death. In the army, he managed to use his skills as a metal worker to allow him the freedom of movement and time needed for political work.

Eventually Jacob was arrested for a minor matter, but his safety was assured because he was favored by the wife of the commanding officer. She gave him an order to build a very complex and ornate metal ornament of her own design and watched over him until it was done, interceding with her husband for Jacob's safety on more than one occasion. The Revolution of 1905 found Jacob a civilian and he returned to Odessa where he resumed work as a labor organizer.

The next years were marked by regular riots and widespread starvation. Jacob was jailed several times. Eventually, money was donated by the rich of Odessa and America to be used to provide food for the starving masses. Jacob persuaded one of the founders of a relief organization to allow him to set up soup kitchens for the poor, and in a twenty-four-hour period he had established a kitchen that served 200. He continued to do relief work until he was tipped off that he was about to be arrested again. He then fled the city to a nearby town, where he went into hiding. There he met and courted Batya, the woman who was to be his wife for forty-five years. She agreed to marry him on the condition that they would leave at once for America. Immediately after their marriage, they fled to Finland and from there booked passage to Milwaukee, where Batya had a brother.

Their story is familiar; they arrived in the United States without any knowledge of English, found themselves in a strange country, surrounded by baggage, with no place to sleep and only fifteen dollars between them. The brother was of little help, and once more Jacob's resourcefulness and determination came into play. Soon, they had a room with a sympathetic family, and Jacob had a job as a sheet metal worker. At once he began night school and studied English. He resumed his work in the union immediately. The couple saved every cent and bought steamship tickets in monthly installments for the family left behind. Within a year, all the brothers and sisters had been brought to America.

Jacob and Batya housed and helped establish them, and matters went well until the crash of 1907. This threw Jacob out of work just as his first child, a son, was born. Since employment was not available, Jacob managed to go into business for himself, and for the next dozen years his fortunes ebbed and flowed. Many times he prospered, and many times he lost everything and began again from scratch. But the story is consistent–he always pulled himself out of defeat, used his craft, cleaved to his beliefs, worked in and for the union, and remained tightly tied to his family.

In 1918, Batya's brother became ill and was advised to move to California. Jacob, Batya, and their four sons followed. Jacob once more established his own business and ran it according to his beliefs, as a cooperative. In time he drew his sons into it and they worked together until he retired at sixty-five.

Jacob and Batya were exceptionally successful in transmitting their values to the sons. None of the boys were given religious educations, but all felt deeply connected with secular Judaism and were active in the Jewish community; eventually they transmitted this to their children. All the sons were highly educated and became successful businessmen or professionals. They established themselves in the city where their parents lived, and stayed there. The sons married Jewish women and drew their spouses and children into the tight-knit family. The family remained close even after Batya died in 1950. Jacob often quoted her last statement to the family, left by her in a letter still read at family occasions. To her husband and children, she wrote:

> All your life you should hold to your friendship with each other; guarding your health; not pursuing great wealth; leading a normal life; doing good deeds for mankind; helping as far as you can the needy.

These were words to live by, said Jacob; "They contained all of the Torah on one foot."

After leaving his business at age sixty-five, Jacob began a second career, organizing elderly Jews into voluntary groups and community centers. For a time, he moved to Miami and continued to work with the elderly there. When he returned to California, he discovered the Aliyah Community Center and devoted himself to it with vigor. There he met Manya, the widow whose children had married into his own family. They married, weaving the family together with yet another strand, and took an apartment near the center, which "became their second home."

Eventually, Manya grew ill and the apartment was too much for Jacob to manage alone. The couple moved into a luxurious home for the elderly which Jacob found sterile and cold. Eventually, Manya needed hospitalization and they were separated until her death, a few years before Jacob's.

Jacob was a symbol, a symbol perfected in death. He was a worker and a socialist, but also a man who had succeeded in the world. He was immersed in the form of Judaism the center members identified with, secular Yiddishkeit and Jewish cultural-ethical tradition. He supported the center and so did his sons and their children, demonstrating their respect for Jacob and his followers, signifying to the members the hope of continuity and providing them with some visibility in the larger world outside.

At every center gathering arranged by Jacob parts of his earlier life were brought in, and these were the same parts which most center members had also experienced. Jacob contributed economically to the physical continuity of the center as an institution, and to the cultural continuity of its people.

Jacob was not only a symbol of and force for continuity. In addition, he was a symbol to them of the possibility of aging as an admirable, serious career. Extreme age had not cost Jacob clarity of mind, determination of purpose, or passion for life. All this he maintained with an air of gentleness and dignity. He was tolerant and generous, and aroused no envy. Refusing to be caught up in factions and discord, he was the people's leader, the symbolic and literal focus of the members' culture, and of their fragile solidarity and continuity.

JACOB'S CEREMONIAL DEATH

All these threads came together the day Jacob died. Let us now examine that ceremony, following in part the scheme set forth by Moore and Myerhoff (1977), which suggests that ritual dramas for analytic purposes may be divided into three major phases: creation, performance, and outcome. Within these broad categories, there are several pertinent subparts, relevant to the case at hand. These are as follows:

I. Creation
   A. Sequences
   B. Style
   C. Dramatic metaphor and symbolic dramas
   D. Implicit and explicit symbolic messages
   E. Antecedents to performance
II. Performance
III. Outcome
   A. Sociological consequences
   B. Efficacy:
      planned
      unplanned

Ceremonial sequences. The explicit plan in the creation of the ceremony specified a format with several ritual elements which had characterized Jacob's five preceding birthday parties. These were:

(a) a *brocha* (blessing), here a traditional Hebrew blessing of the wine;
(b) welcome and introduction of important people, including the entire extended Kovitz family, those present and absent;
(c) a festive meal of kosher foods served on tablecloths with flowers and wine, paid for mostly by the family but requiring some donation by members to avoid the impression of charity;
(d) speeches by representatives from the center, the sponsoring Jewish organization under which the center operates, local and city groups, and each of the Kovitz sons;
(e) entertainment, usually Yiddish folksongs performed by a member of the family;
(f) a speech by Jacob;
(g) a donation by the family of a substantial sum to the center for its programs and for Israel;
(h) an invitation to those present to make donations to Israel in honor of the occasion, and
(i) birthday cake, birthday song, and blowing out candles.

The design had a feature often found in complex secular ritual dramas. Within it, fixed, sacred elements alternate with more open, secular aspects, as if to lend authenticity, certainty, and propriety to the open, optional sections. In the open sections, modifications, particularizations, and innovations occur, which tie the fixed sections more firmly to the situational details at hand, together providing a progression which seems both apt and traditional. In this case, for example, the brocha is followed by the meal, the meal by a toast, the toast by a speech, a speech by a song, then a song by another speech, and so forth. The brocha, songs, donations, and toasts are fixed and predictable; they are unvarying, ritual elements, and symbolic acts. The personnel, as representatives, are also symbolic, signifying the boundaries of the relevant collectivities and the social matrix within which the event occurs, but the specific contents of their speeches are less predictable, although they inevitably reiterate certain symbolic themes.

In this case, the repeated themes of the speeches touched on the character, accomplishments, and personal history of Jacob; the honor he brought to his community and family; the honor the family brought to their father and their culture; the importance and worth of the attending center members; the beauty of Yiddish life; the commonality of all those individuals, organizations, and collectivities in attendance; the perpetuity of the group and its way of life.

Ceremonial style. The style of the ceremony was another ritual element, characteristic of Jacob's previous parties. It was a style which is generally found in secular, public festivities among strangers—jovial, bland, and familiar. The tone was set by a master-of-ceremonies (Jacob's son, Sam), who directed the incidents and the participants, cuing them as to the desired responses during the event and telling them what was happening as the afternoon unfolded. Despite his seemingly innocuous and casual manner, the style was a precise one, reaching for a particular mood—enjoyment in moderation and cooperation, unflagging within a regulated time frame. In such events, things must be kept moving along, for always in ritual if a lapse occurs, self-consciousness may enter and the mood may be lost. This is especially important in secular rituals, attended by strangers or people from different traditions to whom the symbols used may not be comprehensible. Ritual is a collusive drama, and all present must be in on it.

In this case, highly specific direction was especially important. The old people are notoriously difficult to direct. They enter reluctantly into someone else's plans for them. For cultural and psychological reasons, they resist authority and reassert their autonomy. For biological reasons, they find it hard to be attentive for extended periods of time and cannot long delay gratification. Programs must be short, emotionally certain and specific, skillfully interspersing food, participation and symbols. The people remain involved when their names are mentioned, when they are praised and identified with the guest of honor. But their importance must not be inflated overmuch, for they are quick to perceive this as deception and insult. Furthermore, the old people must not be excited too greatly, for many have serious ailments and heart conditions. Perhaps it was the intense familiarity with their limits as an audience, or perhaps it was the uncertainty that underlies all secular ceremonies that caused the designers of this event to provide in the master-of-ceremonies a very directive leader who frequently told the audience what was occurring, what would come next, and reminded them of what had occurred, reiterating the sequences, as if restatement in itself would augment the sense of tradition and timelessness that is sought in trial.

Metaphor and symbolic dramas. The affair was called a birthday party, but in fact it was a metaphor, cross-referencing two domains, one, the secular birthday party, and the other, a sacred and traditional celebration, a *simcha* (for a lengthier discussion of the importance of guiding metaphors in the creation of secular rituals, see Myerhoff, 1977). The son, Sam, said in his speech, "You know, Pa doesn't think a birthday is worth celebrating without raising money for a worthy Jewish cause." Thus, the event had a more ambitious purpose than merely celebrating a mark in an individual life. The birthday party metaphor was used because it symbolized the people's membership in a secular, modern society. As a simple birthday, it had little significance to them. None of them had ever celebrated their birthdays in this fashion. Indeed, it was the custom to remember the day of their birth by celebrating it on the Jewish holiday closest to their actual birthday, submerging private within collective celebrations. More importantly, the event was called a simcha, a *yontif*, a *mitzvah*—elevating it to a blessing, a special holiday, an occasion for good deeds. The birthday, then, became a cultural celebration and an opportunity to perform good works in a manner which expressed the celebrants' identity with the widest reaches of the Jewish community, including Jews in Israel, and needy Jews everywhere in the world.[3]

The birthday party was also an occasion for staging two basic messages: continuity and honor. Continuity was made explicit in the ceremony's emphasis on the perpetuation of the community beyond the life of individual members. This was signified in two ways, both of which were innovations and departures from Jacob's usual birthdays. First, temporal continuity was signified by the presence of a group of college students, brought into the center during the year by a young rabbi who sought to promote intergenerational ties. He decided that the young people would serve the birthday meal to the elders as a gesture of respect. That a rabbi was there with them was incidental and unplanned, but it turned out to be important. The second innovation was Jacob's announcement that he was donating funds for his birthday parties to be held at the center for the next five years, whether he was alive or not. This donation would provide for events in which members would be assembled for what would probably be the rest of their lives, thus they had some assurance that as individuals they would not personally outlive their culture and community.

The significance of one man's life was enlarged and extended through the use of the birthday party metaphor, linked to a simcha. The party was a vehicle for dramatizing the fact of continuity. In addition, the same event was an occasion for the enactment of honor. The desire to present oneself as an honorable person is surely universal, though of course the specific contents, forms, and occasions in which such honor may be demonstrated varies greatly from culture to culture. The center people, cut off as they are from mainstream society, from younger people and family, have few chances to present themselves and their past accomplishments to the world for approbation. Their marginality and isolation is so profound, their opportunities for being seen, heard, recognized, and acknowledged so limited that among them the desire for attention is absolutely urgent. It might be said that attention from outsiders is one of the critical scarce goods in their society. Attention coming to them from within the group does not meet their need for visibility. Because they are disdained and rejected as a group by the dominant society, establishing their worth to each other is less important than making it evident to more powerful people outside their community. Moreover, they cannot trust each other to remember their worth, since they know their peers, like themselves, will soon be gone. Thus they eagerly seek opportunities to present themselves to the world, to more powerful and younger people especially, in the best possible light.

In this setting, the opposite of honor is not shame, but invisibility. Without public occasions which allow them to show themselves, no one knows they exist. It is more painful to them to be completely ignored than it is to be seen in a bad light, or to be ridiculed or shamed. Among them, much behavior occurs which could be construed as irrational, as showing off, foolish, petulant aggressive, until one realizes that it is motivated by their fierce human drive to be *noticed*.

In this situation, then, it is not surprising that people use ritual and ceremonial occasions of every sort as opportunities for making themselves visible and, if possible, dramatizing their worth. This is the ubiquitous subtext in every drama in which they take part. Since all the center people live in what Moore (this volume) has called limited-term arenas, there are no naturally occurring chances for them to publicly point out the accomplishments of their earlier lives. In societies or social settings in which the elderly are living among those who know their histories—children and neighbors who have been participants in, or at least witnesses of the elder's life—visibility and honor (or dishonor) are axiomatic. Everyone knows what others have been and done. Then the elder may reap the measure of his or her desserts. And when one is deserving, he or she may bask in respect for fulfilling valued cultural ideals, enjoying the esteem of having children well-raised and well-treated, reaping as one has sown the rewards or punishments of one's life work. Honor is there, perfectly clear, manifested formally and informally in the normal course of social life. But among the center people, there is no one to attest that an individual has lived well or badly. The traditional values in terms of which people might assess their own and others' merits are not self-evident. Nearly always, successful, allegedly devoted children are absent. Indicators of previously accumulated worldly success have in most cases eroded. Those who have retained some wealth are discouraged from displaying or even using it in this community, except for philanthropic purposes. It does not gain them esteem; on the contrary, more often it alienates them from the others. If a man has been a good worker, or a woman has been a faithful, devoted wife or housewife, if one has labored for good causes, there are almost no opportunities for showing it, or for transforming it into public honor. They can and do tell one another about such past accomplishments, but these self-proclamations gain them little. Even those accomplished in learning, secular or religious, have to struggle strenuously to demonstrate their knowledge to others, particularly because this knowledge is so rarely deemed useful in their present circumstances.

Among the elderly in such limited-term arenas, where social continuity is ruptured and long-standing social relations are not cumulative, opportunities for dramatizing lifelong accomplishments and personal honor are rare and precious. Jacob's birthday party was an occasion for the presentation of his life and his worthy deeds and ideals. As such, it was a dramatization of his honor, in which his cultural and individual value was portrayed, thus publicly interpreting and validating his past and present existence.

Metaphor and symbolic dramatizations are not uncommonly encountered in rituals of all sorts, but they are especially important in innovative, non-repetitive, nontraditional ceremonies attended by strangers, from different cultural backgrounds drawn together in an ad hoc assembly for a unique event. Then it is necessary to clue in all those involved as to what is occurring, and here metaphors which bring in some familiar common experience are very useful. Metaphors provide the idiom, the vocabulary, so to speak, from which ritual ingredients may be extracted to flesh out the performance. Since rituals are by definition enactments, and since they dramatize some issues which are invisible, specificity is essential for achieving conviction.

So too, symbolic dramatization makes manifest some invisible concerns. It is one thing to simply state that an individual is an honorable person. But ritual goes beyond this by providing opportunities for people to enact their claims, wishes, identities, beliefs, and the like. Thus, rituals fuse the dreamed-of and the lived-in orders, as Geertz (1965) has put it. The *experience* of the invisible order is only possible when enactments occur. Herein lies their persuasive power. In ritual, doing is believing, and "doing" results in a drama, of greater or lesser intensity.

In this case, the metaphor is a birthday party; the symbolic dramas are proclamations of continuity and honor. Naturally, other rituals present other messages and use other metaphors.

Symbolic messages: implicit and explicit. Symbols carry implicit messages, accompanying but distinguishable from the overt communications consciously included by designers of a ritual. These implicit messages are part of the creation of a ritual but not necessarily clearly planned or controlled. The following are the *planned* symbols included deliberately within the ceremony. Other symbols with other meanings were spontaneously brought in when the ceremony was interrupted by Jacob's death, and they will be taken up later.

Many of the symbols deliberately employed have been mentioned: Every Yiddish word was a symbol, evoking a deep response. The man Jacob, his character and values, and his entire family were significant symbols, standing for success, fulfillment of Judaic ideals, and filial devotion. The dignitaries and the publics they represented, too, were among the symbols used, including physically absent participants who were referred to. The birthday metaphor with cake, candles, and gifts, the presence of a master-of-ceremonies and "guest of honor," and the tone of the program were also used symbolically, drawn from and referring to American, contemporary secular life. Also important were the symbols for the widest extension of Judaic culture and its adherents, in the form of the brocha, and the references to Israel and to the performing of mitzvot. The presence of small children and young people symbolized the continuity and perpetuity of Judaism. The traditional music, and especially the foods, symbolized and evoked the people's childhood experiences as Jews; they were the least ideological and possibly most powerfully emotional of all the symbolic elements that appeared in the ritual.

Mention has been made of the symbolic significance of many of the key figures involved in the ceremony. Two additional important people must now be introduced—these were the center director, Abe, and the president, Moshe. Abe was a sixty-year-old second-generation assimilated American of Russian-Jewish parentage. A social worker, he had been with this group a dozen years and knew the people intimately, usually functioning as their guardian, protector, interpreter, and mediator. He, along with Jacob and his sons, developed the format for the ceremony and helped conduct it. The president, Moshe, was a man of eighty-two, with a Hassidic background.[4] He was a religious man with a considerable religious education and a Yiddishist. It was to him that questions about Judaism and its customs were likely to be referred. After Jacob, he was the most respected man in the group and one of Jacob's closest friends.

Antecedents of the ritual. Everyone at the center knew that Jacob had been very sick. For three months preceding his party, he had been hospitalized in an intensive care unit, and three weeks before, at his request, he was removed by his son, Sam, to the latter's home so that he could be "properly taken care of, out of the unhealthy atmosphere of a hospital." Before, Jacob had always resisted living with his children, and people interpreted this change in attitude as indicative of his determination to live long enough to come to his birthday party. The old people were aware that Jacob had resolved to have the party take place whether he was able to attend or not. People were impressed, first, because Jacob had the autonomy and courage to assert his opinions over the recommendations of his doctors—evidently he was still in charge of himself and his destiny—and, second, because Jacob's children were so devoted as to take him in and care for him. But most of all they were struck by his determination to celebrate his birthday among them. They were honored and awed by this. They followed closely the daily developments which preceded the celebration: details concerning Jacob's health, the menu for the party, the entertainment, all were known and discussed at length.

As the day grew close, much talk concerned the significance of the specific date. It was noted that the celebration was being held on Jacob's actual birthday. The parties had always been held on Sundays, thus the date and day coincided only every seven years. Surely this was no accident. March, in itself, was especially important. In the Hebrew calendar, it is a month of major holidays. Moreover, they said, in March Moses was born and died, and he was said to have died on his birthday.

A week before the event, there was talk that Jacob had died. Many who were in touch with him denied it, but the rumor persisted. Two days before the party, a young woman social worker, and a close friend of Jacob's, told the college group that she had dreamed Jacob died immediately after giving his birthday speech. She also told many people that Jacob's sons were advising him against coming to the party, but that he would not be dissuaded. Nothing would keep him away.

The atmosphere was charged with excitement before the party had even begun. Abe, the director, was worried about the old people's health, and the effects on them of too much excitement. There were those who insisted that on the birthday they would be told Jacob had died. Jacob's friend Sarah said, "He'll come all right, but he is coming to his own funeral."

And what were Jacob's thoughts and designs at this point? It is possible to glimpse his intentions from his taped interviews with a son and a grand-daughter. In these, common elements emerge: He was not afraid of death but he was tormented by confusion and disorientation when "things seem upside ways," "not the way you think is real." Terrible thoughts and daydreams beset him, but he explained that he fought them off. "I have always been a fighter. That's how I lived, even as a youngster. I'd ask your opinion and yours, then go home and think things over and come to my own decision." In one of the tapes, he described his battles against senility and his deter-mination to maintain coherence by writing, talking and thinking. He concluded, "I was very depressed in the hospital. Then I wrote a poem. Did you see it? A nice poem. So I know I'm still living and I have something to do. I got more clear-headed. I controlled myself."

Jacob had always controlled himself and shaped his life, and he was not about to give that up. Evidently he hoped he might die the same way. "I'll never change," were his last words on the tape.

It was difficult for Jacob to hold on until the party and to write his speech, which seemed to be the focus of his desire to attend. Its contents were noteworthy in two respects: first, his financial donation and provision for five more parties, whether he was there or not, and second, his statement that whereas on all his previous birthdays he had important messages to deliver, on this one he had nothing significant to say. Why, then, the desperate struggle to make this statement? The message, it seems, was that he could and would deliver it himself, that he was still designing his life and would do so to the end. The preparations and the manner of the speech's delivery conveyed and paralleled its message.

The Performance of the Ritual

The day of the party was fair, and celebrants came streaming toward the center out of their rented rooms and boarding houses, down the small streets and alleys several hours too early. That the day was set apart was clear from their appearance, the women in white gloves, holding perfectly preserved purses from other decades, wearing symbolic jewelry, unmistakable, often expensive gifts from their children—golden medallions bearing grandchildren's names, "Tree of Life" necklaces studded with real pearls; Stars of David; and the golden letter "Chai," Hebrew for life and luck. All were announcements of connections, remembrance, and worth. Glowing halos from scarves and bright hats colored the ladies' expectant faces. Men wore tidy suits polished with use, and overfrayed, starched shirts.

The center hall, too, was festively decorated and people were seated formally. At the head table was the Kovitz family and around it the dignitaries. Jacob, it was learned, was behind the curtain of the little stage, receiving oxygen, and so the ceremony was delayed for about half an hour. At last he came out to applause and took his seat. Music called the assembly to order and people were greeted with "Shalom," Hebrew for peace. Jacob was presented as the guest of honor, then introductions followed, referring to the Kovitz family as *mishpoche* (extended kin), finally extending the term to include all those assembled. By implication, all present were an extended family. Each member of the Kovitz family was named, even those who were absent, including their academic titles and degrees, generation by generation. The assembly was greeted on behalf of "Pa, his children, his children's children, and even from their children." The religious brocha in Hebrew was followed by the traditional Jewish toast, "*L'chayim*," to health and life. Sam set out the order of events in detail, including a specification of when Jacob's gift to the center would be made, when dessert would be served (with speeches), and when the cake was coming (after speeches), and so forth. The announcement of procedures was intended to achieve coordination and invite participation. The audience was appreciative and active. People applauded for the academic degrees of the family and for the regrets from family members unable to attend, and recognized the implicit messages of continuity of tradition, respect from younger generations, educational accomplishment, and the dramatization of filial devotion and intense familism.

The meal went smoothly and without any public events, though privately Jacob told the president, Moshe, that he wished people would hurry and eat, because "malakh hamoves, [the Angel of Death, God's messenger] is near and hasn't given me much time."

As dessert was about to be served, Sam, as master-of-ceremonies, took the microphone and began his speech, in which he recounted some biographical details of Jacob's life and certain cherished characteristics. He emphasized his father's idealism and social activism in the old country and in America, and spoke at some length about the courtship and marriage of their parents. Though their mother had died twenty-four years earlier, she remained a strong influence in keeping the family together, he said.

During Sam's speech, Jacob was taken backstage to receive oxygen once more. People were restive and worried, but Sam assured them that Jacob would soon return and the program would continue. Eventually Jacob took his seat, leaning over to tell one of the young people in English, and Moshe in Yiddish, that he had little time, and wished they would hurry to his part of the program, for now he said, "Ich reingle sich mutten malakh hamoves." (I am wrestling with the Angel of Death).

The progression was interrupted briefly when those in charge recognized Jacob's difficulty in breathing and gave him oxygen at his seat. A pause of about ten minutes ensued. The thread of the ritual lapsed while people watched Jacob being given oxygen. Moshe and Abe were worried about the impact of this sight on the old people. The previous year someone had died among them, and they had been panic-stricken. But now all were rather quiet. They talked to each other softly in Yiddish. At last Sam took the microphone again and spoke extempore about his father's recent life, filling the time and maintaining the ritual mood until it became clear that Jacob was reviving. Sam told the group that maybe his wife's chicken soup—proper chicken soup prepared from scratch with the love of a Yiddishe mama—had helped sustain Jacob. This was received with enthusiastic applause. Most of those in the audience were women, and their identity was much bound up with the role of the nurturant, uniquely devoted Jewish mother. In fact, the earlier mention of the importance and remembrance of the Kovitz mother had been received by many women as a personal tribute. They also appreciated the appropriateness of a daughter-in-law showing this care for a parent, something none of them had experienced. This set of symbols—the chicken soup, the Yiddishe mama, the inclusion of the name of the family matriarch, the reference to the maternal role—clearly struck a deeply resonant emotional chord.

Sam went on to explain that, since leaving the hospital, Jacob had "embarked on a new career, despite his age." Jacob was teaching Sam Yiddish and had agreed to stay around until Sam had mastered it completely. "Since I am a slow learner, I think he'll be with us for quite a while," he said. This, too, was full of symbolic significance. The suggestion of new projects being available to the old, and of the passing on of the knowledge of Yiddish to the children was an important, highly symbolic message.

Sam went on, extending his time at the microphone as he waited for a sign that Jacob was able to give his speech. By now Sam was improvising on the original format for the ritual. He made his announcement of the gift of money, half to the center for cultural programs, half to Israel, reminding the audience that Jacob did not believe a birthday party was worth celebrating unless it involved raising funds for deserving Jewish causes.

Still Jacob was not ready, so the microphone was turned over to Abe, who improvised on some of the same points, again and again touching important symbolic themes. He, like Sam, referred to Jacob as a stubborn man and to the Jews as stiff-necked people, tenacious and self-determined. He reassured the assembly that they were important people and would be remembered, that outsiders came to their center to share their simcha and appreciate their unique way of life. They, he said, like Jacob, would be studied by scientists one day, for a better understanding of the indivisibility of mental and physical health, to see how people could live to be very old by using their traditions as the basis for a good and useful life. He finished by emphasizing Jacob's most revered qualities: his devotion to his people, his learning and literacy, his courage, and his dignity. He was an example to them all. "And," he went on, "you, too, you are all examples."

At last the sign was given that Jacob was ready. Abe announced the revised sequence of events: Jacob's speech in Yiddish, then in English, then dignitaries' speeches, then the cake. Jacob remained seated but began his speech vigorously, in good clear Yiddish.[5] After a few sentences, he faltered, slowed, and finished word by word. Here are selections from his speech in translation:

> Dear friends: Every other year I have had something significant to say, some meaningful message when we came together for this yontif. But this year I don't have an important message. I don't have the strength. . . . It is very hard for me to accept the idea that I am played out. . . . Nature has a good way of expressing herself when bringing humanity to the end of its years but when it touches you personally it is hard to comprehend. . . . I do have a wish for today. . . . It is this: that my last five years, until I am 100, my birthday will be celebrated here with you . . . whether I am here or not. It will be an opportunity for the members of my beloved center to be together for a simcha and at the same time raise money for our beleaguered Israel.

The message was powerful in its stated and unstated content, made even more so by the dramatic circumstances in which it was delivered. Jacob's passion to be heard and to complete his purpose was perhaps the strongest communication. He was demonstrating what he had said in the earlier interviews, that he sustained himself as an autonomous, lucid person, using thinking, speaking, and writing as his shields against dissolution and senility.

Jacob finished and sat down amid great applause. His and the audience's relief were apparent. He sat quietly in his place at the table, folded his hands, and rested his chin on his chest. A moment after Sam began to read his father's speech in English, Jacob's head gently fell forward, then back, and his mouth opened slightly. Oxygen was administered within the surrounding circle of his sons as Abe took the microphone and asked for calm and quiet. After a few moments, his sons lifted Jacob, still seated in his chair and carried him behind the curtain, accompanied by Moshe, Abe, and the rabbi.

Soon Abe returned and reassured the hushed assembly that a rescue unit had been called, that everything possible was being done, and that Jacob wanted people to finish their dessert: "Be assured that Jacob knew the peril of coming today. All we can do is pray. He's in the hands of God. His sons are with him. He most of all wanted to be here. Remember his dignity and yours and let him be an example. You must eat your dessert. You must, we must all, continue. We go on living. Now your dessert will be served."

People complied and ate quietly. Regularly Abe came to the front to reassure them, with special firmness when the fire department siren was heard outside. He explained at length all the steps that were being taken to save Jacob, and concluded, "He's very delicate. Your cooperation is very beautiful. Jacob wants us to continue. You heard his speech. We all have a date to keep. Out of love and respect for Jacob we will be meeting here for the next five years on his birthday. We will be here, you will be here, whether to celebrate with him or commemorate him. They are taking Jacob away now. The hospital will telephone us and we will tell you how he is doing."

People complied and continued eating. There were many who quietly spoke their certainty that Jacob was dead and had died in their midst. The conviction was strongest among those few who noticed that when the rabbi and Moshe left Jacob behind the curtain, they went to the bathroom before returning to their seats. Perhaps it was only hygiene, they said, but it was also known that religious Jews are enjoined to wash their hands after contact with the dead. Hence, the gesture was read as portentous.

The room was alive with hushed remarks. "He's gone. That was how he wanted it. He said what he had to say and he finished."

"It was a beautiful life, a beautiful death."

"There's a saying, when the fig is plucked in due time, it's good for the fig and good for the tree."

"Did you see how they carried him out? Like Elijah, he died in his chair. Like a bridegroom."

"He died like a *tzaddik*." (A tzaddik (plural, *tzaddikim*) in Hassidic tradition is a saintly man of great devotion, often possessing mystical powers.)[6]

"Moses, also, died on his birthday, in the month of Nisan."[7]

Order was restored as the dignitaries were introduced and removed. Again the ritual themes reappeared in the speeches: Jacob's work among senior citizens, the honor of his family, his exemplary character, and so forth. A letter to Jacob from the mayor was read and a plaque honoring him proffered by a councilman. Then a plant was given to his family on behalf of an organization, and this seemed to be a signal that gifts were possible and appropriate. One of the assembled elderly, an artist, took one of his pictures off the wall and presented it to the family. A woman gave the family a poem she had written honoring Jacob, and another brought up the flowers from her table. The momentum of the ritual lapsed completely in the face of these spontaneous gestures. People were repeatedly urged by Abe to take their seats. The artist, Heschel, asked what would be done about the birthday cake now that Jacob was gone. He was rebuked for being gluttonous. With great difficulty, Abe regained control of the people, reminding them sternly that the ceremony had not concluded. There remained one dignitary who had not yet spoken. This, Abe pointed out, was insulting to the group he represented.

Abe was improvising here, no longer able to utilize the guidelines of the birthday metaphor. The ceremony threatened to break apart. In actuality, Abe was worried about letting people go home without knowing Jacob's fate. It would be difficult for him to handle their anxieties in the next few days if they were left in suspense. And no one wanted to leave. The circumstances clearly called for some closure, some provision of order. The last dignitary began to talk and Abe wondered what to do next. Then the phone rang and everyone was still. The speaker persisted, but no one listened.

Abe came forward and announced what everyone already knew. "God in his wisdom has taken Jacob away from us, in His mystery He has taken him. So you must understand that God permitted Jacob to live 95 years and to have one of his most beautiful moments here this afternoon. You heard his last words. We will charter a bus and go together to his funeral. He gave you his last breath. I will ask the rabbi to lead us in a prayer as we stand in solemn tribute to Jacob."

People stood. About a dozen men drew yarmulkes (skull caps) out of their pockets and covered their heads.

The Rabbi spoke: "We have had the honor of watching a circle come to its fullness and close as we rejoiced together. We have shared Jacob's wisdom and warmth, and though the ways of God are mysterious, there is meaning in what happened today. I was with Jacob backstage and tried to administer external heart massage. In those few moments with him behind the curtain, I felt his strength. There was an electricity about him but it was peaceful and I was filled with awe. When the firemen burst in, it felt wrong because they were big and forceful, and Jacob was gentle and resolute. He was still directing his life, and he directed his death. He shared his wisdom, his life with us and now it is our privilege to pay him homage. Send your prayers with Jacob on his final journey. Send his sparks up and help open the gates for him with your thoughts.[8] We will say Kaddish.[9] 'Yatgadal v'yakadash shmay raba. Magnificent and sanctified be the great name of God.' "

The ritual was now unmistakably over, but no one left the hall. People shuffled forward toward the stage, talking quietly in Yiddish. Many crossed the room to embrace friends, and strangers and enemies embraced as well. Among these old people, physical contact is usually very restrained, yet now they eagerly sought each other's arms. Several wept softly. As is dictated by Jewish custom, no one approached the family, but only nodded to them as they left.

There were many such spontaneous expressions of traditional Jewish mourning customs, performed individually, with the collective effect of transforming the celebration into a commemoration. Sarah reached down and pulled out the hem of her dress, honoring the custom of rending one's garments on news of a death. Someone had draped her scarf over the mirror in the ladies' room, as tradition requires. Heschel poured his glass of tea into a saucer. Then Abe took the birthday cake to the kitchen. "We will freeze it. We will serve it at Jacob's memorial when we read from his book. He wouldn't want us to throw it away. He will be with us still. You see, people, Jacob holds us together even after his death."

Finally, the center had emptied. People clustered together on the benches outside to continue talking and reviewing the events of the afternoon. Before long, all were in agreement that Jacob had certainly died among them. The call to the rescue squad was a formality, they agreed.

Said Moshe, "You see, it is the Jewish way to die in your community. In the old days, it was an honor to wash the body of the dead. No one went away and died with strangers in a hospital. The finest people dressed the corpse, and no one left him alone for a minute. So Jacob died like a good Yid. Not everybody is so lucky."

Over and over, people discussed the goodness of Jacob's death and its appropriateness. Many insisted that they had known beforehand he would die that day. "So why else do you think I had my *yarmulkah* with me at a birthday party?" asked Beryl.

Heschel commented, "After a scholarly meeting it is customary to thank the scholar. Jacob was a scholar and we thanked him by accompanying him to Heaven. It's good to have many people around at such a time. It shows them on the other side that a man is respected where he came from."

Bessie's words were, "He left us a lot. Now the final chapter is written. Nu? What more is there to say? The book is closed. When a good man dies, his soul becomes a word in God's book."

It was a good death, it was agreed. Jacob was a lucky man. "*Zu mir gezugt*, it should happen to me," was heard from the lips of many as they left.

Outcome

Sociological consequences. Two formal rituals followed, the funeral, attended by most of the group (which as promised arrived in a body on a chartered bus), and a *shloshim*, or thirty-day memorial, held at the center.

At the funeral, the young rabbi reiterated his earlier statements, concerning the "electricity" he had felt emitting from Jacob just before he died, describing how Jacob used his remaining strength to make a final affirmation of all he stood for, and, the rabbi added, at the last moment of his life Jacob–surrounded by all the people he loved–believed in God. (Others disagreed with this and were certain that Jacob died an agnostic. They didn't confront the Rabbi on the matter, however; said Heschel, "If it makes the Rabbi happy, let him believe it.")

In his eulogy, Jacob's son Sam said: "In our traditions there are three crowns—the crown of royalty, the crown of priesthood, and the crown of learning. But a fourth, the crown of a good name, exceeds them all."

Spontaneously, at the graveside, without benefit of direction from funeral officials, many old men and women came forward to throw a shovelful of earth on the grave, sometimes teetering from the effort. Each one carefully laid down the shovel after finishing, according to custom. Then they backed away, forming two rows, to allow the Angel of Death to pass through. They knew from old usage what was appropriate, what movements and gestures suited the occasion, with a certainty that is rarely seen in their present lives. Moshe, one of the last to leave, pulled up some grass and tossed it over his shoulder. This is done, he explained later, "to show that we remember we are dust, but also that we may be reborn, for it is written: 'May they blossom out of the city like the grass of the earth.' "

A month later, the shloshim was held. In it, a final and official interpretation of Jacob's death was forged and shared. He was a saint by then. He must be honored, and several disputes were avoided that day by people reminding one another of Jacob's spirit of appreciation and acceptance of all of them and his wish for peace within the center. The cake was eaten with gusto as people told and retold the story of Jacob's death.

Funeral and shloshim were the formal and public dimension of the outcome of Jacob's death. Informal, private opinions and interpretations were also part of the outcome. These were revealed in subsequent individual discussions, informal interviews, casual group conversations, and a formalized group discussion on the subject. On these private casual occasions, people said things they had not and probably would not express in public, particularly about matters that they knew might be regarded as old-fashioned, "un-American," or "superstitious." In confidence, several people expressed wonder and some satisfaction at what they regarded as the divine participation in the event. One lady said with a chuckle, "You know if the Lord God, Himself, would bother about us and would come around to one of our affairs, well, it makes you feel maybe you are somebody after all."

Said Sarah, "I wouldn't have believed if I didn't see with mine eyes. Myself, I don't really believe in God. I don't think Jacob did neither. If a man talks about the Angel of Death when he's dying that don't necessarily mean anything. Everybody talks about the Angel of Death. It's like a saying, you know what I mean? But you gotta admit that it was not a regular day. So about what really went on, I'm not saying it was God working there, but who can tell? You could never be sure."

Publicly, the subject was chewed over at great length. Debate is a cherished traditional form of sociability among these people. And this was certainly a proper topic for a pilpul (literally "pepper," referring to the custom of lively scholarly argument about religious texts). A kind of pilpul was held with a group in the center which had been participating in regular discussions. One theme considered by them in detail was the young social worker's dream in which she anticipated the time and manner of Jacob's death.[10] Dreams, they agreed, must be carefully evaluated, for they may be sent by God or the demons, and as such are not to be taken as prophecy on face value. After much discussion, one of the learned men in the group said that perhaps the young woman should have fasted on the day after the dream. This assures that the previous night's dream will not come true.

Heschel quoted a Psalm in which King David prayed to God "to know the measure of his days. The request was denied because God decreed that no man shall know the hour of his death" (Psalm 39:5). This troubled the group. Did Jacob know the hour of his death? Could it be that God granted Jacob what he had denied King David? Why had a young girl had the dream? She knew nothing of these matters. Why had it not come to one of them, who understood the significance of dreams? After an hour or so of disagreement, only two points were clear. First, that the news of the dream had received widespread circulation before the birthday party, and, second, that it added to people's readiness to participate in a commemoration instead of a party. It made what happened more mysterious and more acceptable at the same time. Did it convince anyone that God had had a hand in things? Perhaps the most general view was expressed by Moshe, who on leaving, said, "Well, I wouldn't say yes but on the other hand I wouldn't say no."

A major sociological consequence of the ritual was its impact on various outsiders. The attending dignitaries were included in the moment of intense community which followed Jacob's death, and were duly impressed. Before leaving, one of the non-Jewish politicians told the people around her, "I have always heard a lot about Jewish life and family closeness. What I have seen here today makes me understand why the Jews have survived as a people." This praise from an official, a stranger, and a Christian, to a group which has always regarded Christians with distrust and often fear, was a source of great satisfaction, a small triumph over a historical enemy, and an unplanned but not unimportant consequence of the ritual.

The events of the day were reported widely in local newspapers and soon picked up by papers all over the country. Members of the audience were given opportunities to tell their version of what happened when children and friends called them or wrote to ask them, "Were you there that day?" The impact on the center members of the dispersion of the news to an outside world, ordinarily far beyond their reach, was to give them a temporary visibility and authority that enlarged their importance, expanded their social horizons, and intensified their communication with the world around them.

Efficacy of the ritual. In discussing the outcome of a ritual, we must inquire about its efficacy, as well as its sociological consequences. How shall we estimate the effectiveness of a ritual? How can we know if it has done its work? These are complex, troubling questions. It is possible to estimate the efficacy of a ritual in terms of the explicit intentions of the performers and creators. But one must go beyond this and inquire, too, about unintended effects, and implicit, unconscious messages carried by the ritual. Rituals are built around symbols, and symbols, we know, do much of their work below the level of consciousness. Thus, one must go beyond asking those involved about their purposes to estimate the success of a ritual.

And, too, we must ask for whom a ritual did or did not succeed. Many publics and audiences are addressed in complex collective rituals. In religious rituals, for example, audiences include the deities and supernatural forces, which, it is hoped, witness and are moved by the performance. Sometimes those most affected by a ritual are not the central subjects but the audience, or even those who were not present but heard about it afterward. Finally, we should take up the long-range as well as immediate consequences of ritual in judging its success, since rituals have an impact which is often long delayed.

But it is not possible in actuality to take up all these questions, for the field worker never has such complete information. And in working with symbols, analyses will never be complete; by definition, sacred symbols are inexhaustible in their range of referents and are boundless in the private messages they convey. Subjects cannot verbalize the totality of their apprehension of symbols because so much of their meaning is not conscious. Inevitably, then, there are blanks in our inquiry, and finally the field worker must take responsibility for making inferences about some of these lacunae, going beyond observed behavior, recorded statements, and "hard" data. Without taking such risks, we lose all hope of understanding the issues which make ritual interesting in the first place. In discussing ritual, an analysis of outcome is always an interpretation, and a provisional one. Here, then, is a provisional interpretation of the efficacy of Jacob's birthday-memorial.

The party was indeed a successful ritual. But it must be said that all rituals, as communicative acts, are efficacious to some degree simply by virtue of being held and being witnessed. They are not instrumental acts, nor are they technical performances, and thus not aimed at concrete results. They must be judged as dramatizations of an attitude toward life, not as literal events dramatizing a piece of life itself. This is seen clearly in rituals held in primitive societies. No one is so unempirical as to think that rain is caused by a rain dance. It is a dance not for, but about rain; in Burke's (1957) felicitous phrase, it is the dancing of an attitude.

The attitude so arranged is one of the basic tasks of all ritual: that of calling attention to a segment of everyday life, making it extraordinary by framing it, setting it apart from the trivial, mundane, evanescent progression of daily affairs. Ritual celebrates, freezes, and frames that which it takes up. If the spirits notice and it rains, so much the better, but the successful outcome of a rain dance does not depend on the weather.

Conversely, a ritual fails when it fails as a communication, either because it is misunderstood or because it does not manage to call forth the requisite attitude of "specialness" and attention from its audience. If people are not sufficiently engaged to suspend disbelief, if they are bored or conspicuously disinterested, the ritual is seen through, as an arbitrary invention instead of an expression of inevitable truth. Then it fails as communication.

Let us take up the question of the efficacy of Jacob's party in two steps: first as a planned, predictable, secular ritual with social intentions and overt symbolic messages; second, as an unplanned event transformed midstream into a different ritual, containing implicit, sometimes religious messages, with meanings that go beyond the social.

As a birthday party, the planned secular ritual, Jacob's ritual could not have failed. It was convincing and clear, and received by the audience with appreciation and cooperation. It demonstrated social and cultural continuity, and provided for perpetuity of the collectivity beyond the limited lifespan of Jacob, the central figure. It honored the man Jacob, his friends, family, and values. It identified Jacob with his tradition, with the history of his people, and extended the relevant community to the widest range of membership, referring to the absent, invisible collectivity of all Jews, through time and space. These intentions were relatively modest and not uncommon for secular ceremonies of this sort. The turning point occurred when Jacob tamed his death, transforming it into a numinous, enormously sacred, powerful drama.

In dying when he did, Jacob gave his last breath to his group, and this was understood by them as a symbolic message of his profound regard for them. His apparent ability to choose what is ordinarily regarded as beyond human control hinted at divine collaboration (though it is unlikely that Jacob intended such a message). Neither did anyone consciously intend to develop the party into a memorial. That was a kind of accident, though an understandable one. The collective, spontaneous response to death in terms of familiar religious practices is not rare. With death everyone has experience, and death rites are among the most tenacious and familiar areas of religious expression. The saying of the Kaddish was spontaneous and fortuitous. A rabbi was present at the birthday party only because of his association with the youth group. Without him, the Kaddish would not have been said, and, strictly speaking, his recitation of the Kaddish on this occasion was not religiously correct. Ritually, psychologically, and socially, however, it could not have been more correct.

Kaddish is referred to as the mourner's prayer; significantly, it says nothing about death. It is the prayer glorifying God's name which is said at the close of synagogue services. It is recited at a person's grave, then, once each month for a year, and each year thereafter on the anniversary of the death. At *Yiskor*, memorial services held in synagogue, Kaddish is also said. These memorials typically emphasize the living, their relationship with the deceased, and the proper manner in which their lives should be conducted. Often included in memorial services is the recitation of Kaddish to include prayers for Jewish heroes and martyrs of all generations, all "who died for the sanctification of God's name." And often a request is made for the name of the departed to "be bound up with all the company of righteous Jewish men and women," with the ancestors, and with those who will yet come. Thus, Kaddish in particular, and Jewish memorial services in which it is said, emphasize continuity, not loss and cessation of life. Through Kaddish, the dead person continues, assured remembrance in the prayers of his/her children.[11] Through Kaddish, a temporary community of mourners is created, an assertion of continuity between all Jews who have ever lost a beloved.

For religious and nonreligious alike, that day Kaddish enlarged and generalized the significance of Jacob's death. At the same time, it particularized his death by equating it with each person's historical, subjective, private griefs, thus completing an exchange between the collective and private dimensions of experience (see Turner, 1971, for a fuller discussion of this process of exchange between the private and collective poles of experience referred to by sacred symbols). When such an exchange takes place, symbols are more than mere pointers to things beyond themselves. A transformation occurs and "symbol and object seem to fuse and are experienced as a perfectly undifferentiated whole" (Langer, 1942). Such transformations cannot be planned or achieved by will; they are small miracles for which rituals reach but which they only occasionally achieve. Transformation carries the participants beyond words and word-bound thought, calling into play imagination, emotion, and insight, and "altering our conceptions at a single stroke" (Langer, 1942). Then participants conceive the invisible referents of their symbols, and may glimpse the underlying, unchanging patterns of human and cosmic life, in a triumph of understanding and belief. Few rituals reach such heights of intensity and conviction. When this occurs, all those involved are momentarily drawn together in a profoundly religious, sometimes nearly ecstatic mood of gratitude and wonder. That Jacob's death was a genuine transformational moment was attested to by the profound sense of community among those present, and the fulfillment that they appeared to have experienced with the recitation of the Kaddish.

I said earlier that in analyzing ritual we must be concerned with the unintended, implicit messages that are conveyed as well as the consciously understood, planned communications. Therefore, in this case, it must be asked what messages were contained in those elements which appeared that afternoon without deliberate planning: Jacob's references to the presence of the Angel of Death, his seeming ability to choose the moment of his death, and the prophecy of his death in the form of the dream? The questions are particularly important because ritual is supposed to deliver a message about predictability and order, and here were intrusions beyond human control, and therefore intrinsically disorderly and unpredictable.

Paradoxically, these very elements of unpredictability made the ritual more persuasive and more convincing rather than less. These surprises came in traditional garb. Prophetic dreams and the Angel of Death were familiar notions. And there were precedents for the timing of Jacob's death in the accounts of the tzaddikim, and in the deaths of Elijah and Moses. Thus, conceptions existed for handling them, and if most people involved claimed not to believe in the religious dogma, neither did they overlook the possibility that religious explanations discarded long ago might warrant reconsideration on this occasion.

Jacob's death revived the idea, or at least the hope, that sometimes people, die meaningfully, properly and purposively. Death is often felt as the final manifestation of helplessness, accident, and disorder, but here death seemed apt and fulfilling. Too often, death flies in the face of human conception, reminding us of our ignorance and impotence. It finds the wrong people at the wrong time. It mocks our sense of justice. But here it did the very opposite and made such obvious sense that it appeared as a manifestation of a higher order and morality.

Had there been no intimations of the supernatural, the death would probably have been frightening, suggesting that Jacob's mortal powers were beyond what we normally regard as possible. The hints that there were other forces at work, besides Jacob's will and beyond his control, made a religious experience of one that might otherwise have been more bizarre than spiritual. Despite the interruption of the party and the radical change of course, the celebration that finally occurred had the very sense of inevitability and predictability of outcome which is the underlying, unstated goal of all rituals.

RITUAL, TIME, AND CONTINUITY

Any discussion of ritual is also a discussion of time and continuity; when the ritual in question deals with death and birth, the themes of time and continuity are thrown into high relief. Ritual alters our ordinary sense of time, repudiating meaningless change and discontinuity by emphasizing regularity, precedent, and order. Paradoxically, it uses repetition to deny the empty repetitiveness of unremarked, unattended human and social experience. From repetition, it finds or makes patterns, and looks at these for hints of eternal designs and meanings. In ritual, change is interpreted by being linked with the past and incorporated into a larger framework, where its variations are equated with grander, tidier totalities. By inserting traditional elements into the present, the past is read as prefiguring what is happening in the here and now, and, by implication, the future is seen as foreshadowed in all that has gone before. Religious rituals are more sweeping than secular ones in this elongation of time and reiteration of continuity. The latter usually confine themselves to remembered human history, whereas the former transform history into myths, stories with no beginning and no end. Then time is obliterated and continuity is complete.

To do their work, rituals must disrupt our ordinary sense of time and displace our awareness of events coming into being and disappearing in discrete, precise, discontinuous segments. That discontinuous experience is our everyday sense of time, used to coordinate collective activities; it is external in origins and referents, and does not take into account private responses, stimulation, states of mind, or motivation. Public chronological time is anathema to the mood of ritual, which has its own time. Rituals attempt to sweep us away from the everyday time sense and from the objective, instrumental frame of mind which is associated with it. By merely absorbing us sufficiently, ritual, like art, lets us "lose ourselves" and step out of our usual conscious, critical mentality. When successful, ritual replaces chronological, collective time with the experience of flowing duration, paced according to personal significance; sometimes this is so powerful that we are altogether freed from a sense of time and awareness of self. This is ritual time, and it must be present to some degree to mount the mood of conviction concerning the messages contained in a ritual.

But ritual is still a social event, and it is necessary that, within it, individuals' temporal experiences are coordinated somewhat. They must be delicately synchronized, without obliterating the individual's sense of an intense personal experience. Ordinary time is suspended and a new time instituted, geared to the event taking place, shared by those participating, integrating the private experience into a collective one. These moments of community built outside of ordinary time are rare and powerful, forging an intense communion which transcends awareness of individual separateness. Continuity among participants prevails briefly, in a sometimes euphoric condition which Turner (1974) has described at length as a state of *communitas*, and which Buber calls *Zwischenmenschlicheit*.

Continuity of self may occur in rituals, especially rites of passage marking stages in the individual life cycle, and this produces yet another experience of time. Personal integration is achieved when the subject in a ritual retrieves his/her prior life experiences, not as past memories but as immediate events and feelings, occurring in the present. Then the person is a child or youth once more, feeling one with the earlier selves, who are recognized as familiar, still alive, coherent. Coherence of the "I," a sense of continuity with one's past selves, is not inevitable, as Fernandez (1974) points out. The chaos of individual history, especially when history has been great and often marked by numerous social and cultural separations, may be acute. The burden of memories weigh heavily on the elderly; the necessity for integration of a life is often a strong impulse. Reminiscence among the old is not merely escapist, not the desire to live in the past (see Bulter, 1968, for a discussion of the therapeutic functions of reminiscence among the elderly). It is often the reach for personal integration, the experience of continuity, and the recognition of personal unity beneath the flow and flux of ordinary life.

Because ritual works through the senses, bypassing the critical, conscious mind, it allows one to return to earlier states of being. The past comes back, along with the ritual movements, practices, tastes, smells, and sounds, bringing along unaltered fragments from other times. Proust was fascinated with this process. His work examines how the past may sometimes·be recaptured with all its original force, unmodified by intervening events. This may occur when the conscious mind with its subsequent interpretations and associations is bypassed. Experiences of past time come back unaltered, often as spontaneous responses to sense stimuli; as Mendilow (1952) describes this process, it occurs when the chemistry of thought is untouched by intervening events and the passage of time (for further discussion of this process, see Myerhoff and Tufte, 1975). These numinous moments carry with them their original, pristine associations and feelings. This is timelessness, and the past is made into present. It is, says Mendilow, a kind of

> hermetical magic, sealed outside of time, suspending the sense of duration, allowing all of life to be experienced as a single moment. . . . These are pin-points of great insensity, concentrations of universal awareness, antithetical to the diffuseness of life [1952: 137].

These "pinpoints of timelessness" are beyond duration and change. In them one experiences the essence of life—or self—as eternally valid; simultaneity has replaced sequence, and continuity is complete.

Conceivably, any kind of ritual has the capacity to retrieve a fragment of past life. Rituals associated with and originating in childhood are more likely to do so, and these especially carry opportunities for finding personal-historical continuity. Two characteristics of these rituals are salient here: first, their intensely physiological associations, and, second, their great power and immediacy, coming as they do from the individual's first emotional, social experiences. They are absolutely basic, arising in the context of nurturance and dependence, evoking the familiar, domestic domain, utterly fundamental, preceding language and conception. In our world of plural cultures, the first domestic nurturant experiences are often associated with ethnic origins, bound up with first foods, touch, language, song, folkways, and the like, carried and connoted by rituals and symbols learned in that original context. Ethnic ritual and symbol are often redolent with the earliest, most profoundly emotional associations, and it is often these which are the means for carrying one back to earlier times and selves.

Consider the statement made by one of the old men present at Jacob's birth-death ritual. "Whenever I say Kaddish, I chant and sway, and it all comes back to me. I remember how it was when my father, may he rest in peace, would wrap me around in his big prayer shawl. All that comes back to me, like I was back in that shawl, where nothing, nothing bad could ever happen."

The Kaddish prayer was probably the most important single ritual that occurred the day of Jacob's death. It was the most frequently and deeply experienced aspect of Jewish custom for the people there, the most ethnically rooted moment, sweeping together all the individuals present, connecting them with earlier parts of self, with Jacob the man, with each other, and with Jews who had lived and died before. The life of the mortal man, Jacob, was made into a mythic event, enlarging and illuminating the affairs of all those present. Here is ritual achieving its final purpose of transformation, altering our everyday understanding in a single stroke. Ultimately, we are interested in ritual because it tells us something about the human condition, the mythic condition and our private lives all at once. It demonstrates the continuity between one human being and all humanity. It does more than tell us an eternal tale; it sheds light on our own condition. This Jacob's death did.

Jacob, when the celebration ended, had become a point from which radiated the enlarged, as well as the immediate, meanings of his life and death, the grand and the minute, the remote and the particular, all implying each other, until continuity had become total unity.

Jacob's death couldn't change the hard realities. But if people lived only by hard realities, there would be no need for rituals, for symbols or myths. The power of rituals, myths, and symbols is such that they can change the experience we have of the world and its worth. Jacob's death rites may be considered an extraordinarily successful example of ritual providing social, cultural, biological, and spiritual continuity. More perpetuation, more connection, more interdependence, more unity existed when the day was over making the oblivion of an individual and his way of life a little less certain than anyone had thought possible that morning.

NOTES

1. Here I am distinguishing between "religious" and "sacred" and treating them as categories which may exist independently or may be joined. Where ideas, objects, or practices are considered as axiomatic, unquestionable, literally sacrosanct, they are "sacred," with or without the inclusion of the concept of the supernatural. Their sacrality derives from a profound and affective consensus as to their rightness; their authority comes from their embeddedness in many realms of tradition. Over against the sacred is the mundane, which is malleable and negotiable. When sacrality is attached to the supernatural, it is religious *and* sacred. When sacrality is detached from the religious, it refers to unquestionably good and right traditions, sanctified by usage and consensus.

2. For a discussion of the role of luck, accident, and personal idiosyncrasies in the lives of the elderly see Simić on winners and losers, this volume.

3. A simcha is a day of rejoicing; a yontif is a special holiday, often a religious occasion. A mitzvah (plural mitzvot) is an obligation which it is a blessing to perform. Often it includes religious requirements; here it refers to charitable works and good deeds.

4. Hassids were a deeply religious, sometimes mystical group which practiced a vitalized, fervent form of folk Judaism in many parts of Eastern Europe during the nineteenth century.

5. All these people are completely multilingual and use different languages for different purposes, with some consistency. For example, political and secular matters are often discussed in English; Hebrew is used to make learned, final points in settling debates; Russian or Polish appear in songs, poems, reminiscences, in arguments and bargaining. Yiddish, the *mamaloschen*, punctuates all the areas, but appears most regularly in times of intense emotion. It is also used most in conversations about food, children, cursing, and gossiping.

For some, Yiddish has connotations of inferiority for several reasons. It was the language of the mundane world, distinct from Hebrew, the sacred language of prayer. And it was associated with domains of childhood, marketplace, and domestic life; women in the shtetl usually knew only Yiddish. It was the language of exiles from the Holy Land living in oppression, and the language of greenhorns in America. For others, the Yiddishists in particular, it is a bona fide language to be treated with respect and used publicly. Careful pronunciation, proper syntax, and avoidance of Anglicized words are regarded as signs of respect for Yiddishkeit. Jacob was always careful in his Yiddish, and this was seen as an indication of his pride in the heritage.

6. It is noted that important Hassids sometimes died in their chairs (Dresner, 1974:25), and it is said that they often anticipated the dates of their death. There is also a suggestive body of custom surrounding the symbolism of the chair which figures importantly in at least two Jewish male rites of passage. In Hassidic weddings it is customary for the bridegroom to be carried aloft in his chair. And an empty chair is reserved for the prophet Elijah at circumcisions; this is to signify that any Jewish boy may turn out to be the Messiah, since Elijah must be present at the Messiah's birth.

7. In fact, Moses died on the seventh of Adar. He did, however, die on his birthday; he was allowed to "complete the years of the righteous exactly from day to day and month to month, as it is said, the number of thy days I will fulfill" (Talmud Bavli Kaddushin 38A). Hence the tradition in folklore that the righteous are born and die on the same day. Elijah did not die in his chair, however. He is believed to have "been taken up by a whirlwind into Heaven" passing out of this world without dying. His "passage" was not a normal death in any event, and this is probably why his death was brought into this discussion. These points were clarified in personal communication by Rabbi Chaim Seidler-Feller, Los Angeles, March 1977.

8. In Jewish mysticism, represented in the Kabbalah, a person's soul or spirit is transformed into sparks after death. For further discussion of this complex philosophy, see Scholem.

9. Kaddish is a prayer sanctifying God's name, recited many times in Jewish liturgy; it is known also as the Mourner's Prayer and recited at the side of a grave.

10. Dreams were very significant among shtetl folk, elaborately discussed and much used in pursuit of symbolic meanings. Four members of the group owned and used dream books which they had brought with them from the old country.

11. One woman described the common custom practiced by her childless aunt and uncle who had "adopted" a young couple to say Kaddish for them after their death. This was often done by those who were childless, had outlived their children, or whose children had completely rejected the religion. These adoptees were known as "our Kaddish," and it was they who were to make certain that the deceased was not forgotten in the prayers of the next generation.

One of the many strong, autonomous women *of the Senior Citizen Center.*

Friendship among women *is especially well-developed in old age among the members of this community. Physical, social and emotional support are exchanged among them in meeting their daily needs.*

The stage in the Senior Citizen Center *is an important site where members can sing, perform, tell stories, and give lectures for whatever audience is available. Here they create an opportunity for visibility and attention and are seen establishing their worth and enacting a personal and collective definition of the meaning of their lives, for peers and for themselves.*

Physical activity and contact *are eagerly sought after; in this culture dancing serves these needs for members. It is one means by which they maintain and reassure themselves of their continuing vitality.*

Celebrations of secular and religious holidays *are opportunities for enriching the meaning of life, punctuating time, and maintaining continuity with the past and with the outside society.*

CHAPTER 6

EL SENIOR CITIZENS CLUB:

The Older Mexican-American in the Voluntary Association

José B. Cuellar

Little is really known about the conditions of aging and the aged among Chicanos. What is the role of the Chicano elderly in the highly complex and urban American society? What is the extent of their influence on, and participation in the social and political life of the family, community, and state? How does the older urban Chicano fare in a society that places a premium on physical strength and attractiveness, sensuality and sexuality, intelligence and learning potential, and independence and productivity?

The answers to these questions have been doubly obscured, on the one hand, by stereotypes prevalent in our society regarding old age in general; and on the other, by idealizations of the Mexican-American family. In the first case, the aged are viewed as chronically ill, socially withdrawn, "about-to-die" members of a deprived group who are increasingly dependent upon others, and who occupy essentially normless, nonproductive positions in our society. In this way, older people are characterized as sharing a dysfunctional and obsolete view of the social and physical world about them, a view inconsistent with today's reality. Thus, there emerges a portrait of individuals with insoluble problems who constitute a burden to both themselves and society. In contrast to this gloomy picture, a commonly held model of Chicano family life portrays an environment in which growing old takes place in the midst of a warm and supportive group of children and grandchildren steeped in an ideology of family solidarity and filial piety. In either case, such unsubstantiated generalizations can only constitute barriers to a better understanding of the real issues faced by aging Chicanos.

Clearly, rigid structural or cultural models are of very limited utility when they are applied a priori in an effort to elucidate real social problems and their solutions. In contrast, a dynamic analytic tool, such as the concept of "aging as a career," can take into account both cultural patterns and constraints, as well as the manner in which real people respond actively to the exigencies of their life situations. Moreover, this conceptual framework makes it possible to subsume a range of various adaptations and behavior since the very idea of a "career" implies a situation in which one can succeed or fail depending on individual ability and initiative expressed with reference to external pressures and historic accident. However, the definition of "success" is not entirely an individual one, but rather one negotiated among peers within a generally shared cultural matrix. In this respect, it would be reasonable to expect that at least in some significant ways the Chicano aged will differ from their non-Hispanic peers.

For Chicanos, there are several avenues by which to achieve some measure of success in old age, some customary and others innovative. The traditional goals include: being moderately healthy; enjoying a good reputation; maintaining positive relations with family members; and having children who are without serious problems and are relatively "successful"—that is, with decent jobs that allow them to take care of their families adequately. In the words of an older informant, "What more can one ask for?" However, a successful career in aging can also involve the adoption of new goals, values, activities, and social roles. In other words, success can stem not only from adapting and adjusting to one's environment, but also from actively responding in a creative way to the contradictions and discontinuities of old age. One manner in which this can be achieved is by the manipulation and full utilization of resources in those social arenas to which the individual has access. Moreover, where such arenas prove inadequate or not viable, new ones can be consciously constructed to better suit existing aims and exigencies. For the urban Chicano in Los Angeles, senior citizens voluntary associations have provided such social arenas, and the rapid proliferation of these age-graded organizations within the Mexican-American community exemplifies the growing need for new settings in which people can frame social relationships in later life. This suggests that, for many older members of the Chicano community, traditional arenas of engagement no longer completely respond to their needs.

It is notable that voluntary associations have become important foci for Chicanos since, outside traditional religious sodalities (*cofradías*), such forms of organization are lacking, for the most part, in Mexican rural society. Thus, their emergence must be explained in relation to the North American historical and social context in which these older people are living out the remainder of their lives.

East Los Angeles is California's largest *barrio*—that is, the most populous concentration of Chicanos in the state. In some ways, it might be characterized as a "city within a city," and as such it comprises an at least partially bounded social and cultural field within an enormous and highly heterogeneous metropolis.

The Chicano barrio of Los Angeles has little in common physically with the low-income, high-rise tenement ghettos or slums of Chicago, Detroit, or New York. There is no concrete jungle inhabited by natives of Mexican descent in Southern California. The barrio, like the rest of Los Angeles, sprawls seemingly endlessly over flatlands, rolling hills, and valleys. Many of its "single-family" dwellings are of the modified Spanish style long traditional in Southern California. The Latin American atmosphere is further enhanced by luxuriant vegetable and flower gardens, and the profusion of subtropical and Mediterranean flora. Everywhere fig, eucalyptus, olive, loquat, citrus, banana, and palm trees give evidence of a benign climate. The barrio's swarthy inhabitants further suggest an almost idyllic Mexican village set down in the midst of a vast urban center. Other physical characteristics lend additional credibility to this view. The streets are frequently unpaved, many buildings are badly in need of repair, and the sewer system is often inadequate. Moreover, in contrast to the Anglo suburbs, barrio residents are highly visible on the streets. Picturesque to the outsider, these superficial manifestations have all too often contributed to the notion that Chicanos are indeed "urban villagers," combining the best of rural life with the advantages of the city in their almost self-contained barrio. Also implicit in this erroneous perspective is the implication that Chicanos are newcomers to the city and its ways.

In Los Angeles, there are actually many barrios with sizable proportions of Chicano residents. Some are over fifty years old; others have been formed only recently. Nevertheless, regardless of their particular history, the very rapid development of Los Angeles into a major metropolis has had tremendous effect on all of them. Freeways have ripped through the heart of East Los Angeles, displacing members of extended families, separating friends and acquaintances, and physically dividing the community. Complete neighborhoods have been destroyed to make way for such manifestations of "progress" as the building of freeways, parking lots, and the Los Angeles Dodgers' baseball stadium.

To the uninformed, East Los Angeles may appear to be a relatively homogeneous, tight-knit, personalized, insulated, kin-oriented "folklike" enclave. But, in fact, it is a highly complex, heterogeneous community of individuals with different characteristics, loyalties, perspectives, and proclivities. In many ways, Chicanos living in the barrios differ more widely from one another than did the "nine Mexican Indians, eight mulattos, two Blacks, two Spaniards, and one Mestizo" who are said to have originally settled Los Angeles in 1781. Nonetheless, by virtue of their shared historical and personal experience, Chicanos share more salient characteristics with one another than they do with the non-Chicano residents of Los Angeles.

An examination of the evolution of Los Angeles in relation to the Chicano experience reveals that the history of the Mexican-American in this city has been unique, and unlike that of other urban populations in the United States. For example, there is little relation between the length of time that persons of Mexican descent have lived in Los Angeles, on the one hand; and their position in the economy, the polity, geographical space, and the social structure within both metropolitan Los Angeles and in the wider Euro-American society, on the other.

Since the violent takeover by the United States of Mexican Los Angeles in the mid-nineteenth century, the city's population of Mexican descent has been relatively ineffective politically, and subjected to economic exploitation, with its concomitant deprivations and social stigma. Although people of Mexican descent have been residents of Los Angeles since its founding almost two centuries ago, and constituted a demographic majority until the latter part of the 1800s, Los Angeles Chicanos still experience a relatively low level of housing, education, income and occupational status, health, and social prestige. Moreover, they have been the recipients of fairly high levels of hostility, suspicion, distrust, prejudice, and overt discrimination.

It is obvious that the experience of the urban Chicano in Los Angeles has been determined by a hierarchy of historical pressures of varying levels of immediacy and geographic specificity, and these include:

(1) The consequences of the sudden and violent European conquest and colonization of Mexico;

(2) the North American occupation and colonization of California, and Los Angeles in particular;

(3) the effects of the extensive and very rapid urban expansion of the Los Angeles area;

(4) the needs of Los Angeles as a Euro-American urban center for a cheap source of labor, a need satisfied by a quasi-colonized Mexican community.

It is only with direct reference to the above-cited antecedents that the contemporary characteristics of the Los Angeles Mexican-American community can be placed in proper perspective. In this respect, these historic foundations should be borne in mind in the context of the following brief description of East Los Angeles and its Chicano inhabitants.

Los Angeles has the largest population of Mexican descent outside Mexico, and the city's eastern portion has historically served as its primary area of settlement and resettlement. It has been estimated that by 1975 nine out of ten residents of East Los Angeles were of Mexican origin. Though East Los Angelenos are spatially highly mobile, this mobility has tended to be circumscribed by the limits of the city. For example, although two-thirds of the population had changed residence during a five-year period, only one-third had moved to East Los Angeles from areas outside the "inner city," with less than two of ten East Los Angeles residents being migrants from outside the metropolitan region.

The slightly more than eight-square mile unincorporated East Central part of Los Angeles County surrounded by the cities of Los Angeles, Monterey Park, Montebello, and the City of Commerce constitute what is known as "East Los Angeles." Since the area has little industry or commerce, housing is one of its most valuable resources, and about half the available land is taken up by predominantly "single-family" dwellings. However, generally it is older and less sound structurally than in the rest of the metropolitan region. More than one-fifth of the housing was reported in need of major repairs, and another two-fifths in need of minor repairs. A majority of the East Los Angelenos rent rather than own their own housing, indicating a lack of control over its disposition and state of repair.

Due to its extent, poverty is a social problem as well as a personal issue in East Los Angeles. More than one in four families lives in poverty; including almost half of the female-headed households, one-third of the households headed by persons under twenty-five, and more than one-fourth of the households headed by persons over sixty-five. Although the average yearly income of East Los Angelenos is higher than that of Chicanos in other parts of California and the United States, it is nonetheless more than $2,000 less than the average yearly income of other residents of the Los Angeles metropolitan area.

The most common economic characteristic of East Los Angeles workers is a less-than-satisfactory relationship to the means of production, characterized by unemployment, underemployment, or undercompensated employment. The unemployment rate for East Los Angeles males remains approximately twice that of other residents of the metropolitan area. Thus, it is not surprising in light of these characteristics that Los Angeles Chicanos have little control over economic resources. Most households remain at, or near, the poverty level. There is a high degree of dependency on public assistance, which appears on the increase, and only a few East Los Angelenos are engaged in the means of production at occupational levels that entail some significant degree of control or economic influence.

Similarly, East Los Angeles Chicanos have limited participation in education, or control over educational institutions as resources. The median educational attainment of all its residents is slightly less than eight years. More than one-fourth are functional illiterates, and East Los Angeles has one of the highest dropout rates in both metropolitan Los Angeles and the state of California as a whole.

As a satellite community and an internal labor colony of metropolitan Los Angeles, East Los Angeles faces a number of issues that complicate the nature of its health care. For instance, a communications barrier exists between health providers and the East Los Angeles Chicanos because people of Mexican descent have been underrepresented in the health professions, and East Los Angeles health facilities are inadequately staffed with bilingual personnel. There is also a lack of community representation at the policy-making level of health care delivery. Thus, there are insufficient and inappropriate health services to meet the needs of the community, particularly its oldest and youngest residents, and consequently the East Los Angeles Chicano has little control over health as a resource.

Although the modified extended Chicano family has been often thought to be a salient resource to its members, almost one of every four East Los Angeles Chicanos under the age of eighteen lives in a home with at least one missing parent. Moreover, because the East Los Angeles family of Mexican descent often does not command sufficient resources to adequately provide for all the needs of its members, a number of extrafamilial social institutions and agencies have been developed to meet those that for one reason or another cannot be met by the family, or are so generalized that they constitute a community problem.

Among the Chicanos of Los Angeles, as elsewhere, the young are in the majority, and the old in the minority. In the Chicano community there are more than three children under five for every person over sixty-five, and three of every four Chicanos are younger than thirty-four. Only five of every one hundred persons of Mexican descent are older than sixty-five. Although these characteristics are fluid, and each year the relative demographic positions of the older Chicano changes, as do the characteristics of the individuals that occupy that status, some continuities persist. The older Chicano is always a member of the Chicano age stratum that has the least formal education, the poorest housing, the greatest number of chronic illnesses, and the least potential for economic productivity and independence in comparison to other groups.

Given the historically based status of the Chicano in Los Angeles, as well as the general status of the elderly in the contemporary urban United States, it is not surprising that the majority of older Los Angeles Chicanos are in need of better health care, housing, transportation, and social services. With limited formal income, probably fixed, and in poor health, the older person of Mexican descent has control over few material or cultural resources of the Chicano community, the Los Angeles metropolis, and the dominant Euro-

American society. For example, many Los Angeles Chicanos over sixty-five report that during the last decade they have faced worsening financial conditions and a loss of physical vigor and vitality.

Because it has been commonly thought that the elderly person of Mexican descent might expect to lay some claims on the resources of his or her offspring and extended family in times of need, it is surprising to find that it is not uncommon for older Chicanos to report that they do not expect financial aid from their families even if they lack enough money to maintain themselves, and they do not expect to live with their children even if they cannot live alone. To some extent, such expectations are grounded in both cultural and social tradition. For example, a number of respondents reported that their parents had never lived with them after they established their own households, nor had they been dependent on them for support. Indeed, most preferred not to live in the same household with their adult children, a majority sharing the cultural notion that older persons should live apart from, and independent of, their offspring.

Who then is responsible for the security and well-being of the aging Chicano? The great majority of those interviewed believed that the responsibility for satisfying the housing, health, transportation, and retirement needs of the elderly belonged to the government, particularly the federal government, rather than to the older person or that person's family. On the other hand, most did not perceive people like themselves as having a great deal of influence on the decisions made by government.

Given the experienced hostility of past political periods and events, as well as the present social conditions, it is not surprising that the majority of older Chicanos do not participate more in the political processes of the dominant Euro-American society. Indeed, less than half the respondents reported being registered voters, and the vast majority did not engage in any type of political activity or approve of most mass "social protest" activities. Still, a majority held some type of both Chicano and age-specific political consciousness, admitting that they gave some consideration to the consequences of their political actions on others of their age group or ethnicity, particularly the latter.

The extent to which older Chicanos are honored, respected, and obeyed within the community of Mexican descent and the wider society may be reflected in the views they hold about older persons like themselves. In this respect, it appears that the older Chicano shares the cultural ideology that has developed about older workers in the Euro-American capitalist urban society. Its basic premises are that the older a person, the more senile, the more wrinkled and ugly, the less sexual and sensual, the weaker and more sickly, and the less productive he or she becomes. Nevertheless, the vision is not an entirely consistent one, and the majority agreed that old people are valuable because of their experience and wisdom. Slightly more than half disagreed that the old are not useful to themselves or others; yet most did agree that the old should retire to make room for the young, and that the old cannot learn as well as the young. They also believed that old people usually suffer from some kind of chronic illness, are apt to complain, are set in their ways and unable to change, and are against reform, wanting "to hang onto the past." It is also significant that more than half of those surveyed over forty-five agreed that old people are sometimes treated like children, and disagreed that older people are not isolated or lonely. Still, paradoxically, most of these older Chicanos reported that they personally hardly ever felt lonely, bored, or afraid, got upset easily, or worried so much that they could not sleep. But almost half of those over forty-five reported that they at least sometimes felt less useful as they got older, that they had much to be sad about; and that things were getting worse.

Older persons of Mexican descent in the contemporary urban United States are not usually found living an indulged and respected life as influential members of the family, barrio, community, or state. The needs of the older Chicano are not being met, especially outside the family. Instead of prestige and respect, the older Chicanos experience the same shame and burden that accompanies old age in contemporary Euro-American society, and as far as the control of resources is concerned, the older Chicanos only hold hopes for power in the future. In this respect, a significant majority felt that there is a need for an active political group of senior citizens, and it is supposed that such an organization might help mitigate the needs and problems of the older Chicano. Still, at the time, only a few were found to be members of any senior citizens voluntary organization. This may be the consequence of several related factors.

First, it may be that older Chicanos have not been attracted to the senior citizens organizations in the community because they are not productive political groups. The majority of senior citizens organizations in East Los Angeles were founded to be explicitly apolitical social organizations, and supported on that basis by such societal institutions as governmental and church agencies, among others. Indeed, the evidence suggests that in most cases senior citizens groups would lose financial support provided by the dominant society's institutions, for example, Los Angeles County, if they encouraged political activism among members.

Second, it may be that more older Chicanos have not joined senior citizens associations because these organizations are not viewed as controlling sufficient resources to adequately satisfy the more pressing needs of older members.

Finally, though there is a long history of voluntary associations in the Chicano community, there may be some cultural rejection of the idea that such arenas should fulfill functions formerly carried out in familial contexts.

Nonetheless, the ethnographic data suggest that senior citizens organizations in East Los Angeles are providing a basis for the mitigation of at least some of the negative losses and discontinuities experienced in aging, as well as for the maintenance of some of the positive continuities associated with old age in the Chicano community. Within the framework of the voluntary association, some older Chicanos have learned new roles, acquired new information, and been socialized into an emergent age-based subculture. The voluntary association has also served as a social arena where its members have demonstrated their competences and abilities, have shared experiences, and have acquired new perspectives as well as some measure of prestige and power through the manipulation of available resources and social interaction.

The fact that more older Los Angeles residents of Mexican descent were not reported members of senior citizens organizations may also be due to the fact that these groups are a relatively recent phenomenon in the Chicano community, and their impact cannot be measured quantitatively. Indeed, the first national association for older persons of Mexican descent and other Spanish-speaking groups was only founded in 1975. Prior to that, there had been no concerted recruiting effort by any such group among members of the Chicano community. Therefore, it is reasonable to expect that the establishment of the Asociación Nacional Pro Personas Mayores (National Advocacy Association for Spanish-Speaking Elderly) will result in a significant increase in the proportion of older Chicanos who are members of a voluntary senior citizens organization. For that important segment of older Chicanos in Los Angeles who were found to be less than satisfied with the contact they had sustained with persons other than family members, the senior citizens organization could provide a viable means of social engagement in later life.

Although in the final analysis we may find that senior citizens associations in the Chicano community serve only the needs of a "deviant" segment of the old-age stratum, the role and function of these organizations merit exposition as an alternative available to older people of Mexican descent.

Voluntary associations have long been a part of the Chicano experience, and of interest to social observers. In this chapter, a discussion of such an organization for Chicano senior citizens will serve to illustrate several processes. First is the development of the role and function of voluntary associations in the Chicano community as affected by significant historical events. Second is the role and function of age-specific voluntary associations in the lives of older persons, particularly in the Chicano community. These concerns will be given substance in the context of what may be termed a "social drama." The immediacy of this illustrative technique will serve to demonstrate how senior citizens manipulate resources and relationships in their attempts to adapt and adjust to the discontinuities and losses associated with aging. A case description of a situation involving conflict will help us understand the effect of cultural ideologies regarding the nature of aging on the behavior of older persons; the role of the organization in satisfying the needs of the elderly; the relationship between prestige, reputation, and status and individual variations in behavior; the creation of new roles and norms for the aged, including a cadre of elites; and the nature of an emergent senior "subculture" in the Chicano community. Taken as a whole, this study should suggest some trends in the redefinition of success and failure in aging as a career for Chicanos, and the effects of both personal initiative and structural determinants.

BEHAVIOR IN AN AGE-GRADED
CHICANO VOLUNTARY ASSOCIATION

The volunatry association of Chicano senior citizens holds a very special meaning for many of its members; it allows them to go places and to see and do things they have never done before in their lives. Some, particularly the women, have never danced or had a drink of alcohol before they joined the club, much less attended a concert or a three-ring circus, visited a museum or a "rose garden," gambled, or seen a Las Vegas casino show. For others, the age-graded club serves as a means of continuing the pursuit of activities they have enjoyed in the past. As one woman explained it, "We are enjoying ourselves because we know we haven't got much time left, so we are going to make the most of it. It's our last fling."

The voluntary association for older Chicanos in East Los Angeles serves different needs for different people. Indeed, it seems that members can be categorized into a variety of types, according to their behaviors within the organization. One such general category is that of *the lonely*. There are two types of lonely senior citizens club members: *the network constructor* and *the companion seeker*. The network constructor uses the voluntary association as a basis for building his or her personal social network. Aurora Carillo is a seventy-four-year-old spinster and a network constructor.[1] She claims the only friends she has are those she has met at the club, and that the club is the only place she goes outside her home. On the other hand, the companion seeker uses the voluntary association to establish a link with a particular individual (or individuals) with whom to share affection, sex, and/or love.

In the East Los Angeles older Chicano community, these two types of lonely club members are attempting to rebuild links with other human beings. In the past, some links were disrupted by the process of generational maturation; some by the practice of neo-local residence by succeeding generations; some by migration, urbanization, and the barrio-annihilating process of urban development; and still others by separation and death. A minority of these lonely persons have been minimally engaged throughout their adult lives, and are experiencing "engagement" for the first time through the voluntary association.

In addition to the lonely individual experiencing social engagement for the first time, there is a more common type of senior citizens club member: *the experience seeker.* Experience seekers are members who are doing things for the first time and enjoying them. They are engaged in new activities and performing the new roles they are learning. Many of the older women fall into this category as do some men, like Mr. Padilla, who is learning to maintain fiscal records, make oral presentations, and participate in the political sphere of the senior-citizen subculture.

Being historically colonized is not without its effects on the situation of the older Chicano. There is a stigma attached to being Chicano. This is often translated into explanations of everyday behavior in the community, as well as within the older Chicano subculture. For example, a number of members defined the present factionalism as the result of nothing more than an inherent characteristic of *la raza* (the race—i.e., the ethnic group) which prevents it from being able to effectively organize. Similarly, the factionalism within the club has often been attributed to "lack of trust," "jealousy," or "envy" between members.

In addition to the specific negative perspectives associated with being a Chicano, those advancing in years must also carry the additional burden of the generalized negative attitude toward old age prevalent in the United States. Thus, growing old as a Chicano is conceptualized mainly in the guise of losses—physiological, social, and economic.

Older Chicanos appear very concerned with the image they project to others. They don't want to appear senile, physically weak, lacking sensuality, ugly, dependent, or nonproductive. But that is the image which is reflected by the wider community and society, and the combination of being old and being Chicano, as well as being a worker, means having less prestige than others.

The voluntary association serves as a means of generating prestige. As a public arena for social interaction, the senior citizens club gives older Chicanos the opportunity to demonstrate their competence and ability to learn new roles. Some members demonstrate their physical strength by dancing every dance, and then bragging about it to anyone who will listen. For instance, one member's reputation comes from not sitting out a single dance during socials.

In Chicano culture, as in the Euro-American society, women are more likely to be thought of as losing their physical attractiveness and their sensuality as they grow older. In American society, old men can be "dirty," meaning sexual, but little attention is given to such issues among older women. Nevertheless, older Chicanas must somehow deal with these physiological needs. Like women elsewhere, they experience the desire to be needed and wanted by the opposite sex. Unfortunately, as the Chicana grows wrinkled and gray, she also has less attention paid to her physical and emotional requirements. Many women in the Chicano community attempt to cover the visible signs of aging by using cosmetics, or dying their gray hair (as do an increasing number of older males). Some older Chicanas and Chicanos use the voluntary association as a social arena to prove their desirability to the opposite sex and their sexual prowess. Success is measured in the number of the opposite sex they can attract.

The problems of the aging female in an urban Chicano community are further aggravated by the early deaths of the males. As in other societies, the majority of older persons in the Chicano community are females. Furthermore, they are facing an "empty nest" at an earlier age, and, as a result, middle-aged Chicanas are finding themselves increasingly alienated. In East Los Angeles, a number of such women have attempted to combat the problems of middle age by joining in senior citizen activities. Unfortunately, this creates conflict. As younger women, they are more physically attractive than the older female members, and thus are perceived as competitors. With this avenue closed, a group of thirty women between the ages of thirty-six and forty-four formed the "Young at Heart Club." The purpose of this club was to "help the community, especially senior citizens, and to discuss our own present and anticipated problems of growing old."

For the older Chicano worker, male or female, personal value is based on the ability to produce, and the most productive are held in the highest esteem. A retired worker does not produce and is dependent on the fruits of past labor or the production of others. Dependence is not valued, and *no* productivity has little worth. However, the voluntary association provides a setting for older workers to seek, recover, or maintain a measure of self-worth. Here, one can acquire a good reputation by demonstrating competence.

Sr. Peralta is a poet. He has written poetry all his adult life. He has the reputation of having the mental ability to compose poems for anyone or any occasion. He often demonstrates this in honor of the birthdays of various individuals, or on important holidays in the senior citizen subculture such as Mother's Day (the most important, judging by the rituals involved), or Cinco de Mayo ("May 5th," honoring Mexico's liberation from France). This seventy-four-year-old retired laborer is widely known as a member of seven organizations. I call him and the others like him *status asserters.* Status asserters use voluntary associations to maintain their reputation of being competent in some particular area.

Mr. Cortez and Mrs. Nava provide examples of another type of reputation seeker who seems to be more typical. This is the *status compensator,* who uses the voluntary association to gain prestige in one social arena to compensate for prestige loss in another. Such a person has already lost a measure of control, or power, with his or her exit from the work force. For many older Chicano workers, the only resources they control outside the family are in their work settings. When they can no longer perform in this arena, their competence is subject to question. Depending on individual initiative and ability, the voluntary association offers an avenue to compensatory resources and power—that is, to a means of building a reputation.

The status seeker is the third type of individual who uses the voluntary association to reflect his self-worth. A good number of individuals have never had much prestige or power until they became a part of the Chicano senior citizens subculture. The experiences related to the idea of status lead us inevitably to the subject of *success* and *failure* in old age. In this respect, because with old age the differences between the objective conditions of individual Chicanos are greatly reduced, and the similarities enhanced, many find themselves in a better position to compete for, and to exercise some measure of control over, resources. In this sense, older Chicanos are "equals" in the social arena, because in terms of the wider society they are all losers to a greater or lesser extent.

Yet, these same losers who act in respect to their need for control of resources and/or prestige are emerging as a group of elites. These elites rise to the top of the older Chicano subculture according to their degree of participation, and to their ability to successfully participate in the subculture's political arena. For example, the situation of conflict and its resolution in the club demonstrates that to stay on top one must be intimately aware of the formal and informal normative rules for behavior, as well as of pragmatic strategies—such as discrediting your opponents in public—for winning power and prestige. However, such "winnings" are limited to the power and prestige available within a subculture based on the age-graded voluntary association.

From another perspective, the differences that distinguish "elites" from other members are those that separate "service providers" from "clients." Given the nature of the organization, these elites play a large part in deciding the kinds of services to be provided, and, thus, the kinds of needs that will be met. It is evident that through the control of resources, the setting of priorities, the establishment of ideological premises about the role and function of the senior citizens voluntary association, and the resultant provision for specific services that the elites are establishing proof of their continued productive contribution to the welfare of the social group.

However instructive, the above skeletal model of the Chicano senior citizens club provides only a partial picture of the myriad ways in which such a voluntary association meets the varied, individualized aspirations of its members. In the final analysis, such abstracted generalizations take their fabric from the ethnographer's detailed observation of ongoing interactions such as the following case history, and only through the exposition of such "real-life" dramas can the richness and complexity of the ongoing socio-cultural process be rendered as a truly credible and human experience.

Mr. Mendoza, as vice-president of the senior citizens club, was in charge of opening the hall before the club's monthly meetings and socials. He once told me that even before he had the responsibilities of a club officer, he would usually show up early because he lived only four blocks away from the center.

On the second Saturday in March, Mr. Mendoza was there early as usual and opened the building. The crowd that had arrived just before meeting time was relatively small. At 1:15 p.m., Sr. Sanchez called the meeting to order after he had appointed members-at-large to take the place of the three missing members of the *mesa directiva* (board of directors). Mr. Sanchez had been elected president of the club at the December meeting, and he and other club officers had been installed during the following month. He had missed the February meeting; therefore, this was the first time that he was presiding as president. Although newly elected, Mr. Sanchez was not new to such an office. He had already demonstrated his ability and competence as president of the Latino Senior Citizens Club for the past two years, and as secretary of the Xochimilco Senior Citizens Club for one year.

At first the meeting proceeded as usual. Following the pledge of allegiance to the flag of the United States and the prayer offered for the deceased, the president called for the minutes of the previous meeting to be read. But before the secretary could read them, Mrs. Salcedo loudly demanded to know why the meeting was being tape recorded. The treasurer, Mr. Barber, rose and explained that it was to help the secretary keep the record straight: "Too many things are said that are later denied. We want to have an accurate record of what is going on." Additional objections to the tape recording were made by other female members but a motion to continue was seconded and passed.

The chairpersons of various committees presented their reports, and among these was Mr. Juárez, co-chairperson of the social committee. As he stumbled through the presentation, he stopped on occasion to beg the general body's forgiveness for his lack of experience with bookkeeping. At the end of his report he apologetically thanked the group, promising that he would try his best to learn as much as he could to better discharge the responsibilities of his new position.

Mrs. Márquez reported that three members of the club were ill, and that cards had been sent to them on behalf of the organization. Moreover, she indicated that they had been called every day, and that she had visited them twice during the past month in her capacity as chairperson of the *comité de salud* (health committee). She then asked Mr. García to present the status of the "death benefits" fund. Mr. García (a board member and past club treasurer) reported that $100.00 had been given to the daughter of Mr. Ayala, a club member who had died during the previous month. Almost as an attempt to settle the disturbed crowd, many of whom appeared to be hearing the news for the first time, Mr. García emphasized that flowers had been sent, and that three of the club officers had attended the funeral. Still, this was not an unusual incident, for it seems that often a member will not hear of the death of another member until a club function, generally after the deceased has been buried.

Following the treasurer's report, Mr. García asked the president for permission to address the general body. Standing in front of the group, he delivered an emotional speech in which he accused Mr. Barber and Mr. Mendoza of fiscal negligence, raising the issue called "the case of the missing petty cash." According to García, Barber and Mendoza, treasurer and vice president respectively, had willfully and maliciously withheld $25.00 in petty cash from Mrs. Nava, the secretary, who needed the money for supplies. Immediately, Mr. Barber and Mr. Mendoza responded by noting that as co-signers on the club's checking account they could not authorize the check without a receipt, and that Mrs. Nava had not turned in a receipt for the supplies she had supposedly bought. Mrs. Nava then immediately countered that she had given the receipt to Mr. Cortez several months before, during his term as president of the club. Mr. Cortez, upon recognition by the chair heatedly responded that he gave the receipt to the former treasurer, Mr. García, suggesting that Mr. García should produce the receipt rather than levy false charges against club officers.

The discussion that followed Mr. Cortez's statements reached such noisy proportions that the president called for order and asked for a motion that the discussion be tabled until the board of directors could examine the issue in detail. The motion was made, enthusiastically seconded, and passed.

But by this time, Mr. García had pulled some papers from his coat and moved to the center of the room. With wide-armed gestures, he waved his hospitalization papers in front of the general assembly. Here was his proof that he was in the hospital, and therefore unable to handle club business as usual during the previous months. His outbreak was met by uncommon silence. His wife then rose and exploded: "You don't care that this man has been sick, and that the illness was in part brought on by what goes on in this club. I'm tired of this. We try our best and you don't care."

"You two are not the only ones who work here," retorted Mrs. Chávez, board member (and vice president of the Latino Social Club). "We all give as much as we can to each other and the club!" Before sitting down, she quietly added, "I don't know, it is only my humble opinion, but I think that what you are interested in is mistreating the characters of Mr. Barber, Mr. Cortez, Mr. Mendoza, and others."

Her husband, the former president of the Latino Social Club, stood, saying: "I know some of you don't like me because you think I talk too much. Maybe I do, but I must say what is right and what is not! Here you are acting like this is some kind of Watergate or something. You are recording everything that is being said, and everybody is accusing somebody else of doing something wrong. *Hermanos y hermanas* (brothers and sisters), we are all acting like teenagers instead of senior citizens. We must trust and take care of each other. If we don't, who will? No one has done anything wrong. Let's go on with our meeting, and forget all this nonsense."

As he sat down, a number of people looked at the clock. It was rapidly approaching 3:00 p.m. Several of the members quietly left, as President Sánchez attempted to secure order by reminding everyone that the issue had been tabled. Looking at the clock, he stated, "In the future, we are going to keep the discussion down to five minutes." But most members were now engaged in private discussions. Above the general murmur, Mrs. Salcedo remarked, "But we are here to be served, and not to serve." This remark was obviously directed against Mr. Mendoza, who now had the floor, and was about to speak in behalf of the club's sponsorship of a youth sports team.

The reactions to this item of new business were mixed and varied. Srs. Cortez, Chávez, and Rodríguez presented positions in favor of the proposal. Sra. Nava, along with Sr. Padilla, and Sra. Juárez, reacted negatively. In turn, each stated that as "old people" they just couldn't afford the luxury of spending money outside the club, and that senior citizen money should be spent on their own activities. Mrs. López, Mr. Cortez's "dance partner," broke her silence by responding: "This club can afford $25.00 to help some community kids."

The motion was made, and the majority of the club members voted to support the team. But in the back, one member turned to another and asked, "I don't understand; what did we just vote for?" The other lady just shook her head. A man in his late forties, standing nearby, said to them: "*Friéguense porque están ancianos*" ("Be damned because you are old"). To which one of the women responded, "What about you?"

"I'm just here to see what I can do," said the former trade unionist from Culiacán, Mexico, "how I can help?"

Meanwhile, more members had quietly departed. As Mr. and Mrs. Chávez walked out the door, he turned to President Sánchez and made a "thumbs down" gesture.

Mr. Sánchez nervously looked at the clock again, and reached in his briefcase to produce a letter. He called for order. When it came, he soberly read his letter of resignation as president to a general assembly that had now dwindled to less than thirty persons, less than half the original number of those in attendance. As Mr. Sánchez made his presentation, Mr. Barber was positioning himself in front of the officers' table. Mr. Sánchez offered three reasons for his resignation. The first was the economic recession, "the inflation" which had caused layoffs at the plant where he was a foreman, requiring that he work more hours than in the past. The second was that his other obligations, as president and officer of other clubs were too demanding. He said that he would rather relinquish his post than perform his duties poorly. And finally, he reported that his wife's health had been progressively getting worse, and therefore he could make no commitment to carry the additional responsibility of the presidency of the club.

The reaction was swift. Mr. Barber, standing in front of the membership as Mr. Sánchez sat back, began to speak as various other individuals vigorously tried to get recognition from the chair. But Mr. Barber's statement was cut short. President Sánchez recognized Mr. Padilla. Sr. Padilla, who appeared surprised by the resignation, asked Mr. Sánchez to reconsider, suggesting that Vice President Mendoza could substitute until President Sánchez could return to his post and responsibilities, as allowed by the club's bylaws. This was rejected by Mr. Sánchez, who said his decision was final and irreversible. With that, Mr. Padilla announced that he was leaving on his vacation shortly, and therefore had to resign his position as board member. Mr. Juárez then rose, and begging the group's forgiveness, resigned his co-chairmanship of the social committee. Mrs. Juárez followed suit.

Sra. Nava, who had been standing waiting to be recognized, asked the members present to refuse the resignation, moving that Sr. Sánchez be given a three-month waiting period before his resignation became final. From his chair, Sr. Padilla asked if Sr. Mendoza would be willing to carry the responsibility for three months as suggested by Mrs. Nava. As President Sánchez shook his head negatively, and Vice President Mendoza stood to respond, Mr. Barber reminded the membership in general, and Mr. Padilla in particular, that the president's decision was final, and that all that could be done was to have Vice President Mendoza assume the presidency according to the bylaws.

Sr. Mendoza stood and waited for the room to quiet. When the members were ready to listen, in a strong voice he stated: "I am here to serve you. If you want me to substitute for Mr. Sánchez, and if Mr. Sánchez will promise to return after three months, I will carry the burden of his post. But if you want me to assume the presidency, I promise that I will do everything in my power to make this the best senior citizens club in East Los Angeles. What we do is up to you."

With that he sat down and waited for the response. Before the applause for Mr. Mendoza's statement had subsided, Mr. Sánchez had closed his briefcase and was walking toward the door. A number of individual members stood and began moving around gathering their personal belongings. The hour was late, and many of the other members, such as Mr. and Mrs. Chávez, were already at the social of the Montezuma Senior Citizens Club being held at the Veterans of Foreign Wars Hall.

As Vice President Mendoza called an end to the meeting, Mrs. López, usually in charge of the raffle held at the end of every monthly business meeting, expressed more concern about not having been allowed to perform her role as raffle organizer than about the "surprise" resignation of President Sánchez.

Indeed, the resignation had not been a surprise to a number of persons concerned. Sr. Sánchez had informed the members of the mesa directiva on the previous Thursday at their regular monthly meeting to organize the agenda for the club's meeting. In fact, most of the issues discussed that particular Saturday afternoon in March had already been discussed among the club officers the previous Thursday. For example, Mr. Garcia had brought up the "petty cash" issue, and all concerned had taken the same positions on Thursday. I found that in fact the club's meetings were frequently simply expanded versions of the Thursday officers' meeting. The same arguments were advanced by the same people with the same positions on both occasions.

The only difference was that, in this case, the only one who had not revealed his position on Thursday was Vice President Mendoza. He had been expected to resign, or temporarily assume the presidency. He provided the only surprise of the day by proposing to accept the presidency. Mr. Cortez had been the most surprised. He had expected that upon the resignation of both Sr. Sánchez and Sr. Mendoza, among others, Mr. Barber would move that new elections be held. According to their plan, this would allow Mr. Cortez a chance to recover the post he had lost to Mr. Sánchez in December.

The events surrounding the March meeting of the club, which I have just described, were the "climax" of a series of maneuvers that had been set into motion the previous summer. What actually had occurred was a prolonged struggle for prestige, power, and the control of coveted resources that accompany club leadership by individuals belonging to two opposing factions that had developed within the organization. Thus, we can observe the process by which individual older persons, depending on their levels of personal initiative and the nature of their needs, manipulate available resources to satisfy their personal aspirations in the context of a voluntary association.

A significant role in the definition of the Chicano senior citizens club as a meaningful social arena is played by this factionalism and the conflict it generates. Thus, rather than constituting a maladaptive feature, such conflict guarantees the vital and meaningful engagement of the elderly participants. It is only in the light of these considerations that what is immediately to follow can be placed in proper perspective.

Late in August, when Mrs. Nava's house meeting to organize the September social acted simply as a screen. Present were Mrs. Juárez, Mr. and Mrs. Padilla, Mr. and Mrs. García, Mrs. Salcedo, and Mrs. Márquez. In addition to preparations for the social, discussion also centered on the problems within the club in general, and particularly on the rumors that several members had been exploited by the leadership. There were also accusations of mismanagement of the club's funds. It was decided the only way to put an end to the problem was to organize a slate of candidates to run in the December election against the incumbents. This would be a break from the tradition of running as individual candidates. Additional meetings were held, with each participant being asked to bring one or two "trusted" members each time. Mrs. Nava took responsibility for the organization of these activities. Mr. Mendoza joined the group in September upon the invitation tendered by Mr. García, after a meeting of the Latino Senior Citizens Club, where they both served as board members.

Two decisions were made in September. The first was to choose the following nominees: Mr. Sánchez for president, Mr. Mendoza for vice president, Mr. Padilla for treasurer, and Mrs. Nava for recording secretary. It was agreed that others would be subsequently nominated to fill positions on the mesa directive, and various committees. The second decision was that formal charges would be brought against the incumbent "offenders" at the next meeting.

The October meeting proceeded as usual, almost without an unanticipated incident. The minor exception came when the *portero* (sergeant-at-arms) read the names of potential members and escorted them to the front of the assembly to be introduced. One of the three prospects was a full-figured, comely woman of forty-five. When she was introduced, Mrs. López and Mrs. Salcedo both stood and asserted that the woman was too young, and therefore not eligible. The "young woman" responded that she was forty-five years old, and therefore eligible for membership. Mrs. López insisted that the minimum membership age was forty-seven and not forty-five. After a short discussion, the membership decided to accept her as a member. The critical argument had been posed by Mr. Mendoza, who had pointed to the woman's strong desire to participate in the club's activities, as well as to the contributions she could make through the contacts she had with "show business" personalities in the area. As a final gesture of good will before sitting down, the woman offered to use her contacts with persons in the Spanish-speaking mass media to give the club free publicity. This was met with general applause, a sign that the group as a whole was acutely concerned with the reputation of their organization. On the other hand, the "threat" that she posed was revealed in the vote; the decision being unanimously supported by male members, and rejected by almost half the females.

When Mr. Cortez called for "new business," Mrs. García stood and accused Mr. and Mrs. Rodríguez—founding members of the association and organizers of club trips and junkets—as co-chairpersons of the social committee, of overcharging the members for the activities they organized, and pocketing the difference. Furthermore, she asserted they were receiving kickbacks from several travel agencies and bureaus. Above the ensuing confusion, Mrs. Nava stood and loudly accused President Cortez of stealing money from club members through the manipulation of the fiscal records.

The accusations took the leaders by surprise, and their first reaction was to proclaim their innocence. Their next reaction was to establish a fact-finding committee composed of present and past members of the mesa directiva. The reaction of the general body was that of shock and disbelief, although suspicions did begin to surface. The ad hoc committee, chaired by Mr. Mendoza, was to review the books and records, and establish whether any money was missing from the club treasury, and whether there was any evidence of exploitation by the Rodríguezes. It would make its report at the next monthly business meeting.

On the second Saturday of November, the ad hoc fact-finding committee reported they could find no evidence of stealing or exploitation on the part of any of the officers. Their recommendation was that the accusations be forgotten, and the members of the *familia* be brought together again.

But President Cortez immediately, and with great drama, handed the gavel to the vice president, Sr. Chávez, and asked the membership to allow him to temporarily step down from the presidency. Once this was granted by the bewildered membership, Mr. Cortez demanded a full apology from his accusers, Mrs. Nava and Mrs. García in particular.

"All I want is justice. I have been unjustly accused of being a thief. This I cannot stand for."

Turning to the general membership, he said: "The investigation has shown that I, and my friends Sr. and Sra. Rodríguez, have been falsely accused of misbehavior. Now I ask you, am I a thief?"

"No!" responded the general body loudly.

"Should I continue as your president? Do I have your confidence?"

"Yes," came the response.

With that, Mrs. García, who had been standing near the back of the meeting hall, addressed the assembly.

"I will never apologize. If you want them instead of me, then stay with them. As for me, you will never see my face here gain."

Then she walked out of the meeting, her husband following behind. This left the gathering in a turmoil. Mrs. Nava sat silently, and listened to the oratories of Mr. Chávez and others calling for an end to the disputes and accusations in the club. Mrs. López addressed the members, reminding them, "People have to clean their own house before they start making accusations against others."

Mr. Martínez, the seventy-four-year-old poet, pleaded for solidarity: *"Como viejos, que nadie quiere, y mexicanos, tenemos que unirnos no dividirnos con tonterías"* ("As old persons, that no one wants, and Mexicans, we must unite and not be divided by silly things"). Sr. Fontana chided the group for acting like teenagers, rather than showing the wisdom of their years. Others appealed for solidarity to counteract the negative effect this situation was having on the "name" of the club. Shortly after, President Cortez called an end to the meeting.

Indeed, because many of the members also belonged to other senior citizens clubs, the "situation" was a central subject of discussion at meetings of other groups in East Los Angeles for a six-month period following the accusations.

The election of club officers was held in December, as is the case with most East Los Angeles voluntary associations. Prior to the meeting, Mrs. Nava made arrangements with Mr. García, club treasurer at the time, for Mr. Sánchez to pay the five months' worth of back dues he owed, thus making him eligible to run for office. The elections were not without incident.

After the votes were counted, Mr. Cortez, after having been given vocal support by the membership at the November meeting, was soundly defeated by Mr. Sánchez, who had not attended a club function for over three months. In her nomination speeches for both Mr. Sánchez and Mr. Mendoza, Mrs. Nava made continual references to their previous experience as officers of other organizations. She also constantly emphasized the need for "new" leadership that would be sensitive to the needs of the members, and not to persons outside the club.

Mrs. Nava was nominated for the office of club secretary by Mrs. García, who had vowed never to return after the November meeting. Mrs. García, during her nomination speech, told of the sacrifices Mrs. Nava had made to help many of the local senior citizens, particularly other club members. She placed the greatest emphasis on Mrs. Nava's past record of involvement with club activities, in spite of her having been a member for only slightly over one year.

Mrs. Nava, along with Mr. Sánchez, Mr. Mendoza, and Mrs. García were elected to the most important club positions. Mr. Padilla, nominated by Mrs. Sánchez, was defeated for the treasurer's post by Mr. Barber. Mr. Barber, nominated by Mr. Cortez, was the only one of the "old" leadership to be retained.

As is customary with most senior citizens clubs in East Los Angeles, the new officers were installed at the first scheduled business meeting of the new year. But, as was also usually the case, with the "Christmas" social having been cancelled due to conflict with New Year's celebrations of various other groups, "regular" business was postponed in order to complete the "installation" ritual.

Although relatively new to the community, the senior citizens clubs have developed fairly rigid rules for the installation of new officers, and the violation of these rules generally results in conflict. The usual procedure is for the outgoing president to contact another president of a "respected" senior citizens group, and formally request that as an official representative of that organization, he or she install the incoming members of the mesa directiva.

On the chosen date, the outgoing president, after calling the meeting to order, asks the membership for permission to dispense with the regular business. He then invites the visiting dignitary to perform the ceremony.

The ushers then bring the newly elected officers to the front of the group, as the sergeant-at-arms reads their names. The ritual leader then has each officer repeat the oath of office, and details their duties and obligations to the association. These oaths and responsibilities are a variation on the oath that all members take upon joining the organization. After all of the new officers are seated at their respective positions at the head table, the outgoing president hands the gavel, as a symbol of authority, to the new president, and declares that each is officially installed. At that time, the new president can officially reopen the meeting, or ask for an adjournment, to be followed by a celebration and club social.

A minor conflict arose at the installation of the new officers in this case because the rules were violated. When Mr. Cortez dismissed the regular business of the club, Mr. Sánchez announced that Mrs. Quiñones, president of a government-supported senior citizens group, would have the honor of performing the installation ceremony. As Mrs. Quiñones moved to take her place at the center of the room, Mr. Cortez blocked her way, announcing it was his prerogative as outgoing president to select the person to conduct the ceremony. Furthermore, as an individual, he could not permit Mrs. Quiñones, who had been openly critical of the association in the past, to be part of any club function, much less an important ritual such as the installation.

Mrs. Quiñones, rather than appeal to the membership for support, as she might have done, walked toward the door. There she was intercepted by Mrs. Nava. After a brief discussion between the two, Mrs. Quiñones left the building, and the ritual continued according to custom.

But rather than ask for an adjournment, the new president, Mr. Sánchez, decided to continue the meeting. After the pledge of allegiance to the flag in English, which was as usual half-muttered by the predominantly Spanish-speaking members, one of Mr. Sánchez's first acts was to request permission to remove the Mexican flag from behind the head table. The rationale given by President Sánchez, a Cuban immigrant, was *"Estamos en Los Estados Unidos y no en México"* ("We are in the United States and not in Mexico"). Mr. García, a Puerto Rican, proposed the motion, and it was seconded by his wife. The loosely structured meeting ended shortly thereafter, with the new president's first and only act while in office having been soundly defeated by an overwhelming majority.

THE VOLUNTARY ASSOCIATION AS A PSYCHOLOGICAL AND SOCIAL RESOURCE

For many older Chicanos, the voluntary association clearly fills a psychological and social void. Undoubtedly, this is in part a response to the erosion of older values and institutions that are no longer totally viable in the context of a rapidly changing urban center. In other words, these clubs provide outlets for universal needs and desires that might otherwise have no adequate mode of realization. Moreover, what is perhaps most significant is that these common-interest groups give evidence of the active role older people may play in shaping their own destinies.

In contrast to people in so-called "traditional" societies, who strive to achieve their life goals in the arenas constituted by unselfconscious and nondeliberate forms of social organization such as the family, the clan, the neighborhood, the village, and the like, the older Chicanos described in this essay have deliberately constructed a social field to meet a number of their most deeply felt needs.

Although in the final analysis, the voluntary association cannot erase for older Chicanos the stigma of 200 years of racial, political, cultural, economic, and social oppression in Los Angeles, it can to a degree compensate for some of the immediate effects of this past history. What is provided is an arena whose activities assume transcendent meaning for the participants through their active engagement and as the result of their mutual definition of the situation as one of significance. Thus, while the age-graded voluntary association cannot increase the real income of its members, guarantee them better medical care and adequate nutrition, or bestow upon them immediate and real political representation in the larger community, it can nevertheless provide them with what is perhaps of equal importance, a feeling of vital engagement in life and a sense of personal worth.

NOTE

1. All names have been changed to preserve the anonymity of the research subjects.

Seniors at club social in East Los Angeles.

Seniors at housing project social.

Club meeting at housing project.

CONCLUSION

Andrei Simić and Barbara Myerhoff

The five studies in this volume have attempted in their analysis of aging to reconcile its culturally stable aspects with its dynamic dimensions, conceiving of each particular cultural niche as a distinct and unique resource subject to manipulation and individual interpretation and misinterpretation. For the most part, in anthropology, cross-cultural comparisons have been drawn in respect to highly visible and ostensibly stable structural characteristics, ignoring aberrant or seemingly idiosyncratic elements. Our chapters have strived to depart from this tradition, and perhaps the very diachronic nature of aging itself tends to favor a historical and processual approach. Needless to say, aging is the result of an individual's passage through time, through the life cycle, through a chain of interpersonal exchanges and relationships, arriving finally at old age, whose essence is the product of a multitude of events, inferences, judgments, choices, and decisions. Thus, we have conceived of aging not as a passive state, but rather as the continuation of a lifelong creative experience by which individuals activate and constantly reinterpret their cultures.

We have sought common measures to assemble, analyze, and compare data from five vastly different cultural backgrounds, measures that would treat not only structure but process and experience as well. From our research, there have emerged three major themes, providing a common vantage point for interpreting the behavior of individuals growing old under a variety of contrasting circumstances: *continuity; the sexual dichotomy;* and *aging as a career.* Though we have opted to analytically distinguish these measures as discrete attributes, as will be seen, they are really inseparable facets of a single, shared, deep structure of aging—that is, aging in its broadest connotation, the inevitable progression from infancy to senescence and final death.

CONTINUITY

Sharp ruptures and dramatic discontinuities may set the aged apart more profoundly in some societies than in others, and within the same cultural milieu some persons more than others. Continuity and discontinuity have both qualitative and quantitative aspects, and they are ubiquitous features of every event system. The very nature of the concept of continuity as a

[231]

criterion of measurement and comparison is diachronic; that is, it relates to process and experience, and as such is of particular relevance in the analysis of aging. In this book, continuity has been perceived arbitrarily in terms of three measurable perceptual points of reference: that of *space,* that of *social relationships,* and that of *ideas. Spatial continuity* makes reference to an individual's relationship, be it actual or symbolic, to certain real, imagined or mythological places. Thus, this connection may not be necessarily of a physical nature, but rather vicarious or existential ties may also link an individual throughout his lifetime to a particular territory or community. Clearly, the idea of space in this respect is interconnected inseparably with the spheres of social relationships and culture. *Social continuity* deals with the permanency, frequency, and intensity of interpersonal relationships as they fluctuate through time. Similar to the case of spatial continuity, face-to-face relationships are not a necessary definitive characteristic since social relationships may be maintained vicariously and symbolically not only in life but in death as well. *Cultural continuity* implies contact with, and access to, a coherent and relatively stable body of ideas, values, and symbols.

The theme of continuity itself is closely associated with those of the sexual dichotomy and aging as a career. Not only can we address ourselves to the specification of general levels of continuity within cultures, but we can also expect that men and women may differ in this respect just as individual differences will also be great.

What does continuity mean for the aged; how important does it become with advancing years; and what particular functions does it assume in later life? For example, are obligations of care and respect on the part of younger people for their elders more rigorously adhered to in societies where high levels of continuity are the rule? In this respect, it has become almost axiomatic in the social sciences from at least the time of the appearance of Durkheim's *Suicide* (1897) that excessive change is socially and psychologically disruptive. On the other hand, anthropologist Paul Bohannan (1963: 387) has suggested the idea of stability and continuity in change, citing the fact that American culture regards change as a stable value unto itself. With this in mind, the analytic separation of these three kinds of continuity assumes particular significance. For example, is it possible to balance excessive change in the cultural sphere by the maintenance of stability in the area of interpersonal relationships or through continuing ties to a personally significant place? Surely this issue is meaningful for everyone; however, for those who are approaching the end of their lives, *interconnectedness,* actual or imagined, becomes a dominant theme, .one vital to their very sense of identity and meaningfulness.

The five societies portrayed in this book vary markedly with respect to the particular levels and kinds of continuity present as generalized characteristics. In two cultures, Chagga and Yugoslav, the life cycles of our informants evidence a great deal of interconnectedness and experiential integration; that is, from infancy onward, there is a relatively undisrupted flow of relationships, and a continuing proximity to familiar ideas and places. Where sharp ruptures have occurred, counterbalancing and stabilizing elements were usually also present, and corrective action was in theory possible, and in many cases did take place. In contrast, levels of continuity in the lives of the Mexican sample from Netzahualcoyotl are significantly lower, though for some individuals all three types are similarly present. The Mexican-Americans of East Los Angeles and the Jews of Venice provide a very different kind of case since both groups have been essentially cut off, though not to the same extent, from the sources of their childhood experience. In both instances, the elderly are also separated by a cultural gap from their more Americanized children. Thus, these aging people, within a great American urban center, are the product of a number of definitive ruptures: migration from their place of birth; separation from the culture that socialized and nurtured them into adulthood; partial alienation within their present cultural environment, and the concomitant severance or slackening of all-important intergenerational ties.

Of course, in not one of these examples is continuity utterly lacking, rather there is a question of differences in pervasiveness, strength, and the particular forms and constellations of those continuities present. In no society studied is there lacking some social and psychological energy brought to bear to maintain or to re-create a sense of connectedness. For some, such as the Chagga, this process involves the nourishment of existing, highly energized relationships and viable institutions; for others, such as the Jews of Venice, the task is essentially retrospective. For all, however, the less tangible aspects of continuity crystallized in the form of memory, ritual, and myth are equally real and important, as are its other, more concrete manifestations. As an aged Yugoslav wrote to an immigrant relative in California, "Forgetfulness creates separation, not time and space." Thus, it is that the need and drive for continuity is omnipresent, but in each of the five cultures considered its realization is achieved in a different way, and with a varying degree of completeness and credibility.

The Chagga exemplify the concept of stability in change, and Moore's subjects have lived out their lives in what she calls "life-term social arenas." They have been able to spend their years in the same villages, with the same kin and neighbors, and though rapid political and economic changes have swept Tanzania, for most, time has run its course in a relatively uninterrupted and consistent flow of events, relationships, and ideas. For instance, with the passing of colonialism, innovation has, as often as not, accommodated traditional culture, and inversely, the accommodation of traditional culture to innovation has not been excessively abrupt. For example, Moore describes older men who have taken salaried jobs in the external world without abandoning the maintenance of their village gardens and fields. Thus, in retirement, outside occupations are simply abandoned while otherwise life continues as in the past. Among the Chagga, continuity is assured by custom, and adherence to custom by inescapable community pressure. What this means for the aged is that in the normal course of events the responsibility for their care will fall to a son who will inherit the plot of land his father lives on. However, the intricate relationships and obligations that bind generations together do not necessarily signify that great affection is present. Rather, continuity is guaranteed by a complexity of factors including the fear of supernatural sanctions and the loss of reputation among one's co-villagers. Nevertheless, while the case histories depicted by Moore reveal a situation lacking any utopian aura, still the aged manage to remain active figures in their society in the context of familiar places, people, and traditions.

The Yugoslav case rather closely resembles that of the Chagga, though the spatial dislocations have been greater. Industrialization and urbanization have been accomplished, for the most part, within the context of traditional mores. Even migration abroad has not, in most instances, succeeded in transgressing the firm moral imperatives that link lineal and collateral kin in close-knit systems of economic and ritual reciprocity. In this respect, emotional attachment to one's place of origin remains vital and intense as long as significant kin remain there. Thus, spatial and social continuity are, in essence, inseparable. Nevertheless, as in the Chagga case, kinship and intergenerational relations are fraught with the fear of lack of fulfillment, and the suspicion that reciprocal obligations will not be adequately honored. At the same time, in spite of such negative aspects, even in distant California, immigrants strive to assure the continuity of generations and the survival of South Slav custom among their own children born outside of Yugoslavia.

Netzahualcoyotl stands out in sharp contrast to the environments depicted by Moore and Simić, since here existence is far more precarious, and the maintenance of ties with the past difficult—and for some even impossible. Most divergent from the Chagga and Yugoslav examples is the striking absence of older people here, and Vélez finds that most of the families he studied are typified by sharp ruptures and breaks with ascending generations. He terms these families "ahistorical." For the most part, migration to Netzahualcoyotl has been one of youth, and this characteristic has shaped the composition of the majority of households. However, Vélez also notes that there are many exceptions, and a number of older people have followed their children in migration, and thus continued to fulfill roles within their kinship networks that are similar to those they previously carried out at home. Though Netzahualcoyotl seems to personify discontinuity, upheaval, disruption, and uncertainty, even this demands a certain routinization of life and an attempt to re-create or reinterpret lost traditions. For example, Vélez has identified cultural continuity perpetuating itself in the realm of the management and manipulation of power. This Mexican slum settlement is typified by a dynamic and often explosive political situation, and aging men and women experience continuity through their continued subjugation to political exploitation, a situation that has characterized their entire lives. In spite of its negative guise, the political arena provides an avenue for participation on the part of the aged within the limits of familiar rules and expectations.

The elderly Chicanos studied by José Cuellar present a complex instance of the interaction of continuity and discontinuity resulting from his subjects' intermediacy between two cultures. As is also the case with the Jews of Venice, these Mexican-Americans face the task of reconciling the demands of two contrasting systems of ideas and values. While the majority had long ago severed direct ties with the communities of their origin, at the same time they have never become entirely acculturated to the Anglo-American society in whose midst they live. Because of this, they have experienced some loss of continuity with their children who are more Americanized. They stand between two worlds, tenuously bound to each. Their continuities are fragile at best, and in retirement these older Chicanos have turned to each other to structure their old age in the context of voluntary associations where new relationships can replicate the functions of old ones, and where cultural continuity phrased in the idiom of ethnicity may be maintained and savored.

Of all those considered here, the elderly Eastern European Jews depicted by Myerhoff evidence the sharpest, most extreme, and all-pervasive discontinuities. However, at the same time, they also demonstrate what is perhaps the greatest concern with continuity. For example, unlike the Mexican-Americans, the culture of their youth has ceased to exist, and there is no possibility of reestablishing ties with the communities of their childhood. These old men and women are the product of the ethnically segregated Jewish settlements of Poland and pre-revolutionary Russia, the traditional shtetls. Even the Yiddish language that once flourished in Eastern Europe, and later in immigrant communities in America, is now threatened with extinction. Thus, these elderly Jews have physically lost contact with a major part of the fabric that constituted their earliest lives. Moreover, for the most part, they have failed to socialize their children to the values and customs of the original culture. In spite of the sharp cleavages that separate one part of their lives from another, these old people have clung consciously and tenaciously to the threads binding them to the past. Though their present lives are the product of momentous changes and tragic ruptures, in the face of all obstacles they have been stimulated to re-create in the context of a voluntary association the cultural environment and values of their youth.

This impetus for continuity can be attributed in part to the particular history of the Jews as a dispersed and pariah people. Here one finds a particular sense of community that has not been associated with a spatial dimension or territorial unity since the Diaspora of the Israelites at the time of the destruction of the Temple. Thus, community has been realized symbolically as the product of religious ritual, and synchronized in time by an intense identification with both past history and a Messianic future. In this way, the elderly Jews of Venice have been able to create a sense of social continuity that transcends the boundaries of their own specific age-homogeneous relationships in the context of a modest voluntary association.

Myerhoff's subjects, like those of Simić, can be seen struggling to create a sense of continuity not only in this lifetime but beyond it. In this respect, she discusses two kinds of continuity, *life-historical* and *spiritual.* Another type of continuity also appears in Myerhoff's case, a particular connection between the first part of life and old age, a condition that may not be uncommon among immigrants who in their declining years find themselves once more poor outsiders and marginal members of society, a situation which did not prevail in their middle years. Thus, the return to one's roots and ethnicity draws a resource held in common with fellow immigrants characterized by shared socioeconomic destinies. In old age, the Jews of Venice have turned as a group to their childhood to draw forth the common ethnic materials for a cultural and social resurrection.

What plainly emerges from these essays is that in later life there is a tremendous impetus toward the maintenance of continuity, and where it is lacking, toward its reestablishment. In other words, in old age, the experience and concept of continuity emerge as a prime value. We can recognize this value, and any value for that matter, because, as Barth has phrased it (1966: 5), "people in real life seek it." As Barth explains, there is always an attempt to maximize value through strategic action with respect to it—that is, to make it the object of transactions between oneself and others. Continuity is not an observable *thing* per se, but rather the inescapable experiential product of a kind of process which ties the events and ideas of one period to those of the next. As a criterion for comparative analysis, continuity is not bound to any specific social or cultural forms, but rather simply provides a measurement of interconnectedness.

THE SEXUAL DICHOTOMY IN AGING

The fact is inescapable that male and female life trajectories differ markedly. This disparity in the aging process provides a very special instance of continuity and change. The question of sex differences in aging is also tied to the more general consideration of the way individuals pass from one status to another, and from one set of roles to another throughout the life cycle. Here, too, looms large the issue of experiential interconnectedness. For instance, is the transition from one social personality to another a sudden or gradual metamorphosis? To what degree are new roles anticipated by the actors, and to what extent have they already experienced them vicariously through close contact with those older than themselves? Does one culture contrast significantly with another as to the specificity with which life's path is plotted for those who will follow it? Finally, what are the sexual variations in respect to all of the above questions?

As was previously hypothesized, all societies seem to be typified by some level of entropy and uncertainty, and, indeed, tolerable levels of disparity between culture and social structure may well constitute the necessary adaptability prerequisite for individual and group survival. Nevertheless, the fit between the cultural code and social structure appears to be observably closer in some settings than others. Among our ethnographic examples, this congruence is relatively high among the Chagga, where the life histories of the aged are typified by the passage from one highly differentiated status with its concomitant role expectations to another. Moreover, this fairly rigid structuring and delineation of the behavior appropriate to given segments of the life span are also highly differentiated according to sex. For instance, in Chagga society, as in many non-Western cultures, husband and wife never sleep in the same bed for a whole night, nor do husband and wife normally eat meals together. Usually after the earliest period of marriage, a man occupies a different building from that of his wife if he can afford to do so, and eats alone or with some other male. One can, in fact, speak of separate male and female subcultures in this part of Africa, and this in turn has deep ramifications for the aging process.

Similar to the Chagga, rigidly defined sex roles typify the Yugoslavs, who experienced centuries of Islamic domination ending completely only during the first part of this century. Stereotypically, according to widespread folk expectations, the South Slav male must maintain a public image of independence, aggressiveness, and self-reliance, and all overt power is accorded him. Ideally, the woman's role is complementary, and even when employed outside the home, her familial position remains traditional. However, to rest with this explanation would be to distort the reality of the manner in which life actually functions. As men and women age, their relationships vis-à-vis each other are gradually transformed, and overt power as often as not increasingly masks the locus of other kinds of authority and control. For instance, while the village bride entering the home of her husband for the first time assumes a subservient position to members of his family, as she becomes older, her influence is increasingly felt through the affectual and moral control she exerts over her children. As Simić's chapter demonstrates, men also undergo a gradual transition in their familial relationships as they age, and the positive affect they previously felt toward their mothers is gradually transferred to their wives in the context of a relationship of greater egalitarianism. One can, perhaps, speak of men reaching social and psychological adulthood only upon the death of their own parents. Moreover, due to the covert power of mothers over their sons, Yugoslav society might be characterized as a *crypto-matriarchy*.

As among the South Slavs, in Netzahualcoyotl women also become more assertive and independent with advancing years, and in old age participate to a far greater degree than men in both familial and nonkinship social arenas. For example, women appear to fare better than men as "followers of children" to the city. An old woman can join in the household and continue her traditional role caring for children, preparing food, assuring harmony and order, and performing as a socializing agent in the lives of adult children. Vélez also describes the manner in which networks of comadres (godmothers) in the external world are transformed into instruments for political and economic action. In contrast, men do not characteristically become engaged in such networks, and as they become older, they participate less actively in social life. The origins of this are thoroughly rooted in cultural paradigms stressing machismo, with its concept that male esteem stems from dominance and aggressiveness. However, with declining physical and mental capabilities, older men experience a diminishing ability to fulfill these ideals. Though Vélez does not spell out the consequences of machismo for older men in detail, there are indications that it may be extremely dysfunctional. Similarly, in Simić's study, the machistic role can be seen as costly for older men, as exemplified by the spiralling disasters that befell his informant, Djole, who in a self-defeating struggle to compensate for his loss of manly powers dug himself deeper and deeper into ruin.

In Netzahualcoyotl, a newly formed urban community, the situation of the elderly has been exacerbated by the uprooting of families from their native villages, and a concomitant disruption of traditional relationships. Moreover, there has been a failure on the part of the younger generation to step into the roles previously occupied by their parents. With the development of new economic vistas, a sense of alienation and exclusion has particularly permeated the lives of older men rooted in an agricultural mentality. Thus, in this burgeoning but poor urban settlement, sharp discontinuities separate not only the young from the old, but also, the women from the men.

José Cuellar also finds that the aging experience for males and females among Chicano elders of East Los Angeles is of a very different order. As elsewhere, a number of distinctions are made between the appropriate roles for men and women; however, with aging, the stereotypic expectations of female behavior remain better defined than those for the male. As in Netzahualcoyotl, women, enjoying the freedom and prestige associated with the status of *abuela* (grandmother), easily assume nurturing and managerial positions within their own families and in respect to coparticipants in voluntary associations. Not unlike the Yugoslav example, this is the natural culmination of increasing prestige and power achieved within their own homes as they grow older. Though the assumption of overt power in nonfamilial arenas is somewhat at odds with traditional cultural proscriptions, nevertheless women easily fill the void left by more rapidly declining male prowess. Moreover, while conflict between Mexican and American norms may create a discontinuity of value structures, at the same time biculturality provides a greater variety of role models for the elderly to whom even traditional culture allowed more latitude than to younger persons, particularly in the case of women. Thus, the voluntary association, a mode of organization almost unknown in rural Mexico outside religious sodalities, constitutes a new kind of nonreligious, nonkinship arena where older Chicanos may become actively engaged with those of similar experience compensating for a diminishing of the family as the only major source of purpose and gratification.

Barbara Myerhoff also observes among her subjects the more tenuous and less clearly defined position of older men. Traditional Jewish women have been accustomed to a lifetime of dependence and powerlessness; however her female informants have accommodated to their marginality by developing new habits to compensate for their peripheral position. This behavior has been highly adaptive to their present circumstances, and thus they have been able to cope with poverty, social insignificance, and isolation more adequately than have men. These women have demonstrated greater skills in establishing social relationships with each other, and have acquired a real sense of their own power and meaningfulness despite negative opinions and treatment on the part of external social entities.

As is the case in Yugoslav and Mexican culture, among the Eastern European Jews the female sense of worth has been determined principally by her nurturant role. However, denied the expected familial outlet for these inclinations, Myerhoff finds that her female subjects have directed it toward one another and those poorer than themselves. At the same time, they have also sublimated their maternalism in the context of Zionism. In contrast, the men's lives have always been tied to external economic or problem-solving matters. Within the East European shtetl, these dichotomous male and female roles would have found ample expression even in old age. However, the discontinuities of migration, first to the East Coast of the United States and then later to retirement in California, have severed these people from the arenas where they would have fulfilled traditional Jewish roles in the normal course of events. Nevertheless, the voluntary association has enabled these very old people to realize partially a cultural continuity stretching back to their earliest childhood, but in this respect, female culture has demonstrated greater adaptability and vitality than male.

Several universals are suggested by these ethnographic studies: The first and most obvious is, of course, that each culture clearly defines appropriate behavior, spheres of influence, and areas of responsibility for men and women; the sexual dichotomy punctuates the entire life cycle and is by and large symbiotic in nature; and male and female life cycles exhibit separate developmental histories. The roles of men and women are determined not only by formal position, but are also the product of sentiment and happenstance, and in each are embedded different kinds of power. For instance, such power appears to be sexually complementary, and where men may have control of property, women may dominate their offspring and control ritual. In each culture considered here, power peaks at different times for men and women, and where power declines for one sex, leaving a vacuum, the other frequently steps in to fill it.

AGING AS A CAREER

The third major organization theme of these studies, aging as a career, constitutes a kind of analogy stressing old age as a period of activity, participation, self-movement, and purposefulness. It also underscores the fact that aging cannot be understood in isolation, but rather must be conceived as the product of a building process typifying the entire life span. Stated another way, old age is not necessarily a passive state, but on the contrary one evoking dynamic responses to its exigencies. Thus, in the context of these essays, we have depicted later years as a time requiring the constant expenditure of effort for sociocultural and physical survival. To live out each day with dignity, alertness, control over one's faculties, and mobility necessitates the output of tremendous energy, and in the most general sense of the word, it is a kind of *work*. The second connotation of "career" assumes a diachronic perspective relating to long-term goals spanning an entire lifetime; that is, it constitutes a process by which the individual builds, or fails to build, a lasting structure of relationships, accomplishments, affect, and respect that will give meaning and validation to one's total life at its close. The construction of such a career involves a kind of storing-up of resources for future use. Some of these resources may be material ones, while others may be intangible, such as knowledge, honor, or a sense of intimacy and commonality with others.

Myerhoff's case of Jacob illustrates the careful accumulation of assets over time to be drawn upon in old age. These assets are many and include the nature of relations with his sons; a life lived in accord with the principles of his Judaic culture; the development of a leadership role among his aged co-ethnic peers and the nurturance of a personal style suitable to this group; and his acquisition of skills and habits that could not be eroded with increasing age—i.e., literary and ritual knowledge, philanthropy, and sociability. Similarly, in Simić's essay recounting the history of three generations of Lazići, Grandfather Mitar's satisfaction in old age can be seen to stem from his careful management of his lineage's material assets over many decades, and his perceptive manipulation of family relationships and traditional Serbian custom.

The idea of aging as a career contradicts the concept of growing old as simply a series of losses to be endured or transcended. Though indeed losses do occur with the passing of the years, gains are clearly accrued as well.

However, these gains are not distributed equally to all, and the analogy to a career in its everyday sense of the meaning also suggests the idea of differential success. These essays demonstrate the fact that in every society the rewards possible in old age depend to a great extent on individual ability, resourcefulness, good judgment, and luck at every point during the life cycle. Obviously, the meaning of success if not the same in every culture or social arena, nevertheless, in every instance some criteria for its realization can be specified. In each of the examples, one can note with varying degrees of specificity what it means to be successful in old age; some of the standards are cultural, others situational; the road to achievement may be clearly marked and unambiguous, or it may be fraught with uncertainty and risk.

This book has striven to define how the aged perceive success in particular social and cultural niches. Among the Chagga, physical viability is extremely important in maintaining one's social relationships. In a primitive country with few means of transportation, those who are no longer able to walk are excluded from all-important interactions, and isolation from one's contemporaries and the inability to participate in cross-generational festivities are signs of failure. In contrast, older Yugoslavs are less dependent on physical agility and competency; rather, their success relates to the careful building of reciprocal relationships over the years with their descendants and collateral kin. Here, the prime value stems from ideas of familial corporacy and the willingness to sacrifice individual desires and rewards for group objectives. Similarly, Chicano elders also tend to measure their success in terms of familial values, and "having done life's work well." However, familial and personal mobility have been severely limited by external social pressures inherent in the cultural gap separating Mexican and Anglo-American society. Thus, one yardstick of accomplishment for older persons in the barrio is the level of skills they have developed in dealing with the dominant society's institutions and customs. These abilities include literacy, bilingualism, and some awareness of the basic tenets of Anglo-American culture. However, the elderly Chicanos described by Cuellar generally lack access to the broader society's institutions, and have therefore redirected their energies to participation in the arenas provided by voluntary associations, where they can strive for excellence, recognition, and self-esteem among their co-ethnic peers. Turning to the study by Vélez of Netzahualcoyotl, values for the aged are even more ambiguous, though those he calls the "followers of children" are still able to rely in part on the family as an arena for accomplishment. Nevertheless, volatile change, separation from natal homes in migration, and social instability have isolated this older generation from the younger, and differentiated traditional from contemporary values. For the aged, the task is thus one of reinterpretation and the integration of conflicting norms, experiences, and relationships.

Perhaps the experience of the elderly Jews of Venice best lends substance to what are surely universal concerns of the aged everywhere. The continued survival of this group collectively and individually is in itself a triumph. Myerhoff describes their everyday life in terms of persistence in the face of substantial odds. Among these old people, the markers of accomplishment are quite commonplace: to be able to get up once again; to prepare and pay for their food, to visit friends, and to "simply walk to the ocean." Their work, in its most basic definition, is to remain autonomous and to continue functioning. This task requires the mobilization of a variety of resources: expert financial management in poverty; knowing how to survive with little; a knowledge of available services and charities; the harboring of diminishing physical strength; and the skill of manipulating obligations with friends and/or family. These old people have become adept at soliciting relationships of care from others relying on a variety of cultural imperatives which they exploit with virtuosity. Finally, the most important resource of all is that which they have generated themselves, the creation of a setting in the form of a voluntary association where they may derive the essential sense of personal and ethnic worth that can only be negotiated with others.

These chapters demonstrate that aging differs little from the rest of life in respect to the fact that one must continue the active management and manipulation of his social and physical environment. Though each culture places somewhat different demands on its members as they grow older, and adorns the concept of success with various visible signs, nevertheless, the aged seek universally a sense of participation, self-esteem, external recognition, and verification of their accomplishments. Unfortunately, in no society do all persons meet with equally good fortune in this quest, nor are all social settings similarly amenable to granting this bounty to their aged.

The theme of aging as a career points not only to the possibility of accruing various levels of success or failure that must be dealt with conceptually in later life, but also to old age as a period of construction and reconstruction in both the psychological and social sense. Myerhoff casts light on a particular aspect of this phenomenon in terms of what she calls *dramas of honor.* In all the works in this book, especially in dealing with situations of change, the elderly can be seen attempting to establish their worth in a variety of ways. For example, in the case of the aged Jews of Venice, where there is an extreme instance of separation from dominant centers of action and visibility, Myerhoff's subjects have attempted to construct arenas in which their cumulative accomplishments can be seen and made dramatically apparent. Thus, for disconnected older people whose lives have been separated from significant long-term witnesses to their accomplishments, it is all the more necessary to stage a dramatization of one's worth. Only by doing so may they "cash in" on the rewards of a lifetime, since their biographies will otherwise be known only to themselves. Depending on the cultural setting, this may be done formally and ritually, or informally in casual gatherings, in drinking bouts, or in the context of everyday activities. In more stable situations evidencing greater continuity, these dramas of honor tend to form an integral part of the life cycle, or of family and public rituals as may be seen in the instance of the Serbian patriline Saint's Day (the slava) described by Simić.

In dramas of honor, older people attempt to mobilize and maximize their accomplishments, portraying their abilities past and present in an overt and visible form to others, sometimes strangers or peers, sometimes intimates and kin, who otherwise would not be able to discern the cues of success. Such dramas assume many forms: Margarita's assertions in her daughter-in-law's kitchen (in Vélez); Siara's recounting of his life story to the anthropologist (in Moore); and the reading of essays and poems by elders in the Aliyah Senior Citizens' Center (in Myerhoff) are all occasions for promoting and dramatizing honor. Those with no opportunities, such as Armando's father in the city (in Vélez) or Djole in the old age home (in Simić), are the most dislocated and tragic figures to appear in this book. Thus, if old age is, as Moore states, a "stockpile," there must be opportunities for publicly mobilizing and calling upon the accumulation of skill, knowledge, kinship ties friendships, allies, descendants, heirs, and obligations accrued throughout a lifetime. Where such opportunities do not exist, they may be created.

The concept of old age as a career seems the almost inevitable product of the anthropological approach, stressing the view of the "native" as an analytic point of departure. The ethnographic materials upon which these chapters are based clearly underscore the discrepancy between the outsider's concept of aging as a series of losses, and the insider's perception of the process as a creative one. Thus, like all stages in life, old age presents not only a series of limitations but also constitutes a set of possibilities which may be elaborated.

THE CULTURE OF AGING: STRUCTURE AND PROCESS

While old people have provided a central concern in this book, they have not been portrayed as existing in isolation or frozen in time; rather, we have attempted to depict them as links between generations, as carriers of both tradition and personal experience, and as such as repositories of a kind of history. We have striven to understand their old age as the product of their total lives as reassembled from their own accounts and those of their children, kin, neighbors, and associates. Our research brings together synchronic field observations, and personal and family histories so as to place the "ethnographic present" in the broader context of social, cultural, and individual progression. In essence, these essays on aging represent an effort to escape from what sociologist C. Wright Mills (1959: 149) has termed "the static qualities of a-historical studies."

It is evident that social and cultural phenomena have both a sequential and a simultaneous nature, and because of this it is necessary to bridge the gap between opposing levels of analysis, that is, between persistent overarching structures and ideas on the one hand, and the manner with which individuals actually deal with them on the other. Our present research has accomplished this in part through intensive field work in the anthropological tradition of participant-observation augmented by more formal techniques such as the use of questionnaires, census materials, the taking of genealogies, and the like. However, equal stress has been directed also to the collection of biographical materials, materials that in some cases span over a century. Moreover, field work was not oriented so much to the eliciting of normative statements from informants as to the recording of detailed descriptions of ongoing social interactions and rituals.

It is curious that the life history approach has been applied so sparingly in anthropology, and almost not at all in social gerontology, in spite of such notable examples of the utility of its application as the controversial studies of poverty among Mexicans and Puerto Ricans by Oscar Lewis (1959, 1961, 1965). Moreover, the obvious advantages of such a microhistorical treatment seem even more relevant to research among the aged, who clearly have more to remember than others. What is perhaps most significant is that these advantages are accrued not only to the investigator but to the subject as well. For the informant, the recapitulation of life's experiences is a great deal more than simply a listing of events; it is also an opportunity to reexperience, evaluate, and order the multitude of perceptions, actions, and relationships that punctuate the past. Thus, the creation of an autobiography can be a way of rendering life purposeful and interconnected, a way to evoke a sense of continuity. Also, it is a rare person who recalls his experiences without imposing some judgments as to their personal and cultural significance.

For the ethnographer, the collection of biographical material, as well as the assembling of data regarding ongoing interactions provides indications as to the nature of the dynamic relationship between real behavior and the generalized structures we label "culture." Moreover, the dimension of time assures that the so-called "holistic" approach on which anthropology so prides itself is rendered truly holistic. For instance, Langness (1965: 50), in discussing the role of life histories in anthropological science, notes that in the absence of such materials the anthropologist may return from the field with a mass of statements about the people and culture, but at best will have learned only a little about a lot of individuals. Similarly, without detailed case histories to be placed in relief against a background of cultural norms and modalities, we can discover very little about those shadowy areas of life where cultural prescriptions and paradigms are vague, incomplete, inappropriate, or even totally lacking. Finally, it is inescapable that static models of abstracted structures and norms lack a sense of immediacy, subtlety, and

artistic vitality. Indeed, a good deal of anthropological work pales by comparison with the manner in which the human experience is often portrayed
novelistically in all of its many overtones and varied hues. Surely such authors
as Chekhov, Kazantzakis, or Moravia provide us with at least as great an
understanding of Russian, Greek, or Italian life as any ethnography. Though
these present essays make no claim of such aesthetic and intuitive genius,
they nevertheless attempt to depict through detailed case histories some of
the nuances of the so-called "cultural experience" (regarding the validity and
uses of the life and case history method, see Van Velsen, 1967).

We have sought to discover the paths followed by the aged, ways of
thinking and coping not readily apparent to the middle-aged social scientist
looking at aging as a misfortune or a cultural wasteland. Each of us worked in
a familiar culture, studying persons set apart from us by their years, and thus
in many ways as initially strange as if they had been members of some totally
alien society. Nevertheless, we were empathetically drawn to them by such
factors as co-ethnicity or long acquaintance with their society, as well as the
knowledge that with luck one day we, too, would find ourselves in their
position.

In almost four years of our studies, we have encountered elderly survivors
wending their way toward the culmination of life, sometimes following
culturally designated routes, and at others traversing terra incognita. For
some, this task has met with satisfaction and success, for others it has resulted
in misery and failure. Old age has not been the same for everyone. Some have
built their future carefully while others have foundered along the way
regardless of the cultural context.

IMPLICATIONS FOR SOCIAL POLICY

Two intertwined and generalized conclusions seem to emerge from these
studies in terms of their relevance for social policy. The first relates to the
variability of the aging process cross-culturally and to the existent philosophy
of even-handed universalism which has traditionally pervaded the American
bureaucratic mentality. The second focuses on the idea of old age as a state
embodying not only debits but positive potential.

These essays demonstrate the myriad forms that aging may assume both
from society to society and from individual to individual. An inescapable
dimension of this is the quality of ethnicity and ethnic identity. In a
pluralistic urban setting such as our own, these questions assume particular
salience. At one time, ethnic differences were commonly viewed as an
impediment to the "inevitable" and "desirable" process of assimilation, that
is, a barrier to Americanization. Similar to old age, ethnicity was widely
viewed by outsiders as a liability, and all too frequently treated by insiders as
a burden of shame. In actuality, the ethnic experience, whether in America or

elsewhere, belies these contentions. Rather, what must emerge is a recognition that ethnic cohesion, like kinship, neighborhood, or common lifestyle can provide a potential medium for the solution of both personal and social problems, a function it has in fact fulfilled in this country for an untold number of generations.

A corollary of this is the notion that whatever is devised and/or given in response to social needs must take into account ongoing social arrangements and must be packaged with human connections attached. In other words, social and cultural ties must be sustained, or conditions created where they may be generated; otherwise we deceive ourselves in our well-intentioned efforts to create a truly human milieu for the elderly to inhabit. If we allow them to live simply as biological creatures without culture and significant social ties, we discount their lives as human beings. Surely, these life histories must reveal that we ourselves will be "they" in a few years, and we had best now begin to attend to our own future.

BIBLIOGRAPHY

ANDERSON, B. G. (1972) "The process of deculturation—its dynamics among United States aged." Anthropological Quarterly 45: 209-216.

ARENSBERG, C. (1937) *The Irish Countryman*. New York: Macmillan.

ARIES, P. (1974) *Western Attitudes Toward Death: From the Middle Ages to the Present* (P. M. Ranum, trans.). Baltimore: Johns Hopkins Press.

BARTH, F. (1966) *Models of Social Organization*. London: Royal Anthropological Institute of Great Britain and Ireland.

BENDIX, R. (1962) *Max Weber: An Intellectual Portrait*. Garden City, N.Y.: Doubleday.

BENEDICT, R. (1934) *Patterns of Culture*. Boston: Houghton Mifflin.

BOHANNAN, P. (1963) *Social Anthropology*. New York: Holt, Rinehart & Winston.

BURKE, K. (1957) *The Philosophy of Literary Form*. New York: Vintage.

BUTLER, R. N. (1968) "The life review: an interpretation of reminiscence in the aged," in B. L. Neugarten (ed.) *Middle Age and Aging*. Chicago: University of Chicago Press.

CLARK, M. (1967) "The anthropology of aging: a new area for studies of culture and personality." The Gerontologist 7: 55-64.

——— (1972) "Cultural values and dependency in later life," pp. 263-274 in D. O. Cowgill and L. D. Holmes (eds. *Aging and Modernization*. New York: Appleton-Century-Crofts.

COWGILL, D. O. and L. D. HOLMES (eds.) (1972) *Aging and Modernization*. New York: Appleton-Century-Crofts.

CUMMING, E. and W. E. HENRY (1961) *Growing Old: The Process of Disengagement*. New York: Basic Books.

DRESNER, S. H. (trans.) (1974) "The deaths of the Hasidic masters (from the Histalkut Janefesh," pp. 24-30 in J. Riemer (ed.) *Jewish Reflections on Death*. New York: Schocken.

DURKHEIM, E. (1893) *The Division of Labor in Society* (G. Simpson, trans.). New York: Collier-Macmillan Ltd.

——— (1897) *Le Suicide*. Paris: Etude Sociologique.

ERLICH, V. S. (1971) "Obespravljena generacija (The disenfranchised generation)." Sociologija 3.

EVANS-PRITCHARD, E. E. (1937) *Witchcraft, Oracles and Magic Among the Azande*. Oxford, Eng.: Clarendon Press.

FERNANDEZ, J. (1974) "The mission of metaphor in expressive culture." Current Anthropology 15, 2: 119-133.

FILIPOVIĆ, M. S. (1964) "Studije o slavi, službi, ili krsnom imenu (Studies of the slava, the service, or baptismal name)." Matica Srpska, Zbornik za Društvene Nauke 38: 51-76.

FREUCHEN, P. (1961) *Book of the Eskimos*. Cleveland: World Press.

GEERTZ, C. (1965) "Religion as a cultural system," pp. 1-46 in M. Banton (ed.) *Anthropological Approaches to the Study of Religion*. New York: Praeger.

——— (1973) "Thick description: toward an interpretive theory of culture," pp. 3-30 in
C. Geertz (ed.) *The Interpretation of Cultures*. New York: Basic Books.

GOLDEN, H. E. (1939) *Hamadrikh, the Rabbi's Guide: A Manual of Jewish Religious
Rituals, Ceremonials and Customs*. New York: Hebrew Publishing Company.

GOODY, J. (ed.) (1971) The Developmental Cycle in Domestic Groups. Cambridge,
Eng.: Cambridge University Press.

HALPERN, J. M. and D. ANDERSON (1970) "The Zadruga: a century of change."
Anthropologica N.S. 12: 83-97.

HAMMEL, E. A. (1964) "Culture as an information system." Kroeber Anthropological
Society Papers 31: 83-91.

HART, C.W.M. and A. R. PILLING (1960) *The Tiwi of North Australia*. New York:
Holt, Rinehart & Winston.

HYMES, D. (1974) "Origins of inequality among speakers," pp. 45-71 in E. Haugen and
M. Bloomfield (eds.) *Language as a Human Problem*. New York: W. W. Norton.

JUNG, L. (1974) "The meaning of the Kaddish," pp. 160-164 in J. Riemer (ed.) *Jewish
Reflections on Death*. New York: Schocken.

LAMM, M. (1969) *The Jewish Way in Death and Mourning*. New York: Jonathan David.

LANGER, S. K. (1942) *Philosophy in a New Key*. New York: Mentor.

LANGNESS, L. L. (1965) *The Life History in Anthropological Science*. New York:
Holt, Rinehart & Winston.

LeVINE, R. A. (1965) "Intergeneration tensions and extended family structures in
Africa," pp. 188-204 in E. Shanas and G. F. Streib (eds.) *Social Structure and the
Family: Generational Relations*. Englewood Cliffs, N. J.: Prentice-Hall.

LEWIS, O. (1952) "Urbanization without breakdown: a case study." The Scientific
Monthly 75: 31-41.

——— (1959) *Five Families*. New York: Basic Books.

——— (1961) *The Children of Sanchez*. New York: Random House.

——— (1965) *La Vida*. New York: Random House.

MENDILOW, A. A. (1952) *Time and Novel*. London: Peter Nevill.

MILLS, C. W. (1959) *The Sociological Imagination*. New York: Grove.

MOORE, S. F. and B. G. MYERHOFF (1977) "Introduction: forms and meanings," in
S. F. Moore and B. G. Myerhoff (eds.) *Secular Ritual*. Amsterdam: Van Gorcum.

MYERHOFF, B. G. (1977) "We don't wrap herring in a printed page: fusions and
continuity in secular ritual," in S. F. Moore and B. G. Myerhoff (eds.) *Secular Ritual*.
Amsterdam: Van Gorcum.

——— and V. TUFTE (1975) "Life history as integration: personal myth and aging." The
Gerontologist.

NASH, ——and——WINTROB (1972)

OLNEY, J. (1972) *Metaphors of Self: The Meaning of Autobiography*. Princeton:
Princeton University Press.

ORNSTEIN, R. E. (1969) *On the Experience of Time*. Middlesex, Eng.: Penguin.

SCHOLEM, G. G. (1969) *Kabbalah and Its Symbolism*. New York: Schocken.

SIMMONS, L. W. (1945) *The Role of the Aged in Primitive Society*. New Haven: Yale
University Press.

——— (1960) "Aging in preindustrial societies," pp. 62-89 in C. Tibbitts (ed.) *Handbook
of Social Gerontology*. Chicago: University of Chicago Press.

SOLZHENITSYN, A. (1969) *Cancer Ward*. New York: Dial.

TRACHTENBERG, J. (1969) *Jewish Magic and Superstition: A Study in Folk Religion*.
New York: Atheneum.

TURNER, V. (1967) "Aspects of Saora ritual and shamanism: an approach to the data
of ritual,' pp. 181-204 in A. L. Epstein (ed.) *The Craft of Social Anthropology*.

London: Tavistock.

——— (1974) *Dramas, Fields and Metaphors: Symbolic Action in Human Society.* Ithaca, N.Y.: Cornell University Press.

VAN VELSEN, J. (1967) "The extended-case method and situational analysis," pp. 129-149 in A. L. Epstein (ed.) *The Craft of Social Anthropology.* London: Tavistock.

ZASHIN, J. (1974) "The fraternity of mourners," pp. 166-169 in J. Riemer (ed.) *Jewish Reflections on Death.* New York: Schocken.

ABOUT THE AUTHORS

JOSÉ CUELLAR received his B.A. in anthropology from California State University (Long Beach) in 1969, and his M.A. and Ph.D. in anthropology from UCLA, where he was a National Institute of Mental Health Graduate Research Trainee. In 1970 he was the UCLA Alumni Association's award-winner for Distinguished Academic Achievement. Cuellar was a National Science Foundation Research Fellow at the Andrus Gerontology Center (University of Southern California) from 1973 to 1975. Trained as an urban anthropologist, he is a specialist in gerontological anthropology, anthropological theory, and Chicano Studies. He is presently Assistant Professor of Anthropology and Chicano Studies at the University of Colorado at Boulder, where he also serves as Director of the Chicano Studies Program.

SALLY FALK MOORE received her L.L.B. (1945) and Ph.D. (1957) from Columbia University, and is Professor of Anthropology at the University of California, Los Angeles. She has taught at the University of Southern California and at Yale, and is Honorary Research Fellow of the Department of Anthropology at University College, University of London. She is author of *Power and Property in Inca Peru* (Columbia University Press, 1958), *Law as Process* (Routledge & Kegan Paul, 1977), and editor with Barbara Myerhoff of *Symbol and Politics in Communal Ideology* (Cornell University Press, 1975) and *Secular Ritual* (Van Gorcum, 1977). She has contributed to numerous journals in her field, and has been studying the Chagga since 1968, with field work in the years 1968-1969 and 1973-1974.

BARBARA MYERHOFF is Professor of Anthropology and Chairperson of the department at the University of Southern California. She received her B.A. in sociology in 1958 from UCLA, her M.A. in human development from the University of Chicago, and her Ph.D. in anthropology from UCLA. She is a Research Associate at the Andrus Gerontology Center at USC in addition to her other duties. Her special interests are in the areas of religion, symbolism, ritual, ethnicity and aging, and youth culture. She is the author of *Peyote Hunt: The Sacred Journey of the Huichol Indians* (1974, Cornell University Press), co-winner of the National Book Award in philosophy and religion. She is the co-author of the Academy Award winning documentary film "Number Our Days" (1977; with Lynn Littman).

ANDREI SIMIĆ received his Ph.D. in 1970 from the University of California (Berkeley), where he specialized in the problems of urbanization and social change in Southeastern Europe and Latin America. He has carried out extensive field work in Yugoslavia, and is the author of a number of works dealing with modernization in the Balkans, including *The Peasant Urbanites: A Study of Rural-Urban Mobility in Serbia.* He is currently Associate Professor of Anthropology at the University of Southern California and a Research Associate at the Andrus Gerontology Center. His interests include the study of Euro-American ethnic groups, and he has served for the past three years as Ethnic Studies Consultant to the Joint Committee on Eastern Europe of the American Council of Learned Societies, and as a consultant to the Portuguese Ethnic Studies Project of Northern California.

CARLOS G. VÉLEZ holds a B.A. in political science and an M.A. in English from the University of Arizona (Tucson), and an M.A. and Ph.D. in anthropology from the University of California, San Diego. His fields of specialization are political anthropology, urban anthropology, applied anthropology, sociocultural change, culture and education, the anthropology of aging, and the anthropology of literature. He conducted field research in Ciudad Netzahualcoyotl, Mexico, from 1971-1974, and he is the author of numerous papers and articles in his fields of interest. He is currently Assistant Professor in the Department of Anthropology at the University of California at Los Angeles.